INDIAN & HOME MEMORIES

INDIAN & HOME MEMORIES

HENRY COTTON

GYAN

Published by

Gyan Publishing House
5, Ansari Road
Daryaganj, New Delhi-110002
Phone: 011-47034999, 9811692060
E-mail: books@gyanbooks.com

Distribution Network
gyanbooks.com
India, USA, Canada, UK, Australia

ISBN: 978-93-7097-337-4 (PB)

First Published, 1911

2nd Impression 2025

Printed at: Gyan Press, Delhi.

INDIAN & HOME MEMORIES
Author: HENRY COTTON

INDIAN AND HOME MEMORIES

Henry Cotton

From a painting by Hugh G. Riviere, presented by the people of Bengal, 1903.

[Frontispiece.

INDIAN & HOME MEMORIES

BY

SIR HENRY COTTON, K.C.S.I.

WITH 19 ILLUSTRATIONS

1911

C'EST ICY UN LIVRE DE BONNE FOY, LECTEUR

PREFACE

I BELONG to an Anglo-Indian family, and am saturated with Indian traditions and associations. My father and grandfather were in the Indian Civil Service before me, and one of my sons is now a member of that Service. I was myself in the Civil Service for thirty-five years. My life in India was not devoid of incident ; I have had the honour to rise to high office, and for four years after my retirement I sat as a Member of the House of Commons.

I have made many friends, and, I am sorry to say, not a few enemies. In these pages, which are an unvarnished record, I submit my memoirs to the judgment of the public, and venture to hope that they may add to the number of my friends and not increase the ranks of those who are enrolled upon the other side.

οὔτοι συνέχθειν, ἀλλὰ συμφιλεῖν ἔφυν.

HENRY COTTON.

September, 1911.

CONTENTS

ILLUSTRATIONS

INDIAN AND HOME MEMORIES

CHAPTER I

ON THE THRESHOLD

THE earliest of my ancestors of whom I have any knowledge was Dr. Nathaniel Cotton, who was born in 1705, and lived a long and useful life at St. Albans, where he died in 1788. In his day he was well known for his writings in prose and verse, and his poems were very popular, running through more than twenty editions. I have in my possession a copy of his works which was once the property of Dr. John Brown, the author of "Rab and his Friends," and that excellent man's appreciative pencil comments are evidence of the high estimation in which Dr. Cotton's writings were held in a past generation. There was a good old custom in our family to bestow a half-crown on every child as soon as it could recite Dr. Cotton's poem, "The Fireside," which begins with these quaint and pleasing verses :—

"Dear Chloe, while the busy crowd,
The vain, the wealthy, and the proud,
In folly's maze advance ;
Though singularity and pride
Be called our choice, we'll step aside,
Nor join the giddy dance.

From the gay world we'll oft retire
To our own family and fire,
    Where love our hours employs;
No noisy neighbour enters here,
No intermeddling stranger near,
    To spoil our heartfelt joys.

If solid happiness we prize,
Within our heart this jewel lies,
    And they are fools who roam;
The world hath nothing to bestow,
From our own selves our bliss must flow,
    And that dear hut, our home."

Dr. Nathaniel Cotton was an eminent mental specialist, and in that capacity had charge of Cowper during that poet's successive attacks of aberration. He had a large family, of whom Joseph Cotton, born in 1746, was the fourth surviving son. This was my great-grandfather, who joined the mercantile service of the Honourable East India Company, was for twenty-eight years a Director, became Deputy Master of the Trinity House, and a Fellow of the Royal Society, and died in 1825. His second son, my grandfather, born in 1783, went to India in 1801 as a member of the Madras Civil Service, and served for fifteen years as Collector of Tanjore. On his retirement in 1830, he became in his turn a Director of the Company, and was Chairman of the Honourable Court in 1843. His wife was a daughter of Captain John Stedman, the author of a curious and valuable old narrative of "A Five Years' Expedition against the Revolted Negroes of Surinam," which was published in 1796. This book, which is in two quarto volumes, contains a remarkable series of illustrations by the author, which were engraved in colour by Bartolozzi, Blake, and others. I am proud of it, not only for its intrinsic merits, which are great, but for the humane and sympathetic spirit towards the sufferings of the coloured people, both aboriginal and negro, which it breathes throughout.

My father, Joseph John Cotton, born in 1813, entered the Indian Civil Service in 1831. He married in 1842 Jessie Minchin, daughter of a barrister who was practising in Madras and held for a long time a responsible office in the Supreme Court. My father served in the usual offices which are held by a civilian, and retired on pension in 1862. I served myself in the Bengal Civil Service from 1867 to 1902, and I have at the present time a son serving in India, who entered the Madras Civil Service in 1893. I represent, therefore, a practically continuous service in the country of five generations, a record probably unique. For more than a century the interests of my family have been wrapped up in India, and I may well write of myself, as I have done in the pages of my "New India": "It is my pride that I am, as it were, an hereditary member of the administration."

Born on September 13, 1845, at Combaconum in Madras, where my father was serving as Sub-Collector, I was brought home by my parents in 1848 round the Cape in one of Green's ships, the *Sutlej*. The voyage lasted six months, owing to a violent storm in the Indian Ocean, which carried away all masts, and led to a long stay at the Cape to refit. My father had taken furlough for three years, and settled himself at Wanstead. Only two things stand out in my memory at that time—the Great Exhibition of 1851, where I remember the crowds round the Koh-i-noor, and the funeral of the Duke of Wellington, which I witnessed from a window on the route.

When my parents returned to India, I was consigned with my younger brother James to a dame's school in George Lane, Woodford, kept successively by the Misses Arundale and by Mrs. Mackenzie, mother of the well-known surgeon and throat specialist, Sir Morell Mackenzie, who was then a young medical student, and of Sir Stephen Mackenzie, a no less eminent physician who was about my own age. The Great Eastern Railway was not yet in existence, and we were driven to and from London by coach. Epping Forest was a great playground, and we were as healthy and happy as children could be without parental care. My little brain was stuffed with an enormous accumulation of hymns and simple poetry, collects and long passages from the Bible, which we had to learn by heart and which I am thankful to say I can still recollect as though it were yesterday.

Throughout my boyhood days during the fifties we spent our summer and generally our winter holidays at the residence of my grandfather, James Minchin, then a Justice of the Peace in Devonshire. He had settled on his retirement in one of the most beautiful spots in that beautiful county. Hamslade House, near Oakford Bridge on the river Exe, about four miles from Dulverton on one side and Bampton on the other, was the most charming home for boys that imagination could have devised. A lovely view down the river valley, magnificent oak woods and dense copses, swarming with hair-streaks, fritillaries, and almost every form of butterfly life ; hills and dales and lanes such as only Devonshire can boast of ; trout-fishing, otter-hunting, stag-hunting, bathing and boating, riding and shooting, butterfly-catching, and birdnesting ; a primitive old church with its old-fashioned pews ; Thomas Nunn, the clerk, with his metallic and mechanical " Aaamun " ; old-world and kindly Parson Parkin ; the village stocks and turnpike gates ; a warm-hearted and simple peasantry, the haymaking in summer and the sunbrowned mowers with their enormous jars of cider ; the roses and the strawberries in the garden ; the icicles in winter of fabulous dimensions ; the plantation and shrubbery and arbours within the grounds, every sign and symbol of rustic simplicity and enjoyment—these are the pleasant memories of my holidays for many years in Devon.

My shorter holidays were passed with a dear and kind old great-uncle, Benjamin Cotton, formerly of the Trinity House, who lived in those days at No. 8, Gloucester Terrace, Regent's Park. From the roof of this house we witnessed the unique display of rockets which were fired off from the top of Primrose Hill to celebrate the Proclamation of Peace after the Crimean War. Dear Uncle Ben was an old bachelor of the most lovable type, and was never happier than when surrounded by nephews and nieces of more than one generation. His favourite nephew was William Cotton Oswell, the African explorer and mighty hunter and companion of Livingstone, who was one of the handsomest and most fascinating men I ever knew, and whom I always regarded with unbounded admiration. Uncle Ben's elder brother, my grandfather, John Cotton, lived in solemn state at No. 78, Westbourne Terrace. He had served in Madras for twenty-six years without ever taking leave to England ; his spotless mahogany dinner-table was a thing of beauty and a joy for ever, and he entertained powdered footmen with calves who stood behind his carriage. Another brother, William Cotton, lived at Walwood in Leytonstone. He was a Director and sometime Governor of the Bank of England, a D.C.L. and F.R.S., and a great supporter of the Established Church, building several churches in London at his own cost. He was the father of Sir Henry Cotton, the Chancery barrister and Lord Justice of Appeal, who was my godfather and from whom I derive my name.

In the spring of 1856 I was entered at Magdalen College School in Oxford, and remained there for more than three years. That was the happiest period of my school life, and I revelled in the ravishing music of the College Chapel, the rural walks and river rowing. James Elwin Millard, D.D., was our head-master. A stern pedagogue I thought him, for, *more Orbiliano*, he was fond of the rod, and we used to go up after school for caning for the most trivial offences—such as running out for tuck for bigger boys—but I learned later on to know him at his true worth, and, though he never could get over his dominie manners, he was one of the kindest and best-hearted of men. He was very High Church : there were morning and evening prayers in a private oratory in the house, and there was a Latin grace before and after every meal. He intoned admirably, and the effect of the Litany in the College Chapel when Dr. Millard and another College Fellow, Dr. Rigaud, intoned the service in a duet—a combination of baritone and alto—with the responses of the school choristers and the great organ in the masterful hands of Stainer, was beautiful beyond expression. The leading choristers in my day were Lewis Stacey Tuckwell and William Corfe, and people used to come from far and near to hear them.

Old Jonathan Sawell was usher of the school, a striking and attractive personality. With ruddy face and white curly hair, he was still the most famous singer at the University, and was in great demand at madrigal concerts. I remember a visit paid to the school by the ex-Queen Amélie, widow of Louis-Philippe, and the half-holiday we got in consequence. Saints' days were whole holidays and much appreciated, none more so than the 1st of

May, the Feast of SS. Philip and James. Never did I miss the daybreak function on the top of Magdalen Tower, when the choir sang their joyous carol and the bells rang again while the tower was swaying to their music. Our amusements were fives, hockey, football, bathing, and, above all, rowing. We played but little cricket—though I do mind me of an annual match with Bradfield—for the whole force of the school spent itself on the river.

I was but a little chap, but I may claim that I showed aptitude in a rowing-boat. I once sculled up the Cherwell in a racing skiff as far as Parson's Pleasure and back, having cut the strings of the row-locks to enable me to unship the sculls at will. I entered for the School Sculls and was beaten but not disgraced by A. J. Toye, afterwards house master at Winchester, a much older and bigger boy than myself. I pulled bow in the school four and still remember the names of the other three boys in the boat, though I have met none of them since—Vincent, Schneider, and Postlethwaite. Schneider was a boy of extraordinary muscular development and the pride of Maclaren's, being the most perfect gymnast I ever saw. He afterwards went up to Trinity, and pulled in the winning 'Varsity boat in a year when Brown, also of Trinity, was stroke. Our river excursions were the cream of our life. Once a year only we visited Godstow at the height of the strawberry season; but Kennington Island, with its apple tart and shandygaff, the Iffley bowling alley, the stretches at Nuneham and the lasher at Sandford, are dreams of delight which linger longest in my memory. I do not forget the walks to Bagley Wood and the Happy Valley, where there were butterflies galore. And there was the bathing at Parson's Pleasure! I took to swimming like a duck to water, and year in and year out we plunged from the trees, indulged in running headers, dived, and floated to our hearts' content. Often have I been down there with Dr. Millard when we had to break the ice to bathe. A famous fat old fellow named Hounslow was our swimming-master.

I am afraid I did not do much work at Magdalen School : it was better for me no doubt that I did not. We were taught on the old lines : King Edward the Sixth's Grammar in Latin ; *Propria quae maribus*, *As in Presenti*, and the Athanasian Creed were learnt by heart, and I could recite several Odes of Horace without knowing their meaning. Still, I got a prize or two and left the school a vigorous and healthy lad.

Among my contemporaries there were Robert Williams and Edward Lee Hicks. With the former I was very intimate, though I do not think I had much in common with him. His manners and tastes were not those of other boys, and he was most unpopular with them. I recall that one Guy Fawkes' Day, when we always had a big bonfire and fireworks in the playground, he was maliciously and badly burned by one of the boys, but to his credit he would not divulge the culprit's name to the authorities. He was extraordinarily clever, with great powers of assimilation and a most retentive memory, but he had no ballast or real strength of character and easily fell into temptation. He was known at College as "Student Williams," from the fact of his being at Christ Church, and, though he took a brilliant degree, he did not easily render himself acceptable at any college for a fellowship. In the meantime he gained an unrivalled reputation as a Greats coach, produced a standard translation of the Ethics, and was at last elected at Merton. I met him again in 1877 when I came home on furlough. He had gone down in the world, but was on the staff of the *Examiner* (which he got me also to join), then in the heyday of its prosperity under Professor Minto. Not long after that he died. E. L. Hicks, it is needless to say, was a lad of another type. He was a town boy who made his way in the school, as he has done ever since, by sheer earnestness and merit. Every boy in the school was proud of his success. Very many years elapsed before I saw him again, but a great affinity of interests and aspirations had united us in correspondence. He was then a Canon of Manchester, and is now the revered Bishop of Lincoln.

My boyish reminiscences of Oxford can hardly pretend to be worthy of record. Dr. Routh had died more than a year before I went to school, but his widow was still a subject of awe to us small boys as she went about in her bath-chair and—shall I say it?—with a heavy moustache. Among the Fellows of Magdalen whom I remember best were Dr. Daubeny, Curator of the Botanical Gardens across the road, and Dr. Bloxam, a benevolent old man who often spoke kindly to us. I cannot remember that the new President, Dr. Bulley, ever noticed us collectively, though, if I do not err, his son was our schoolfellow. Dr. Pusey and Dr. Burgon were the great men of the University whom we were taught to venerate, and I recall them both very well. A potent influence in the University was Dr. (afterwards Sir Henry) Acland, who had married Sarah Cotton, daughter of my great-uncle William of Walwood. They were both of them very kind to me, and their house in Broad Street was a home where I passed many pleasant hours with their children, whom, I am sorry to say, I have not met since. Among all the Oxford dons of that day—and I do not forget Dean Liddell of Christ Church—Dr. Acland was, I think, the most striking and intellectual-looking. Among younger dons I received kindness at the hands of Meyrick of Trinity, and among seniors from Salter of St. Alban Hall. But I confess that the greatest hero in Oxford to my boyish eyes was Thorley of Wadham. This was not the learned don who afterwards became Warden of the College, but Thorley the 'Varsity stroke, who also stroked the Wadham eight and brought them to the head of the river. I once had tea in his rooms.

My mother returned from India in 1859 after an absence from England of eight years. She belonged to the sect of Plymouth Brethren, and my father's tendencies were in the same direction, though he never broke off from outward conformity with the Low Church party. It was natural, therefore, that they should take exception to the High Church associations of Magdalen College School, and we were at once removed from there to become day-boarders at Brighton College. The change was a very complete one, and certainly I was sorry to leave Oxford. My brother after one year left Brighton for Winchester, where he won a scholarship, and I did not remain there for more than eighteen months. But I have very pleasant recollections of Brighton also. The College was then a flourishing institution and, after the manner of schools, it had gained in reputation from its cricketing prowess. My heroes were no longer wet-bobs, but men like the elder Cotterill, son of the Bishop of Cape Town, and lately Headmaster of the College; E. B. Fawcett, who long held the world's record for throwing the cricket-ball; and Denzil Onslow, whom I knew very well later in life in India and at home, all of whom got their cricket blues at Cambridge.

The Headmaster of my time was the Rev. John Griffith, and the Vice-Principal was "Joey" Newton, in whose house I lived for my last term. But the most famous of all our staff was George Long, the special classical master, whose name will always be associated with the Dictionary of Greek and Roman Antiquities, his great editions of Cicero, Cæsar, and other classics, and his translations of Plutarch and Marcus Aurelius. He was born with the century and a contemporary of Macaulay at Cambridge, with whom he divided classical honours. He was a most inspiring teacher, and it was from him I first learnt the love of classical literature. I remember well how he used to sit on the table, with his legs dangling, and how he slapped his thighs when he was endeavouring to make his points plain to our unworthy wits. I was too small a boy to have come under his particular notice, but I record gratefully how much I owe to him. Among the masters was the Rev. Edward Comerford Hawkins (father of the distinguished novelist Anthony Hope), in whose class I was for one term, whose character and influence were wholly beneficial, and whose friendship I made later on when we were fellow-members of the Savile Club. I was only a short time at Brighton College, but when I left I was up for promotion to the Sixth Form, and was really keen on my work.

I took no great part in the school games, but I joined the school Cadet Corps which was formed in the very earliest days of the Volunteer movement. I took an intelligent interest in the Farnborough fight between Sayers and Heenan, and I became fairly proficient in gymnastics, singlestick, and fencing. In fencing, indeed, I attained the position of school champion, after a hard bout with Willie Gill, a very close friend, who shortly afterwards passed into the Royal Engineers. He plucked bright honour for himself, not only professionally, but by his famous marches and travels in Persia, China, and elsewhere, and won the Royal

Geographical Society's gold medal. There was a legend about him which enjoyed more truth than legends usually possess, that he inherited an ample fortune from an old gentleman to whom he showed the courtesy of some casual attention when they had accidentally met. He perished with Professor Palmer in a very tragic manner at the hands of Bedouins near Mount Sinai.

The head of the school was J. M. Image, who went up to Cambridge with a scholarship, became a Fellow of Trinity, and has since, I believe, devoted himself to scholarship and teaching at the University. Among my contemporaries were E. L. (now Sir Edward) Bateman, whose statistical services at the Board of Trade will never be forgotten by Free Traders, and whom I did not meet again till after the lapse of fifty years; Clement Colvin, who became Secretary of the Public Works Department at the India Office; and Augustus Raymond Margary, a charming young fellow, who joined the Consular Service in China, and greatly distinguished himself as the pioneer of a big enterprise in geographical research, making the march from China to Burma. He was murdered in 1875 in Chinese territory near Bhamo, just as he had accomplished his task. Then there was Edward Carpenter (of course known as "Chips"), another classmate who has devoted himself in a life of self-sacrifice to every kind of social and humane endeavour.

But among all my contemporaries the one who impressed himself most upon us by his character was Julius Elliott. He was the youngest son of the Rev. H. V. Elliott, at that time a very well known and popular preacher in the Kemp Town end of Brighton, to whose church I went with my parents on Sundays. His elder brother, Sir Charles Elliott, also an old Brighton College boy before he went to Harrow, was afterwards one of my kindest and best Indian friends. Julius was quite at the top of the school and, possessing great physical strength with plenty of brains and a large heart, was the *beau idéal* of a school prefect. His hammer-throwing and putting the stone we deemed prodigious. He was another of my schoolfellows of great promise who died all too soon. He was an intrepid mountaineer, and made the third ascent of the Matterhorn, and the record of his climb in his own handwriting still hangs, or did hang till recently, as a framed archive in one of Seiler's hotels at Zermatt. He lost his life two or three years later in a terrible fall from the final *arête* of the Schreckhorn, on which, with undue temerity, he had unroped himself from his guides.

Brighton College enjoys a splendidly healthy situation, so close to the glorious sea on the one hand and to the rolling downs on the other, and among my schoolboy reminiscences none is fresher than those of the early mornings when I used to swim out and battle with the waves ; while, as regards the downs, I associate them chiefly with a collection of butterflies. The downs then swarmed with clouded yellows —both *Hyale* and *Edusa*—and blues and skippers of every kind and beauty, and one half-holiday afternoon my brother and I became the possessors of a Bath White—*Pieris daplidice*—which I caught, not because I knew it at the time to be that rare species, but because I was attracted by its dark colour and exceptionally strong flight. We did not know the value of our find till we were coming home, and a gentleman we met on the road asked to inspect our captures and promptly congratulated us on our success. Our friend was the eminent artist and naturalist Mr. Harrison Weir. Another delight was to go up to the racecourse in the evening and sugar the posts with some treacly stuff, a process which always resulted in the attraction and eventual capture in little pill-boxes of a number of moths. One day I caught in a clover-field a solitary genuine locust of huge dimensions, and the Bath White and the locust are still in my possession.

While I was at Brighton my father came home on leave, preparatory to retiring from the Service. He settled at Clifton, in days before the College was in existence, and it was then I went to live in "Joey" Newton's house during my last term at Brighton. After that I left school for good. It was my misfortune to be afflicted in boyhood with a very serious impediment in my speech, and in the summer of 1861 I was sent to a specialist in stammering of the name of Hunt, who lived at Orr House, near Hastings. I can vouch for the fact that I was a bad stammerer when I went and a very bad one for some years after I left. But it is also a fact that during the period I was at Orr House I never stammered at all. The cure consisted in healthy outdoor exercise; the continual recitation in the woods or on the seashore, in a loud voice, of poetry, of which fortunately I possessed a remarkable stock I had already learnt by heart; the strengthening of the diaphragm, and chest expansion, until one could stand punches in that region with indifference; and especially physical control over the tongue, the tip of which when speaking was always to be in contact with the lower teeth. These are all of them excellent prescriptions, and they were faithfully followed by me; but, still, I am afraid Dr. Hunt thought me an impostor. There were several fellow-sufferers during my stay, including one lady, some of whom were horribly bad, and among others was the youthful Lord Goderich, now second Marquess of Ripon. He was the youngest inmate of the establishment. As I have said, my stammering recurred as soon as I left, and for many a long day I found it a simply intolerable nuisance. When I grew to manhood it ceased, though I have always been, and still am, subject to a natural hesitation in speech.

CHAPTER II

THE DAYS OF MY YOUTH

IN the autumn of 1861 I was sent to King's College, London. My father, of whom I had seen nothing during his nine years' absence in India and who was without an opportunity of studying the natural bent of my character and disposition, had made up his mind that I should become a civil engineer, and I was accordingly entered as a student in the Applied Sciences Department. But there I felt myself a veritable fish out of water, and I fear that I neither understood nor profited by a single thing I was taught for a whole year by such able professors as Clerk Maxwell, Smalley, Grainger Hall, and others whom I have forgotten. I worked in the workshop, but only succeeded in damaging myself with my tools. I went down with classes to learn something of practical engineering at the Stratford Railway Works, but took in nothing that I saw. The year was wasted as far as that special department was concerned.

But in the meantime I was slaving secretly even into the small hours at English History and at English and Classical Literature. I bought cribs and with their aid read Homer, Thucydides, and Aristophanes. I made myself familiar with Arnold, Lingard, and Macaulay, and specialised in Blaauw's "History of the Barons' War." The consequence was that I did not lose much ground in general knowledge, and at the end of the year was allowed free scope for my natural inclinations in the General Department. I was then seventeen years of age, sound in wind and limb, and though my education had been desultory in the extreme and I had acquired nothing but a smattering of anything, I had at least developed a taste for books and study. I was placed in contact with a number of studious and clever young fellows of my own age. And I had the advantage of exceptionally capable and brilliant professors and teachers.

The Principal of the College was the Rev. Dr. Jelf, Canon of Christ Church. He was a great divine, who expounded to us Bishop Jewel's "Apologia" and the Thirty-nine Articles. He may have exercised an influence over the students in the Theological Department, but upon us his influence was *nil*. He is best remembered at the present day for his action in removing the Rev. F. D. Maurice from his professorship on the ground of unorthodoxy in the matter of perpetual punishment, an incident which led to the publication of the following lines when it was proposed to set on foot a testimonial fund on the occasion of his retirement from the Principalship :—

"Who was it raised a holy shout
And, all for conscience' sake no doubt,
Turned dear Professor Maurice out?—
My Jelf!

Who is it that has only gibe
And scorn for all the bigot tribe,
And to this fund will not subscribe?—
Myself!"

Fortunately Dr. Jelf was surrounded by a staff of a different calibre. There was Professor Edward Hayes Plumptre, afterwards Dean of Wells. Many a generation of King's College men have had reason to be grateful to him for his kindly care during their student life and his subsequent interest in their careers. None more than I. Nothing could have exceeded the warmth of his sympathy, the kindliness of his monitions, and the example of his single-minded devotion to learning and practical piety. He was my lifelong friend. Through Dr. Plumptre I was placed in contact with his brother-in-law, the saintly Frederick Denison Maurice ; the erudite and accomplished Miss Anna Swanwick, translator of Æschylus and Faust ; Dean Stanley, whose lectures on the history of the Jews I attended by special permission at Queen's College for Ladies in Harley Street ; and made other friends to whom I shall refer later, such as Sir George Grove and Charles Kingsley. Dr. Plumptre was for thirty-four years connected with King's College and resided at the time when I was there in Gloucester Road, Regent's Park. A most liberal-minded man, he took the keenest interest in all the political and social movements of the day.

The Professors of Classical Literature were the Ven. Archdeacon Browne, who retired to the living of Weston-super-Mare, and afterwards the Rev. J. G. Lonsdale, Fellow of Balliol. The former was an aristocratic-looking man and an elegant scholar, to whose refined taste my Latin verses must have been a pain and grief. Professor Lonsdale was more than a most accomplished scholar ; he was one of the most delightful and lovable of teachers. Under them as lecturer was Charles Henry Olive Daniel, then a very young man from Oxford, with fair hair and a light golden moustache, who made himself a very friendly companion, and I still possess the carte-de-visite photograph he gave me when he left to go back to his old College of Worcester, where he is now the well-known Provost. The Professor of

English Literature was John Sherren Brewer, a man of uncommon learning and force of character. With the face of a Socrates, he had also Socratic methods of teaching, and it was a proud moment when any of us were held up for good by him in essay. His hobby was Bacon, and I had good reason to be grateful to Brewer later on when I was called on to write an essay on Bacon in the Indian Civil Service examination, and scored full marks. His erudition and industry found a congenial home in the Rolls and Record Office. Our professor in English History was Charles Henry Pearson, Fellow of Oriel, who afterwards went to Australia and eventually became famous as the inventor of the "Yellow Peril." He delivered his lectures in a very monotonous, high-pitched note and was an acknowledged authority on the Norman Period. During his illness for one term his place was taken by Robert Samuel Wright, also of Oriel, who had been a scholar of Balliol and became in due course one of the most learned Judges of the Queen's Bench. He was a great friend of "Student Williams" and so took an interest in me.

It would have been a poor return if with all these advantages of tuition I did not profit by them. My association with Dr. Plumptre and a natural tendency in that direction induced me to plunge most ardently into theological studies, and I won without much difficulty the Divinity Scholarship at King's College in 1863. It seems strange now to recall with what avidity I assimilated Jewel, Hooker, and Butler, and burrowed into Tischendorff's "Synoptic Gospels." I was always a very diligent biblical student, and it was this speciality which led to my intimacy with George (afterwards Sir George) Grove, who was at that time Secretary of the Crystal Palace, but who was also busily engaged in editing Smith's "Dictionary of the Bible." A study of Blunt's "Undesigned

Biblical Coincidences" had led me to collect many more coincidences of a similar type, and these were communicated through Plumptre to Grove. I had also with infinite trouble compiled for myself a dictionary of every proper name in the Bible, with a reference to chapter and verse, and so it may be that I was able to give some help to Grove in his great work. I often visited him at Sydenham, and it was through Grove that I got to know Kingsley.

Grove wrote—I may be allowed to quote his words — "You will like Kingsley immensely and I feel sure he will like you." That great man, like myself, suffered from an impediment in his speech, and it was fellow-suffering that brought us together. I went down for a week-end to Eversley and have still in my possession—though it is much mutilated by white ants—a letter from Kingsley on stammering and its cause and cure. Kingsley did not stammer in the pulpit, and I have never stammered when making a speech, but it was in ordinary conversation that we both broke down, especially, as Kingsley said, in speaking to servants.

In those days stammering played such a painful and prominent part in my daily life, and the letter from Kingsley to which I have referred is so interesting, especially to those who suffer from our common infirmity, that I do not think I need make any apology for reproducing it.

"You need not," he wrote—his letter is dated from Eversley on the 24th of October, 1863.—"be the least nervous with us who are accustomed to stammering. The details you give are just what I want. They are singularly like those of my own case. Your stammering seems of that mental kind which has puzzled Hunt and so many. It all depends upon the will of the patient after he has learnt the rules of speech. These you have learned by your success while with Hunt. You have now to examine what changed circumstances, mental and physical, occurred when you left Hunt. For to some change the relapse is plainly due. Did you recur to any unwholesome habits, *e.g.*, giving up exercise and sitting stooping over a table? Did anything upset your nerves? Did you begin reading too hard? Did any mental anxiety overtake you? And so forth. The former would loosen the diaphragm and otherwise weaken the organ, the latter would injure the regular and full flow of nerve force from the brain to the organs—a matter on which we know nothing save that it can happen, just as body and mind react on each other. Sexual excess will do it, and, on the other hand, over-reading or over-hunting will do it, and both for the same reason that the nerves are weakened, probably by defect of phosphorus. Think over these things and let me know all you can tell me. The stammering with servants is curious, very curious. It is my worst trial. Is it in your case from speaking too fast and with an empty lung? Or is it from fear of exposing yourself? You must look into these matters. I believe the best cure is Hunt's: to hold your head up, fill your lungs deeply once or twice, and look the person straight in the face. If you hold your head down, you are done for. Speak slow; I never break down now save from speaking fast."

The Divinity was the only scholarship I won at King's College, but I got the College prizes in History, Literature, and Classics. I had no pretensions to being anything of a scholar; my knowledge of Greek and Latin was most discursive and desultory, and my compositions in prose and verse were full of inaccuracies. I was not unconscious of my deficiencies, and in my endeavour to remedy them I sought, in 1864, the assistance of a private tutor, Orlando Haydon Hyman, who was the most extraordinary man I had ever met. He was, I believe, a nephew—I thought at the time a son—of Benjamin Haydon, the painter who astonished London early in the last century with his gigantic canvases, but who, in spite of the considerable share of genius he undoubtedly possessed, was always a failure and at last perished miserably by his own hand. Orlando, as he said of himself, came from Jericho. When I knew him he was Senior Fellow of Wadham, but he never revisited the University. His frame was gaunt, his face sallow and I fear often unwashed, and his dark hair and beard touzled and grizzled. He was always lying down on a couch, and his room was full of cats, two or three of whom would be lying on the couch with him. He had been Ireland Scholar in his day—his knowledge of the literature of Greece and Rome was wonderful and his memory amazing. He would recite from the minor speeches of Demosthenes as readily as from Homer and Horace. It was his habit to tear out and throw on the floor the pages of a book as fast as he read them. He would read a column of the *Times* and remember *verbatim* all that it contained. He was, indeed, a singular and erratic genius with a light vein of mordant humour but withal overflowing with the milk of human kindness. I think he enjoyed my visits to him, for he used to talk and gossip by the hour and I listened to him with wonderment. It is impossible that I could not have learnt much from him, but he could not make me a scholar, and a scholar I never became.

Powerfully influenced as I was by my teachers and two or three older men with whom I was privileged to associate, I yet owe more to the companions of my own age. It was no ordinary set among whom I was thrown at King's College. There was William Thistleton-Dyer, afterwards the eminent botanist and Director for many years at Kew Gardens. But I only knew him slightly, for his interests were not in the same groove as my own. Among others whom I knew better were Gerardo Acha Ceballos, a gifted young Spaniard, a Basque of the Basques, of whose subsequent career and fate I know nothing, but I am confident if he had lived he would have made a name for himself in Spain ; and Ernest Edouard Naville, the famous savant and Egyptologist, whose sweet disposition was reflected in his grave and kindly countenance, and whose passionate devotion to his studies foretold the distinction he was destined to attain. I have seen him but once since, and though our lives have lain in widely different spheres our old affection poured forth as though there had been nothing to interrupt its course. There was Edward Heath, a man of magnetic attraction and great talents. He took the first place in class and at examinations without an effort. I do not know what has become of him ; his dignified appearance would always have commanded attention, and his abilities would surely have won for him a front position in any career ; but he was as modest and self-retiring as he was able.

There were many others who have won a name and fame for themselves. The late Edmund Widdrington Byrne, afterwards Mr. Justice Byrne, is another whom I never met again, but we were most intimate friends and rivals in many an animated debate. He was always a Conservative and I was always a Liberal, and we led opposite sides in the Debating Society, the war between the North and South in America affording unlimited subject for discussion. It is needless, perhaps, to say that I was on the side of the North. Henry John Hood, now a Registrar in Bankruptcy, of winning and silvery eloquence, and beloved of all. William Kingdon Clifford, the most brilliant of men and mathematicians, and as good, when I knew him, in classics as in mathematics. At that time he was firmly held in the theological stage, and it was believed among us that he wore under his clothes a girdle of iron for a penance, and that he used to scourge himself as a discipline. Be that as it may, he was speedily emancipated. His career at Cambridge and afterwards was meteoric ; but he, too, alas ! died early, and I only saw him once again, when he looked ill and prematurely old, before his lamented death. The late William Henry Corfield, afterwards well known in London as the highest authority on hygiene and public health. Sir Charles James Lyall and Richard Stephen Whiteway, who in those days lived with me like brothers. Lyall, who passed with me into the Indian Civil Service, and was best man at my wedding, was a man of encyclopædic erudition, and after a most distinguished career in India became Judicial Secretary in the India Office. Whiteway followed us into the same Service a year later.

Then there was one whom I have reserved to the last, but who comes first in my mind's eye—Evan Buchanan Baxter, who dazzled us all by his brilliancy and was the idol of his friends. Born at St. Petersburg and bred in the South of Russia, where his father was an official in the Education Department, he was, when he came to King's College, a stranger to England. He was an accomplished linguist, speaking many tongues. Though he knew no Greek when he came over, he won a scholarship at Lincoln College, Oxford, the first time he tried. But after one year of residence his father died, he had to return to Russia, and the whole plan of his career was cancelled. He left Oxford and came back to King's College in the Medical Department. There he won all the scholarships he could get, and finally took his medical degree at London University with the best record of his time, carrying off the gold medals for medicine, midwifery, and general proficiency.

PROFESSOR EVAN BUCHANAN BAXTER, M.D.

From a crayon drawing by John T. Nettleship, 1874.

[To face p. 36.

None of us impressed his contemporaries so deeply and so permanently as Professor Baxter. But it was not his abilities, exceptional though they were, which have left the most lasting memory upon his surviving friends. It was the unrivalled charm of the man, the quivering sensibility reflected in his face and every gesture, his personal sympathy, and affectionate and trustful character. He became an eminent physician and an ideal teacher of medicine, holding for eleven years the chair of Materia Medica and Therapeutics at King's College.

I became an Associate of King's College in 1864, but I lingered on within its walls until it became absolutely necessary to make choice of a profession. It was my own desire to prosecute my career at Oxford. But that was not to be, and it is very doubtful how far I should have succeeded there. My brother James at Winchester was always destined for the University, and my father did not see his way to sending me there as well. He was right : James had all the makings of the scholar he afterwards became : I had none of them. And so it was suddenly decided in the spring of 1865 that I should go up for the Indian Civil Service examination in June. I confess that my own thoughts had never led me in that direction. It is true that we were emphatically an Anglo-Indian family. My great-grandfather had traded in the East ; three times at least he had been to India and China in command of an East Indiaman ; Fate had treated him kindly, and the pagoda-tree had yielded a rich reward. My grandfather had entered the Service long before the days of Haileybury, but my father was a typical Haileybury man. I had uncles and cousins by the dozen who had served in the Indian Civil Service or in the Indian Army. If there was ever a young man saturated with the associations of Old John Company, it was I, and yet I had never looked on the Indian Civil Service as a career. My thoughts were all wrapped up in the pleasure and prospects and ambition of a life at home. But my father, if he was wrong when he wanted to make me a civil engineer, had now become a far better judge of my qualifications and qualities than I was myself. I went up for the examination without any cramming; the only subjects I took up were essay, English history and literature, and Greek and Latin; the general, and somewhat discursive, character of the questions was all in my favour, and I passed well. My friend Lyall, who had just taken a first in Mods, came out top of the list. The following letter from him may well close this chapter :—

CHAPTER III

TWO GOLDEN YEARS

THE two years between my passing in the Indian Civil Service examination and my departure for the East will always stand out as a red-letter period of my life. When I passed I was at the impressionable age of nineteen, and we were subjected to special half-yearly examinations in Indian languages, Indian history and law, and political economy, to test us in the progress we were making to prepare ourselves for our future career. I hope I did not neglect those important studies, but I won no prizes in them and was content to hold the place in the list I had already gained without attempting to improve it. I must plead guilty to the fact that, when I was interviewed by two members of the Civil Service Commission, Sir Edward Ryan and another, after I had passed the last of these examinations, Sir Edward gave me a grave but friendly warning that I should do little credit to myself in India if I did not display more industry there than I had done during the past two years. But indeed those were not wasted years. I was already surrounded by troops of friends who had done much to mould my character, and during those years I made many more.

There was no idea at that time of sending selected candidates to join one of the Universities, and I took chambers in London at No. 8, Featherstone Buildings,

Holborn, in order to be as near as possible to Baxter, who was living with his friends John and Edward Nettleship in the top flat of No. 2, Bedford Row. John Trivett Nettleship was then an articled clerk in a solicitor's office, and did not burst his legal trammels until after I had left for India. But his whole soul was burning with enthusiasm for art and poetry, and with his great conceptions and splendid imagination—a simple and courageous man, strong and gentle, and a true friend if ever there was one—he was assuredly the hero of this period of my life. Time and distance afterwards wrought their work and I saw but little of him in later years, but he stands before me always as the best and most tried of comrades. He attained fame and honour in due course as a great animal painter, but his skill in execution and technique was not equal to his conceptions, and it may be that his ultimate reputation will rest more on his drawings and pastels than on his paintings.

Edward Nettleship, the eminent oculist, who retired all too soon from the practice of his profession, was also my very intimate friend, and through them I made the friendship of their brothers, Henry Nettleship, afterwards Corpus Professor of Latin at Oxford, and Richard Lewis Nettleship of Balliol. It was, indeed, a wonderfully gifted family, and their mother, to whom the sons were devoted, and who settled later on at Oxford, was one of the dearest of old ladies. I was always rather afraid of Henry, for he was a good bit older than myself, and did not encourage confidences ; but Loo, as we called him, who was a little younger than I was, and whose modesty and simplicity of life were only equalled by his profound scholarship, I knew extremely well. He had just won a scholarship at Balliol, and was carrying everything in the University before him. To Balliol he devoted all his powers, and many is the generation of undergraduates who will acknowledge their indebtedness to his influence and teaching. He perished on Mont Blanc, overtaken by a storm and frozen with cold, to the infinite regret of innumerable friends. I know of few more pathetic touches than the record of his last hours in the ice-bound cave of frozen snow, singing old Balliol songs to his guides to cheer their spirits as long as strength and breath remained.

Then there was Arthur O'Shaughnessy, the musical and tender poet of nature and of love. I remember as well as yesterday his expressive face and sensuous charm of manner. The "Epic of Women," with its characteristic illustrations by Jack Nettleship, was the first-fruit of his muse. Most beautiful poem I thought it, but it is his later lyrics that are better known, and it was not till after his premature death that his fine and passionate genius received adequate recognition. He was an assistant in the British Museum, employed on the uncongenial duty of looking after stuffed insects and reptiles. I often visited him there and at home, where he lived with his mother. There was a mystery about his parentage, and we had our ideas on the subject.

Richard Foster Craig was another of my friends who died in his early prime. He was a clerk in the House of Commons and as accomplished with his pencil as with his pen. With him I visited the House once or twice, but I do not remember whose Member's ticket it was that enabled me to be present during one of the debates on the Reform Bill, when I heard Gladstone speak. As it happened, the occasion was one of no particular importance. Then there was Alexander Stuart Murray, of the Department of Greek and Roman Antiquities in the British Museum, a little man of quiet and engaging manner, very Scotch, and with a drooping red moustache. He lived with Baxter and the Nettleships when they moved over to new quarters in Rugby Chambers close by. In this case the employment was congeniality itself, and he became the recognised authority in England on Greek sculpture, terra-cotta, and archæology.

Most of the friends I have mentioned in this and the previous chapter were members of a literary society which used to meet in my rooms at Featherstone Buildings. Many a long evening have we sat and talked and smoked together there. The enthusiasm of youth was behind us, and if to some extent we were a little mutual admiration coterie, who will dare to cast a stone at us? It was there Jack Nettleship read in outline the papers which were afterwards his well-known Essays on Browning's poetry. I do not hesitate to say that if he had devoted himself to literature he would have become one of the best-known writers of the day. It was there Sir Charles Lyall laid the foundation of his learned studies into Persian poetry and Alexander Murray expounded the mysteries and charm of Hellenic art. It was there I limned the ideals of Indian life I afterwards endeavoured to realise. From a list of thirty-eight papers read there which I still have in my possession I find that John Nettleship held forth on the Prayer Spirit, on Courage, on Sordello, and on Saul; Sir Charles Lyall on the Reign of Law, Ali Hazin, and Hafiz; Dr. Murray on Greek Art and Pheidias, the Death of Æschylus, and Greek Painting; Sir Edmund Widdrington Byrne on Cattle Plague, the Beasts that Perish, Cyclos, and Might is Right—a queer agglomeration of subjects which I protest did not do him justice; Professor W. H. Corfield on Volcanoes in Auvergne; Professor Baxter on Quid Vita? and Mazzini; R. S. Whiteway on Dupleix, the Antiquity

SIR HENRY COTTON.

From a photographic study by Julia Margaret Cameron, 1867.

[To face p. 42.

of Man, and Thackeray; Arthur O'Shaughnessy on Art Criticism; Richard Craig on Rabelais, and Landscape Painting in its Relation to Poetry; while I was responsible for essays on such varied topics as Slavery in the United States, with which I appear to have opened the ball at the inauguration of the Society, Our Policy in India, English Poetry, a Day's Mountaineering, Hyder Ali, Religion and Progress, and Marriage.

We all had frugal minds, more perhaps from necessity than choice, and I generally dined for a shilling at Izant's in Holborn, and lunched off rolls and coffee at Button's, an old coffee-house now swept away. Another dining haunt was the Scotch Stores near Oxford Circus, where there was a very favoured tap of ale, and on Sundays we frequented the "Rainbow" or occasionally Simpson's in the Strand.

Like all young men, we were very fond of the theatre. As a boy I had often been to the Princess's, where Mr. and Mrs. Charles Kean were the lessees, and I well remember Kean as Louis XI. and as Wolsey; but in these later days the principal Shakespearean parts were taken by Phelps of Sadler's Wells, Ryder, Fechter, and Kate Terry, and above all, Helen Faucit, whose reappearance as Rosalind and Imogen roused all playgoers of that time to the wildest excitement. I cannot say how many times I went to see Sothern as Lord Dundreary in "Our American Cousin," which was certainly one of the most amusing creations ever placed upon the stage. His David Garrick was also a wonderfully fine piece of acting. Toole and Webster at the Adelphi, Buckstone and Mathews, Compton and Chippendale at the Haymarket, Miss Herbert in her revival of Sheridan and Goldsmith at the St. James's, and Kate Terry, wherever she went and whatever part she took, never failed to attract me as their humble and devoted admirer. The Boucicaults with the "Colleen Bawn" and "Octoroon," the screaming burlesques of Byron and Burnand, the higher class comedies of T. W. Robertson which were just beginning at the Prince of Wales's Theatre with their brilliant galaxy of young actors, John Hare, Squire Bancroft, George Honey, Marie Wilton—these were surely attraction enough to a young playgoer, though there was hardly one theatre then where ten are to be found now. We generally slipped into the pit, where there were not the long *queues* which now wait outside, and paid a shilling for our entertainment. Nor was the gallery of the Opera House altogether unpatronised, and from this coign of vantage I have heard Mario and Grisi; Giuglini, the ill-fated and glorious tenor of a fleeting season; and Titiens and Patti in their prime. Of all my memories of Patti commend me to Dinorah in the shadow dance!

And then when we had a little money in our pockets we used to drop in together for supper at Evans's in Covent Garden, and met with many a jovial welcome from Paddy Green. There was no charge for admission, and if there was rather a fancy price to pay for supper, it was well worth it, and the hot, mealy potatoes crushed from their skins into your plate by the napkin-handed waiter were the dream of a *gourmet*. It was said that the singing boys at Evans's were choristers from the Pro-Cathedral, but whoever they were they sang divinely, and "Integer Vitæ," "Ma Charmante Gabrielle," and glees and madrigals in profusion poured forth to our vast delight from their young throats. I speak of Evans's only as I knew it for two years, and confidently assert that never was a vestige of impropriety allowed, and no women were admitted within its cellar walls. I met there Artemus Ward and Home, the spiritualist, and I remember that Jack Nettleship surreptitiously sketched them both. Artemus Ward joined the staff of *Punch* and gave lectures at the Egyptian Hall, but he was no particular success in either capacity. Home once told me that he was sure I possessed remarkable mediumistic faculties, an observation which alone proved him to be a humbug if nothing else ever did.

In 1863, two years before the period of which I am now writing, I paid my first visit to Switzerland. I had gone up to spend a few days with the Aclands at Oxford, when I met Dr. Millard, who had always been very kind to me since I left his school, and he asked me if I would go for a walking tour with him and his brother in the Alps. The idea, of course, took my fancy immensely ; my father consented, and I went off with them about the middle of July in that year. Dr. Millard and his brother, the Rev. Frederick Maule Millard, also a Fellow of Magdalen, were both of them climbers and members of the Alpine Club, an institution which was then in its infancy. I was a mere lad not yet eighteen, with no experience of mountaineering, but they took the risk of my going with them with as little hesitation as I did.

Switzerland possessed then a charm and a romance which it has now largely lost. There were no palatial hotels at any of our mountaineering haunts ; the Bär and Adler at Grindelwald and old Seiler's Mont Cervin and Monte Rosa at Zermatt were little more than châlets ; no railways and no *funiculaires* had penetrated into those sacred preserves. The Swiss Alpine Club had built no comfortable and furnished huts for the accommodation of the luxurious tourist. There were no ropes or chains or ladders to help you over a troublesome piece of rock. We rejoiced to sleep in the open, *sub Jove frigido*, and thought ourselves lucky to put up in a cow-loft. Our hotel expenses would not be more than five francs a day per head, and we had no luggage other than our knapsacks. Chamois were then quite common, and it was a beautiful sight to see them sailing along over the snow slopes. So were chamois hunters, delightfully rugged fellows with great crampons on their heels, and I remember gratefully how two or three of them came clattering down the rocks on one occasion to rescue us from an uncomfortable corner on which we had found ourselves on the Clariden Grat. They had stowed away their dinner in their caps—a gruesome sight—and were quite pleased with the franc apiece we gave them as *bakhshish*.

We did plenty of climbing on this tour, beginning with the little Sentis as a breather and ending up with Mont Blanc on the 15th of August. That was the most cloudless day I have ever known in the Alps, and we were an hour and a half on the summit, with an uninterrupted view in every direction. The enthusiastic folk of Chamounix turned out *en masse* on our return, firing salutes, cheering, and loading me with flowers, as I was supposed to be the youngest climber who had then made the ascent.

Among other trips we made the attempt to climb the Galenstock without guides, and I had a narrow escape from an accident when I fell some three hundred feet down a steep *arête* and, bounding over a *bergschrund*, carried my companions, who were standing at its jaws to save my tumbling into it, down a further slope. The Millards had preceded me without mishap, and when they called on me to glissade as they had done, I, who had not learnt that art, accomplished this catherine-wheel performance. All the breath was knocked out of Dr. Millard's body, and my nose was bleeding and the palms of my hands were burnt from friction with the snow, but no real damage was done, and we were little heroes at the Furca Inn that evening. Another minor incident which might have been an accident occurred as we were coming down the Breithorn, when there was, I think, the most tremendous thunderstorm I have experienced. The claps were continuous, re-echoing from bluff to bluff, snow was falling, and clouds surrounded us. We were roped together, and one slipped and we all came down with a run, but the guide—Moritz Andermatten was his name—managed to stop us just in time.

It was inevitable that I should seek the first opportunity of going to Switzerland again, and I did so in 1866 with Jack Nettleship and Charles Lyall as my companions. Jack and I were determined to leave no stone unturned to make ourselves fit for real work at once, and went into training with a vengeance. In the early mornings we used to walk the streets barefooted to harden our feet, and often have I pounded round Regent's Park like a tramp with shoes and stockings under my arm. We both made ourselves pretty fit, and so it was that two or three days before we started I walked over from Clifton to Weston-super-Mare and back, with a heavy knapsack on my shoulders, while Jack walked from London to Brighton on the same day. Lyall was so strong that he had really no need to train at all. We began this tour with the Titlis, and then made the Oberland our headquarters, having the good luck to pick up Christian Almer as our guide for the season. That wonderful guide was then at the zenith of his powers, and his son Ulrich, a lad of fifteen, who afterwards rivalled his father's reputation, accompanied us on some excursions to learn his work. We did many famous peaks and passes, including the fourth ascent of the Schreckhorn, which had first been climbed by that intrepid mountaineer, Leslie Stephen, some five years before. I bathed in the lake at the Grimsel, and my recollection is that most persons will find that cold enough, but I capped that experience by a swim in the Märjelen See at the Eggischhorn, and by playing among its icebergs.

At the Eggischhorn we came across William Henry Gladstone and Charles Stuart Parker, and I did some very good climbing with them. They were my companions when I made the ascent of the Aletschhorn and back in one day from the Eggischhorn hotel. This is a good test of endurance, and it was the first time it had been done. Old Wellig, who was the landlord of the hotel, gave me a fine ice-axe in memory of the day. It served me well in my time, and afterwards reposed in Nettleship's studio. Gladstone used to talk in the most delightfully unassuming way about his father and John Stuart Mill and others of the Olympian gods whose names I worshipped. He was then a vigorous, well-built man, and jumped across crevasses with a degree of confidence and activity which we did not all possess. In later days, in conversation with his father, when I mentioned this qualification the great statesman replied, "I could jump better than William, but he beat me at running." C. S. Parker was a Don of University College, and a typical Don too: he was afterwards for many years Member for Perth, and became a Member of the Privy Council. I connect the Eggischhorn also with the Rev. Newman Hall and his wife. The former had made the ascent of that simple peak, but was involved in difficulties coming down, when I came to his rescue, and he declared that I had saved his life.

But my most memorable day in the Alps was undoubtedly the 1st of September, 1866, when Jack Nettleship and I climbed the Mettenberg without guides. It was the experience of that day which formed the subject of the paper on "Mountaineering" which I read before the Featherstone Society. It was raining and stormy when we started at daybreak, and both Christian Almer and Melchior Anderegg protested against our folly. Of course we were fools not to follow their advice, but on we went, and when we had passed the little Stieregg Châlet and were on the slopes of the mountain we were wrapped in impenetrable mist and heavy falling snow which did not leave us for hours, and I know not how many breakneck dangers we incurred and how narrowly we escaped. For a long time we could see nothing, and were clinging and climbing with infinitesimal foothold on slippery rocks, springing across waterfalls which seemed to fall from nowhere to nowhere, and worming our way in through *cheminées* and round cul-de-sacs, along the narrowest of ledges, and flattened on the mountain-side, but continually ascending. At last when the weather cleared up a bit and we could see the summit, it was so late in the day that we knew we could not get there, and so had no alternative but to go back, and that fortunately we were able to do by a much easier route than that by which we had ascended. We were a dead failure; but we did not think so, and we bore the reproaches of good old Almer and our friend Lyall with equanimity.

It will be noticed that my two experiences of mountaineering without guides were neither of them without adventure, and that in neither of them did we succeed in getting to the top. I do not, therefore, advise others, unless they are far better and wiser climbers than we were, to venture on similar risks; but unless they do so I can confidently say that they will not share in the exhilaration of the supreme and golden hours that linger longest in memories of the Alps.

On my return to England I was elected in due

course a member of the Alpine Club, and at times I have regretted that I resigned its membership when I left for India. But my mountaineering days were over, for I never found leisure or opportunity for climbing in the Himalayas. Sir Leslie Stephen was then the President, and my admiration for him, with his splendid record and delightful sense of humour, was unlimited. The secretaries were Hereford George of New College, always willing to hold out the hand of fellowship to a young member; and A. W. Moore of the India Office, who attained distinction in the Political Department and whose premature death was a sad blow to his many friends. I highly appreciated the compliment when I was invited as a guest to the Jubilee Banquet of the Club in 1907, which I thoroughly enjoyed, and where I had the pleasure of meeting again old Alpine veterans whom I had not seen for years.

I suppose it must have been due to the fact that my mind was still unsettled about India, or at least that there was still an imperfect realisation on my part that I had definitely embarked on an Indian career, that at this period I allowed myself to nibble at scientific studies in which I had never previously taken the smallest interest. In addition to attending certain medical lectures at King's College such as those of Rymer Jones—who was stone deaf—on Materia Medica, I attended a long course of lectures by Professor Huxley on Comparative Physiology which he delivered during the autumn of 1866 at the School of Mines in Jermyn Street. There were forty-five lectures in all, and I have my notes of all of them. That was labour lost, but I have the most vivid recollection of Huxley as a lecturer. He would begin with absolute punctuality by the clock, speaking with amazing fluency and clearness, never hesitating for a word and never repeating himself, and would wind up with equal punctuality exactly at the expiration of the hour. His skill with the chalk and blackboard, suiting the action to the word, was almost as remarkable as the lecture itself. He was certainly the most wonderful lecturer at whose feet I ever sat. I felt that I was listening to a great man. At the conclusion of this course, which would have placed me on the lines of being a scientist if anything could, I had no longer any doubt that I had no more taste for science than for engineering.

At the same time, I was not idle in other directions. The British Museum was close at hand, and there I spent hours in study. I read at home. I may claim to have known my Tennyson and Browning, Swinburne and Morris—all at least that they had written up to the time of my leaving for India—as well as any other man of my age. My ideas on India were being largely based on John Malcolm Ludlow's "British India: its Races and its History" and "Thoughts on the Policy of the Crown towards India." Those books, written at the end of the fifties, were far in advance of any contemporary writings on the subject, and it is a pleasant duty to acknowledge my indebtedness to their author, whose ninety years have not obliterated his sympathetic and liberal instincts. A book that produced a profound impression on me was Buckle's "History of Civilisation," and from that I passed through the medium of Mill's essays in the *Westminster Review*, afterwards separately republished, to the "General View" and "Catechism" of Auguste Comte.

In this course of reading I collaborated with Baxter, and together we attended the lectures on Positivism which were given by Dr. Richard Congreve at Bouverie Street, Strand, in the spring of 1867. Assembled there together was a very small but noteworthy audience, including George Eliot, George Henry Lewes, Cotter Morison, Godfrey and Vernon Lushington, Frederic Harrison, Edward Spencer Beesly, and John Henry Bridges. In later years I came to know most of these very well, and Dr. Congreve was destined to exercise a lasting influence over me through a constant and regular correspondence extending over nearly thirty years. But at that time we listened only and did not venture to obtrude ourselves. I can only say that Comte's writings produced on our receptive minds something of the effect that Chapman's Homer wrought on Keats :—

> "Then felt I like some watcher of the skies
> When a new planet swims into his ken;
> Or like stout Cortez when with eagle eyes
> He stared at the Pacific—and all his men
> Look'd at each other with a wild surmise—
> Silent, upon a peak in Darien."

As my days in England drew to a close, I made other friends, and it came to pass that the whole current of my life was turned into another channel. I was brought into close connection with the Camerons of Freshwater and the Prinseps of Little Holland House. Mrs. Cameron and Mrs. Prinsep were two of a large family of sisters, daughters of James Pattle of the Bengal Revenue Board, who went out to India as long ago as 1790. The former met and married in Calcutta Charles Hay Cameron, then Legal Member of Council, who was associated with Macaulay in the preparation of the Indian Penal Code and survived until the close of the nineteenth century as the last of Bentham's personal disciples. The latter married Henry Thoby Prinsep of the Indian Civil Service, also a Member of Council and afterwards for a quarter of a century a Director of the Honourable East India Company, and a Member of the Secretary of State's Council of India. Mr. Prinsep when I knew him was a grand old man, and a very storehouse of Indian knowledge, from whose lips I learned at first hand of the mysteries of the Patni Sale Regulation of 1819, which he had himself been mainly instrumental in passing into law. Mr. Cameron, with his beautiful white hair and flowing beard, was one of the most distinguished-looking men I ever met. His words were always wise, and I loved to listen to his conversation of days long gone by.

Julia Margaret Cameron, as she liked to subscribe herself in fine, bold characters, was a remarkable woman. Visitors were attracted to her hospitable home at Freshwater no less by her own talents than by the reputation of her venerable husband. She was well known for her bold innovations in the art of photography. The intrinsic merit of her pictures appealed to the public taste as much as the interest associated with their subjects. The Poet Laureate and Sir Henry Taylor were among the earliest of her successes, and after these came portraits of Browning, Carlyle, Darwin, Sir John Herschel, Herr Joachim, and others distinguished for intellectual gifts or personal graces. In due course she produced a series, quite unique in their suggestiveness, of heads and groups and of imaginative representations of individual personages in literature and history. After a daring fashion of her own she forfeited the sharpness of outline which ordinary photographers strive for, by placing her sitter far out of focus and subjecting the plate to an unusually long exposure ; but the secret of her genius, the study of pose and feature and artistic arrangement of drapery and subject, has not been transmitted to her imitators or successors. Colnaghi's Gallery was the recognised place of exhibition for her pictures season after season. Mrs. Cameron's singular ardour of enthusiasm, the energy with which she flung herself into whatever she undertook, her forgetfulness of self and readiness to help others, her rare warmth of heart, expansiveness of sympathy, and old-fashioned directness of expression, endeared her to all who came in contact with her. There are few of her friends who do not possess some memorial of her in the products of her art, which she was wont to distribute with characteristic and lavish generosity. The railway-station waiting-rooms of Lymington and Brockenhurst still are—or at least were till lately—decorated by her pictures which grace their walls. In later life she went, accompanied by her husband, to Ceylon, where as a young man Mr. Cameron had himself been employed in the reorganisation of the public service, and there they both died.

Sarah Prinsep was endowed in large measure with all the charms and attributes of character of her accomplished sister. A more kindly and sympathetic soul, a more motherly woman, I never met. Her home at Little Holland House—long ago pulled down and built over—one of the most lovely of London residences, with its frescoed walls adorned with the handiwork of George Frederick Watts, and beautiful gardens, was then the centre of an artistic circle to which I was privileged to have access. I only know Watts, "Il Signor," as he was reverentially called, very slightly. But it was within those walls when she was staying there with Mrs. Cameron, that I wooed and won the fairest of fair young girls who became my wife on the 1st of August, 1867, and who has since been my devoted companion and helpmate for better and for worse through many years of vicissitudes and successes, sorrows and aspirations, clouds and sunshine. A halo of tender affection

LADY COTTON.

From a photographic study by Julia Margaret Cameron, 1867.

hangs in my memory over Dimbola Lodge in Freshwater Bay and the quiet village church where we were married, over Little Holland House, and every link and association of all the hours of happiness which must always be inseparable in my mind from the names of Cameron and Prinsep.

It was at this time that I met Tennyson and others of Mrs. Cameron's friends. Hallam and Lionel were then boys who had not gone to school. They were present at our wedding, for which the Laureate lent us his carriage to drive over to Yarmouth. I met Lionel, in failing health, many years later in India, which he was visiting with his wife, and it gladdened him to talk of Freshwater and Farringford and Alum Bay. Of the great poet I can only say "*Vidi tantum*," and my recollections of him are of the ordinary type, with his great cloak and deep gruff voice and volumes of tobacco smoke in his den at the top of the house. He welcomed me cordially when I was at home a few years later, but I was rather taken aback by the "Well, and how do you like India?" which was his first utterance and not lacking either in depth or gruffness. *Ore rotundo* he used to read and recite his own poetry, and those who were privileged to hear him can never forget the effect he produced. His wife was a sad invalid at this period.

Sir Henry Taylor, who lived a great deal at Bournemouth for his asthma, was perhaps Mrs. Cameron's greatest friend; there was certainly no one whom she admired more, and he was known in the household as Philip, with reference to his greatest and best known dramatic creation "Philip van Artevelde." His figure was a singularly striking one, and his grand countenance and majestic beard lent themselves in a very marked measure to the illustration of Mrs. Cameron's art. Some of the set groups of Sir

Henry Taylor and my young wife, such as "Esther and Ahasuerus," were among the happiest of her successes. "'God speed thee well' used to be said by the clerk in the village churches in the north in my youth on such occasions, and it is what I say with all my heart." That was the message he sent to us on our marriage.

William Allingham, too—the Boswell of Tennyson, though he did not write his Life, and something more, for he was no mean poet in himself—I often used to meet at this time. He was unmarried then and lived at Lymington, where he showed us many attentions. Robert Browning I did not know personally; his intimacy with Jack Nettleship, based on Nettleship's famous essays, had not then begun, and I only met him later in life at Society functions, where he was usually surrounded by a bevy of fair admirers. Carlyle I never met to speak to, but I travelled with him more than once in an omnibus, and had the satisfaction of paying him the respect I owed to the author of "Hero-Worship."

The days of my youth had now passed, and it was a sharp and somewhat jarring contrast when I was suddenly plunged into the isolation and monotony of Indian official life. In those days at least there was a disillusionment about India which it was necessary to live through. But how quickly did this feeling disappear and how rapidly did all one's interest become absorbed in that country and in the welfare of her people! To India the whole of my mature life has been devoted, and when I retired, after thirty-five years of official service, I did so with the profoundest regret, for I owe a debt to India I can never repay. But still my memory loves to linger on the joyous hours of my early manhood, and I can well apply to them and to Jack Nettleship and all the other friends of youth the stirring words

ESTHER AND AHASUERUS. (PORTRAITS OF SIR HENRY TAYLOR AND LADY COTTON.)

From a photographic study by Julia Margaret Cameron, 1867.

GEORGE FREDERICK WATTS, R.A.

From a photographic study by Julia Margaret Cameron, 1866.

[To face p. 56.

he inscribed to me on the fly-leaf of my copy of his "Essays on Browning":—

"To my friend; in the memory of whose communion with me for two golden years,

"The doubtful years untried
Seem fair to us and fortunate
In spite of death, in spite of fate."

CHAPTER IV

INDIA AT LAST

OF our voyage to India there is little to be said. We picked up the steamer at Marseilles, having stopped in Paris for a few days to visit the Great Exhibition of 1867. A further train journey awaited us in Egypt, from Alexandria to Cairo, and again from Cairo to Suez. The Suez Canal was not then open, and indeed was not used by the P. & O. Company for mail traffic until some years after the occupation of Egypt in 1882. Cairo, where we stayed at the rather rickety old Shepheard's Hotel, was our first real glimpse of the East. There we visited the splendid mosque, and heard for the first time the Muezzin's sonorous call to prayer. We had time and enough to see the sights, for we were detained nearly a week, pending the arrival of a connecting steamer at Suez. The P. & O. boats then were very unlike the comfortable floating hotels they have since become. The old *Pera* and *Mongolia* did very well when they made their nine knots an hour. We carried all our live-stock on board, and not for one moment could we escape the noise and smells of the cattle-pens and hen-coops. The luxurious smoking-room of the present day was conspicuous by its absence, and the hottest part of the deck, where little demons with scarlet cummerbunds and puggeries ran about with small balls of fire, was the portion of the ship set aside for smokers' use. Wine bills troubled us not ; beer and wine, with the one exception of champagne, were *compris*. Ice, however, was unknown, though ices were handed round as a treat on Sundays.

We made a long stay at Aden, giving us plenty of time to go on shore as well as to watch the diving boys, and our next halt was at Point de Galle in Ceylon, for Colombo was not then a port of call. The glimpse we caught of the cinnamon gardens seemed to us the most beautiful vision we had ever seen. Coming up the Bay of Bengal, we ran down a country brig full of Mecca pilgrims, but happily the crew and passengers were saved and brought on by us to Calcutta. We left London on the 23rd of September, 1867, and the pilot boarded us at the Sandheads in the mouth of the Hooghly on the 29th of October. This was the date on which under the rules then in force my Indian service began, and we counted it an auspicious omen, for it was also my wife's birthday.

We landed in Calcutta on the next day ; but landing was by no means the simple arrangement it now is. There were no jetties in '67, and we were ignominiously carried on shore on the backs of coolies who waded through soft and most disgusting mud. We had no friends to meet us, and our first experience was to find that the only two hotels then in Calcutta—Wilson's (now the Great Eastern) and Spence's—were full to overflowing. It was after much delay and only through the kindness of one of our fellow-passengers, who was able to vacate his rooms and stay with a friend, that we got shelter at all at Wilson's. This was not a good start, but we had reason to be thankful.

Our arrival in Calcutta was signalised by a tremendous and continuous downpour of rain, which on the night of the 1st of November culminated in one of the most terrific cyclones on record. No such storm has raged in Calcutta since, though, three years before, on the 4th of October, 1864, there was a gale quite as violent and much more destructive to life and property, inasmuch as it was accompanied by a tidal wave which flooded the country and carried away entire villages. On this occasion we were spared the tidal wave, but the force of the wind was appalling, and great damage was done. Big trees were torn up by the roots, and the wretched dwellings of the poor were levelled to the ground. In the crowded suburb of Alipore, which surrounds the Lieutenant-Governor's residence, not a hut remained standing. The spacious Maidan, when we arose next morning, was strewn with dead crows and fallen trees. We were safe in a well-built hotel, but the noise and fury of the storm all night were beyond description. The massive shutters, known as *jhilmils*, banged and clattered outside the windows until they were blown bodily away and fell with a crash into the street. The windows were bursting open, and I was up all night barricading them with our trunks and boxes. It was, too, the opening night of the Opera Season in Calcutta, and there were direful tales of horses and carriages blown over, and of men and women in their finery crawling on hands and knees through the blinding rain and tempest. I have had experience in other parts of the country of two more cyclones of a similar nature, but it may be imagined that the shock of this storm on the first night after our arrival stands in my memory as the worst. It seemed a strange and terrible land that we had come to, and it so happens that from time to time in India my wife and I have borne our full share of the cataclysms of Nature—earthquakes and floods and storms. But of these in their place.

We were, as I have said, friendless in Calcutta. For nearly a month we lived at first in the hotel and later in Mrs. Box's boarding-house. At last a Member of Council arrived from Simla, Mr. Noble Taylor, who had been a friend of my father's in Madras, and to whom I had a letter of introduction. He invited us to stay with him for a few days at his house in Elysium Row. Two other Members of Council were chumming with him, bachelor fashion, Henry Sumner Maine and William Nathaniel Massey.

Sir H. S. Maine, one of the greatest jurists of his day, whose treatise on Ancient Law I had been studying as a text-book at home, was Legal Member of Council for no less than seven years, but, despite the mass of legislation for which he was responsible, and the admirable minutes and University speeches he placed on record, he has left a smaller reputation behind him in India than many lesser men. His manners were dry and unsympathetic, and I do not remember that we ever received a word of encouragement or welcome from him.

There was more of human nature about Massey, who had been for a short time M.P. for Tiverton, and who had come out to India as Financial Member in succession to Sir Charles Trevelyan. But he was never very happy at his work, and had the reputation of doing no more of it than he could help. Stories, more or less amusing, were current about him, of which I give one. His Assistant Secretary was R. H. Hollingberry, an excellent official but addicted to writing portentously long notes. The question of a gold currency—started, by the way, by Sir William Mansfield, at this time Commander-in-Chief—was on the *tapis*. Old Hollingberry sent up a memorandum of about a hundred pages on the subject, concluding with the modest hope that the Honourable Member would read it, and that it might be of help to him. On which Mr. Massey minuted: "Certainly not! If Mr. H. can summarise what he has to say in three or four pages, I will consider it."

The third of the party, our host, Mr. Noble Taylor, was a civilian whom I remember only as being somewhat pompous and official in manner. Probably he was not more so than other Calcutta big-wigs, but that was the impression he left on us. He was being trounced at the time in all the newspapers for a habit of conveying his daughter's pony between Simla and Calcutta at the public expense, and the cost of a single journey was said to be more than the value of the pony. Such was the gossip of the hour which I recall during this month of waiting. Certain it is that we carried away with us no particularly pleasant memories of this house of Honourable Councillors, who were none of them inclined to take any interest in a young and unknown couple on the threshold of official life. We were uncommonly glad when marching orders—for some reason or other unduly delayed—arrived, posting us to Midnapore.

CHAPTER V.

THE INFLUENCES OF THE SIXTIES

IT is hardly necessary to say that the India of the sixties was very different from the India of to-day. The surroundings were different, the associations were of another character. The Father of the Bengal Civil Service when I went out was Sir Donald Macleod, then Lieutenant-Governor of the Punjab, who had arrived in India in 1828, while one of its oldest members was Arthur Grote, brother of the great historian. Many changes had occurred since they had started on their careers in the days of Lord William Bentinck. The Sikhs had been subdued after a fierce struggle, great provinces like the Punjab, Oudh, and Lower Burma had been annexed, the momentous rule of Lord Dalhousie and its consequences had come and gone, the Mutiny with its horrors and stern repression, the transfer of the administration from the Company to the Crown—these were memorable vicissitudes, but such changes are not comparable to those which have taken place during the forty years since those old veterans retired. There was no change during the long period of their service in the relations between the rulers and the ruled. There was no change in those relations during the earlier days of my own service.

The old spirit still brooded over the surface of the country: New India was in the womb of the future. There was no awakening of the East, no sense of growing nationalism among the races and communities : still smouldering were the hopes and aspirations of a later age. The seed had, indeed, been sown by the efforts of men like David Hare, by the teaching of the early missionaries, among whom Dr. Duff was pre-eminent, by the educational policy of Macaulay, by the educational dispatch of the Board of Directors in 1854, which was drafted by Mill, by the establishment of Universities in 1857, and, above all, by the Magna Charta of the Queen's Proclamation of 1858 ; but there were then no signs of a harvest.

The men of my time were the inheritors of the old ways and old traditions. Sir John Lawrence was the Governor-General. His grey moustache and rugged features and rough-and-ready manner are not easily to be blotted from remembrance. I had come out to India with an immense admiration for his vast services to the country, and that admiration I have never lost. He was one of the greatest of Viceroys, and I do not willingly say anything in derogation of his fame. Yet it is the plain truth that he was not free from the faults and failings of his generation. He was a strong man, but he was vulnerable. He came from the Punjab, an older man than Nicholson, who was his subordinate. These men had been trained in a hard school, and they meted out summary justice with an iron hand. *Sic volo sic jubeo, sit pro ratione voluntas*. That was their motto, and they acted on it to the uttermost.

The Punjab influence has never been a good one when extended to other provinces, and frontier methods have always been a source of danger in their facile application to general use. The cult of Nicholson had become a fetish. How many stories were we not told of the exploits of these heroes of India with stick and whip! I remember one circumstantial story, which was in free circulation, that young fellows at Lahore used to hang about the door of the church which John Lawrence frequented, because they knew that on some pretext or other the Chief Commissioner would be sure to hammer his syce (or groom) before driving home, and they wanted to see the fun. It was public property that as Governor-General he was not exempt from the old vice. And if these things were done in the green tree, what would be done in the dry?

I am bound to say that this pernicious practice of striking natives, and especially domestic servants, prevailed as a common and general habit during the whole of my residence in India. I believe and trust that it is far less common now. It was much less common at the close of my service than it was in the early days. But it was always a gross and flagrant evil. I remember once when I was walking through the streets of an up-country city with a high official, and a few miserable petitioners blocked the way by throwing themselves prostrate before him and endeavouring to clasp his feet, he struck them right and left with his stick, and thought nothing of it. On another occasion when I had ventured to remonstrate with a distinguished officer for striking a lazy or careless gardener, I was met with the reply that there was no harm in it, and that everybody did it. When I retorted that I did not, I was told that I was the only man he had ever met who could say that. These are not reminiscences on which I love to dwell, but they serve to illustrate how subtle and unconscious is the poison of demoralisation in Anglo-Indian life.

Ten years had elapsed since the Mutiny, but the Mutiny was, in the early days of my service, a living memory in the minds of all. That memory was not a benign influence on the future career of the young civilian. When I first arrived in the country, it was duly enjoined on me as a matter of vital importance that I should insist on all the outward and visible signs of deference and respect which Orientals with a leaning to sycophancy, resulting from generations of subjection and foreign rule, are only too willing to accord. Although I was a very *chota* (small) sahib, and posted only to the humble office of Assistant to the Magistrate and Collector of a district, I was early taught that, though I might be but a fly on the wheel of the official hierarchy, I was, in the eyes of the people among whom I lived, a representative of the Government and entitled as such to rights and privileges on no account to be foregone.

Such was the atmosphere in which we lived; we were directly encouraged to assume an attitude of a patronising and superior character, which was obviously inimical to the best influences which should be exercised in the service of the State. The old Haileybury tone still pervaded the Civil Service, and the new class of competitioners to which I belonged and who had their spurs to win were easily attracted into the prevailing current. Nor was there any deterrent from the Indian side; nothing could exceed the obsequious and cringing demeanour of the old class of Indians, especially those about the Law Courts, with whom mostly we were brought into immediate contact. It was, in fact, a demoralising environment into which we were thrown, and I am not ashamed to say that I succumbed to it.

CHAPTER VI

MY FIRST STATION

In 1867 there were only 3,000 miles of railway in India. In 1910 there were over 32,000 miles. This expansion of the railway system has revolutionised the country by itself. There were then several hundreds of miles wanting to complete the communication between Calcutta and Bombay. The only railways in Bengal were the trunk system of the East Indian Railway and the Eastern Bengal Railway, which had its terminus at Kushtea.

There was no railway to Midnapore. The only way of going there was by budgerow or country boat as far as Uluberia, and from that point by palanquin journey of about twelve hours. The palanquin or palki bearers were a wonderful service, and performed prodigies of endurance. With swinging and rapid gait and a weird sing-song intonation, varying from a high to a low cadence, in the stillness of the night, some carrying flaming torches, and others with baggage poised on a bamboo slung across one shoulder, they made their way along in a manner which, if it became tedious on repetition, was to young folk who experienced it for the first time full of excitement and romance. That was the common method of progression in those days, and even in Calcutta every one went about in a palanquin who could not afford to keep a trap.

On arrival we were met with the most cordial of receptions from our Magistrate and Collector, my immediate official superior, William James (now Sir William) Herschel, son of one of the greatest of astronomers and grandson of another. He invited us to stay with him, and his house was our home. We can never forget the kindness he showed us, and he has always been one of our truest friends. His warm-hearted welcome soon blotted out the rather discouraging impressions of Indian life we had brought with us from Calcutta. He was a fine-looking man, clean-shaven then, in the prime of life and full of decision and character. He had earned a high reputation as Magistrate of Nuddea during the indigo troubles. Although he remained at Midnapore only for a short time after we joined, he exercised a powerful influence over me, for I had the greatest regard for him, and have always thought myself very fortunate to have started my career under his guidance. I have often observed how much the life of a young Assistant is moulded by the first Magistrate under whom he serves. It is far more important for an Assistant to be posted under a good Magistrate than it is to get a good climate, or what is called a good District.

At this time, and for many years previously, Sir William Herschel was actively engaged in working up the system of identification by finger-prints. Acting on purely empirical lines, he lost no opportunity of experiment, and my own thumb impressions were taken by him often enough forty-three years ago. He urged it upon the Government, being convinced of its value, but the idea was not accepted. It was not until 1892 that any official trial was given to the system. I was then Chief Secretary under Sir Charles Elliott, and it was on Herschel's suggestion from England that I placed myself in communication with Mr. Henry and Mr. Holmwood, who were respectively at the head of the Police and Registration Departments in Bengal. Sir Francis Galton's book on Finger Prints, which I had received from Herschel, was placed in their hands, and their energy and co-operation, with the aid of Galton's methods, ensured for the system an immediate and brilliant success. Its subsequent development is due to Mr. (now Sir Edward) Henry, the present Commissioner of Police in London. But to Herschel must undoubtedly be accorded the credit of being the first to grasp the truth that finger-prints afford an irresistible proof of identity, the perception of the simplicity with which they can be brought to bear on fraud, and the conviction of their enormous efficacy in the cause of justice. It was Sir William Herschel who initiated the system, Sir Francis Galton who placed it on a scientific basis, and Sir Edward Henry who has organised its use in a practical manner which is now universally recognised as the most decisive and certain method of identification.

The district of Midnapore adjoins the Province of Orissa, which in 1867 was slowly recovering from the effects of the terrible famine of 1866. That famine had found the Government unprepared. There was no famine code then, and the signals of warning and methods of famine administration which are now in use had not been devised. It came on the authorities like a thief in the night, and I remember how one of the local Magistrates told me that his first knowledge of the existence of distress was when he found an old woman in his bathroom eating his soap. The famine was severely felt also in Midnapore, through which runs the main trunk road to Orissa. Railways and steamers have now transformed the conditions of communication, but at the time of which I write all the pilgrims to Juggernauth into the number of cattle-hides which were exported still to be witnessed the ghastly spectacle of unburied skeletons. It was a common practice for pilgrims to measure their length on this road as an act of penance or expiation, and I have seen scores and scores of them lying down, rising erect, lying down again, and so wearily and painfully crawling along on their way to the holy shrine. Devotees have been known to spend months and even years on this measured progress from their distant homes to Pooree. I have seen them thus even in Calcutta by the side of the "Red Road," along which the beauty and fashion of the city were disporting themselves on their evening drive.

On the transfer of Sir William Herschel from the district he was succeeded by Herbert Reynolds, who, with his wife—a bright and kindly body if ever there was one—have also remained from that time to this among our best and dearest friends. Reynolds had passed into the Civil Service with distinction in the first year of competitive examinations. He was Newcastle medallist at Eton and a brilliant scholar at Cambridge, and though by taste and temperament he had none of the active qualifications which are required to make a good district officer, his natural abilities were so great that he easily supplemented those deficiencies, and was, in fact, one of the most efficient and resourceful Magistrates I have ever known. But it was not until he was drafted a few years later on into the Secretariat that he found full scope for his powers, and when he once got to Calcutta no subsequent Lieutenant-Governor could ever spare his services from the headquarters of the Government.

Under Reynolds I learned my work rapidly and thoroughly. For more than a year I was in charge of the Treasury, an admirable training from which I profited much. I was occasionally placed in charge of the District jail, which at that time had not been delegated to the executive control of a medical officer; I had my share of duty on municipal and educational committees, and all kinds of miscellaneous revenue work and correspondence were entrusted to me. As officer in charge of the jail I had to superintend executions, a function which ought not to have been imposed on an officer so young as I was. I have a horrible recollection of a case in which the rope broke, and the unfortunate victim was hanged a second time. All the while I was at Midnapore I was also taking up criminal cases on a small scale and, after I had gained a little experience, rent cases, which were still tried under Act X. of 1859 by revenue officers and had not been transferred to the Civil Courts.

I was never a good linguist, but I learned to speak Bengalee fluently and Hindustani colloquially, and could write and read the Bengalee and Persian characters with facility. It was much easier to learn the vernacular languages then than it is now. All the ordinary work of the office was done in the vernacular; very few of the clerks knew English, and the pleadings in court were always in Bengalee. Nowadays all this is changed: an English-speaking class of court officials has come into existence; the pleaders or *mukhtars,* who knew no English in my day, now all plead in that language, and the young civilian is no longer compelled, as it were, to think and speak in the vernacular if he is to transact any business at all. For my part, when I was in charge of a Subdivision a year or two later I did the whole of my office work in Bengalee except correspondence, and for weeks and months together spoke no other language while in office.

Even at this time I sought, as far as it was possible

for me to do so, the company and society of educated members of the Indian community, and I made many friends among them. In particular I recall the name of Baboo Ram Okhoy Chatterjea, a Deputy Magistrate, who, I believe, is still living in extreme old age at Benares, the Holy City, to which pious Hindoos retire in their declining years. He was a Brahmin of high caste belonging to a race of learned Pundits, and he had taught himself English in middle age. From his lips I learned much, not only of office work, but of the religious life of the people and of social and domestic customs. I well remember the impression created on my mind when, walking out with him, the Hindoos whom we met would accost me with the respectful gesture they will always accord to official rank, while they would prostrate themselves and rub their foreheads in the dust before my companion. To him they rendered a genuine obeisance ; to me they showed a sign of artificial respect only. The sense of official relationship was entirely swallowed up by the stronger feeling of social subordination. I was permitted to attend the services of the Brahmo Samaj and have been a witness there of the remarkable degree of religious intensity of which the Hindoo spirit is capable. Both among Brahmos and others I carried away with me from Midnapore many friendships which were never severed in life, though few, very few, of my contemporaries still survive.

My eldest son was born at Midnapore, and that is another link which must always bind me to my first station, which, strange to say for one who has travelled in Bengal as much as I have, I never revisited. It was a quiet station then. The great canal works were in course of construction under James Kimber, who was afterwards for many years chief engineer to the Calcutta Municipality. The most noteworthy resident was William Terry, who had been for forty years in charge of the important silk and indigo interests of Messrs. Watson & Co. within the district. He and his good wife were the depositaries of all local tradition, and dispensed open-handed hospitality in the old style. Lawn tennis had not been invented, but of course there was a station club with the usual amenities, and a very poor old racquet court where we played. With great pains we organised an ice club, of which I was secretary, but the only way we could get ice was by bullock-cart from Calcutta, a distance of seventy miles, and the amount available for distribution was often sadly insufficient. The hailstorms in the hot weather were a feature of the district, and we used to rush out with pails and buckets to collect the huge hailstones which fell, often as big as pigeon's eggs, to replenish our scanty ice supply.

Unusual excitement was aroused on one occasion when Captain (afterwards Sir James) Johnstone arrived with a herd of about a hundred elephants which he had caught by Kheddah operations in the jungles of Keonjhur and was convoying to the Government depôt, which was then at Barrackpore. Johnstone was one of the finest fellows I ever met in the East ; he was at this time employed in very congenial work as Superintendent of the Keonjhur Tributary State, which had lately broken out in open rebellion against its ruler, and afterwards won a great reputation by his intrepid conduct in troublous times on the North-East Frontier, where he was in charge of Manipur, a State with which I also was destined to come in contact.

I drove a buggy—dogcarts did not come till later—and rode a horse, but I was always an indifferent horseman. There was no polo then. In no kind of field sports did I ever take an active part. I have been out pig-sticking, but I did not enjoy it. Even snipe-shooting—to which the whole Anglo-Indian world is addicted—presented no attractions to me. On rare occasions I have shot a snipe. I had a gun and a rifle and a revolver which I had brought out from home, but made as little use of them as possible. Midnapore swarmed with monkeys, and my wife once found a big *hanuman* or *lungoor* grimacing before the mirror on her dressing-table. I rushed for my revolver and took several shots at it on a tree where it had taken refuge, but I am thankful to say that I missed it every time. I once lowered myself to the level of shooting a pariah dog which had not done me any harm, and the anguish of the poor brute haunted me for days. I have shot an alligator, and that I did with some satisfaction, for within it were found the bangles and ornaments of women and children it had eaten. I never indulged in big-game shooting, though it was not for want of opportunities.

But with all this feebleness of disposition, as most will deem it, I vow that I was not a whit behind any of my contemporaries in admiration for the heroes of my early days—Frank Simson and George Morris, a relative of my own, Fraser MacDonell, Ross Mangles, and Charles Buckland ; these men were the idols of the younger members of our Service, household words among us for their prowess in the camp and field, as mighty hunters with spear and gun, as men renowned for their fearlessness and valour. Above all, our pride was in Fraser MacDonell and Ross Mangles, who were both of them decorated with the Victoria Cross for conspicuous gallantry in the attempt to relieve the little house at Arrah. All these I knew very well in after days when I was closely associated with them in official life, and I am bound to say of one and all that their merits as officials were great ; but whilst I was at Midnapore they were names only—names to be uttered with bated breath as one and another told stories of their exploits.

I served an apprenticeship in Midnapore of nearly twenty months ; not an unprofitable one, I am sure, for I learned much, and there is little alloy in my memory of those days ; but for some time I had been looking forward to a transfer in the ordinary course to more independent duty, and it was with unfeigned pleasure that I received an intimation from Government in July, 1869, that I had been posted to the charge of the Subdivision of Chooadanga in the Nuddea District. The charge of a Subdivision is the prize to which all young Assistants aspire, and I was delighted when I obtained it. There, indeed, I was ushered into a new life, and gained many experiences both good and bad.

CHAPTER VII

A STRONG MAGISTRATE

CHOOADANGA! Our home for nearly three years. The name conveys no idea to the Anglo-Indian of to-day unless he realises vaguely that there is a railway station of that name, with a dull outlook, on the way to Darjiling. Then, however, it was one of the best known of Bengal Subdivisions, and I was deemed a lucky fellow to have got it. At first sight certainly it was not attractive; Charles Lyall, who came down from Allahabad to spend a Christmas with us, called it a rat-hole. Our little bungalow and the adjoining court-house were dumped down in the midst of rice-fields; our evening walk was along a road with rice cultivation on either side; we had no trap, for there was no driving road; there were no trees to relieve the tedium of the prospect except a solitary peepul or two about our own compound, and there was not another white face within ten miles. Yet we were very happy at Chooadanga. My young wife had a brave heart and possessed her soul in patience, though I was away at my work every day and all day, leaving her alone. There were compensations; another son was born to us, and the care of two little children was a source of unceasing delight and engrossing occupation. If our life was monotonous it was not devoid of incident, and if we had no immediate company, at least we were on the railway in touch with Calcutta. Studded too over the neighbouring country were the hospitable and spacious homes of many an indigo planter with whom we were on very friendly terms, and whom we often visited. That was the distinctive feature of Chooadanga; it was the principal centre of the indigo industry in Lower Bengal, and that was its attraction to young civilians in comparison with more humdrum places, where very likely there were no other white people at all.

I was in charge of a Subdivision with an area of 440 square miles and a population of about 240,000 souls. A Subdivision is a division of a District. A District—more resembling a French *département* than an English shire—is the unit of administration everywhere in India. This arrangement of Districts, with a population of from one to three millions, and an area of from one thousand to five thousand square miles, over each of which a single officer presides, in whom all authority is centralised, and who is himself the hand and eye of Government, is a vigorous administrative conception organised with consummate skill by our predecessors more than a century ago. But it is a form of administration adapted only to autocratic rule, and for many years has been weakening perceptibly from its inherent inapplicability to an environment where changes are becoming rapid. There were symptoms of decay even in my time, and a desperate attempt to galvanise it into fresh life was made by our new Lieutenant-Governor, Sir George Campbell. He was supported, as was natural, by Civil Service opinion, and there was no more strenuous advocate of the patriarchal form of government, or one-man rule, than James Monro, the District officer of Nuddea, of which Chooadanga was a Subdivision.

James Monro was no ordinary man. He was

endowed with great abilities and force of character, exceptional industry and knowledge of his District, and a magnetic personality. After his retirement from the Service he made a name for himself during the eighties as Director of Criminal Investigations at Scotland Yard and as Commissioner of the Metropolitan Police. When I served under him he was in his prime, a terror to evildoers, a sleuth-hound in the detection of crime, fearing nothing, daring all things, deliberately straining every section of law and procedure, and falling many times under the correction of the High Court for irregularities and even worse transgressions. He was known among a certain class as the *keute*, or black cobra, Sahib, and was the ideal of what is called in official language a strong Magistrate. He was my official superior. I was then very young, only twenty-four years of age, and I confess that I admired him greatly and was completely carried away by the glamour of his achievements. The wise and sober example of my late chiefs, Herschel and Reynolds, was soon supplanted by the influence of a more brilliant and more dangerous guide. I had early made up my mind that whatever happened I would get on in the Service—I was full of youthful ambition; I, too, would win the reputation of being a strong Magistrate.

At that immature age I was, like all other members of the Civil Service—and as they still are up to the present time—vested with magisterial powers beyond comparison greater than those possessed by young men of the same age under any civilised Government. Uncontrolled by public opinion and from the nature of the case with little judicial experience, it would have been strange if I had not been led into occasional errors and sometimes into abuse of power. That must be the obvious result of a system which is to blame. I exercised first-class powers under which I could sentence up to two years' imprisonment, impose a fine of a thousand rupees, and inflict whipping up to thirty stripes. I remember to have been very pleased when I was entrusted with these powers. I was, in fact, too young to have been invested with them, and to some extent, therefore, may plead to have been the victim of a bad system. But I cannot rest my defence there. Severity is often taken as the mark of strength, and as this is a page of confessions I make bold to confess that I was harsh and severe in my administration of justice. I was too fond of convicting and of long sentences, some of which were fortunately modified or reversed on appeal, to my own personal annoyance, but others which ought to have been were not. There can be no doubt that I was frequently unsympathetic in my dealings with the people. I hope and believe that wherever else I have served in India I have not failed to leave behind me a name honoured and loved ; but I can make no such boast here. I made friends as I have always done ; I certainly did that, but I think I was feared rather than loved, and my general attitude was not one to inspire affection.

I indulged freely in the practice of sentencing men to be whipped as a judicial punishment. The Indian Whipping Act was passed in 1864 and is one of the disastrous consequences of post-Mutiny legislation. It is still in force, though I am thankful to say it has lately been modified, and some of its worst provisions have been repealed. The number of judicial floggings which used to be inflicted in India is appalling ; in 1878 it amounted to 75,223. That was a record, but even up to recent times it has always been excessive ; in 1900 it was 45,054 and has rarely been below 20,000 in any year. There are now hopes of better things, and the effect of recent legislation, supported by the growing expression of public opinion, which has become a power now whatever it may have been in the seventies, will undoubtedly be to reduce the number within more moderate limits. The way of flogging was and is to tie a man up by his hands and legs to a wooden triangle so that he cannot move and then to inflict the punishment on his bare buttocks with a rattan. I have often seen men with their skin cut to pieces where the rattan had fallen. I have seen men faint away insensible from pain, and I have heard of authenticated cases of men who have died under the lash. The triangles in Bengal are an unpleasant feature outside every criminal court, and they used to accompany me into camp. It is painful to me to make these admissions. I do not like to dwell on the subject, for it is exceedingly horrible, and I simply loathe this form of judicial punishment. It is impossible to conceive of a more brutalising procedure, and it is with shame and sorrow I record that I was addicted to it. I can only plead that the scales very soon fell away from my eyes and that ever after in my service, in whatever office I held, I did my utmost to discourage it.

The prince of indigo planters in the nineteenth century was James Hills. As a boy in 1815 he was shipwrecked off the coast of Orissa on his first arrival in India, and very soon after that date he acquired the concern of Neechindipore, which, long since passed into other hands, must always be associated with his name. Working at first in a semi-official partnership with old John Company, and afterwards through the vicissitudes and triumphs of an indigo career, he experienced during a long life more than the usual oscillations between success and failure. He was at Neechindipore—known to all as Neech—during the whole of our stay at Chooadanga. The most hospitable of men, we were always welcome under his roof ; and the annual Durga Pujah festivities, when the courts were closed for twelve days, for which his guests would arrive from Calcutta and elsewhere, were the rendezvous of all the planters and officials of the District. He was very partial to my wife and myself, and like all old men delighted to gossip of the past. It was in the early twenties that Marjoribanks—one of the last of the Commercial Residents of the Company, who enjoyed a salary of £5,000 per annum and lived in a magnificent house which cost £10,000 and was sold on his retirement in 1828 for £200—was a partner to the extent of a quarter share in the concern. Then Shore was Magistrate and Ogilvie Collector of Nuddea, and the Hon. Mr. Ramsay, an uncle of Lord Dalhousie, was Resident at Maldah.

Two generations of the official hierarchy had passed away since those days. Then the planter ruled in his own kingdom and his word was law. The ryots gave him ten bundles of indigo for the rupee. Three or four thousand maunds of dye were not unfrequently consigned for sale to one of the great indigo marts at Calcutta. In five years fortunes were made, and in as many they were lost. At one time there was stabling for seventy horses in the Neech compound. On one occasion the Magistrate had heard stories he did not like, and sent out a special detachment of police as a precautionary measure. These men Hills quietly attached to himself as a bodyguard and personal escort. Of *lathial* stories (a *lathi* is a kind of quarter-staff) and stand-up fights, of battles where the hired *brajobashi* (upcountryman) fought with a determination which would have done honour to the Company's ranks in a campaign ; of hair-breadth escapes where the planter, waylaid by a band of spearmen, only saved himself by the fleetness of his good steed; of armed hosts attacking out-factories and levelling them with the ground; of whole bazars plundered by one party, with retaliation as effective from the other—of all such anecdotes of the olden time there was no man who had greater store, and who had more lived in the scenes he loved to narrate. His power in my time was practically unlimited, and it was ever exercised for good. The tenants of the estate looked with an extraordinary and almost idolatrous reverence upon the true *burra* (big) *sahib,* who was an old man, as they would tell you with characteristic exaggeration, when their grandfathers were children. During the inundation of 1830, did not Mr. Hills, at a cost of one lakh of rupees, get rice from the East and seed for our cold-weather crops and support us into another year? So they used to talk among themselves; and so it was in later days, when circumstances had gone hard with the concern, that I have known the headmen of some of the interested villages to club together and declare that they would sell everything they had rather than it should come to pass that they should pay their rents to another landlord.

This time-honoured old Scottish gentleman was as esteemed and trusted by the officials of Government as he was respected by his people. The records of violence, the planter's opprobrium through which he had lived and of which, it must be admitted, he was not ashamed had left him unstained. His sterling benevolence and good sense had marked him through successive administrations as an exceptional member of a class in which so favourable an exception was but too uncommon. His generous hospitality, his frank and open deportment, his ready reception of the European traveller, his irreproachable courtesy, his kindness to the countryfolk who would daily flock to ask his advice or aid, had endeared him to all who knew him and have left a memory in the hearts of those who were fortunate enough to be honoured with his intimacy and confidence which time cannot efface.

Mr. Hills left India at the close of 1872, and died in England soon after his retirement. His sons and daughters—and there were many of them—were all worthy of their father. There must be few men of my standing in India who had not the good fortune to know one or more who bore the name of Hills. Archie, the eldest, who was originally destined for the Army, was, like his father, for half a century an indigo planter in Bengal. The best of good fellows, an unrivalled horseman, and the most famous pig-sticker who ever lived, his lot fell unfortunately upon the decaying days of the industry. From Lord Mayo and Bill Beresford downwards, all the great pig-stickers of my time learned all they knew from Archie Hills. He never rode out without a hog-spear in his hand, and was the first man who ever speared a leopard from horseback. Bob Anderson did it afterwards, and Lionel Inglis at Dacca. But there was a personal charm about Big Archie—so called, not because he was a big man, for he was not, but to distinguish him from a cousin of the same name—which placed him head and shoulders above all the other sportsmen and planters of his time. Then came Jimmy—now so well known as General Sir James Hills-Johnes, V.C.—his father's special pride, the lifelong friend of Lord Roberts, and with his fellow-gunner, Henry Tombs, the hero of one of the most striking exploits at the Siege of Delhi. There was Jack Hills of the Royal Engineers—Sir John Hills, K.C.B.—burly, brusque, and good-natured, who commanded the sappers at Candahar and won fame and honour at a time when all in authority were not so determined and level-headed as himself. There was Bobby the Calcutta indigo broker, an old Rugby boy ; great at cricket and other games, pig-sticking and polo, he excelled at everything. And poor Geordie ! another Royal Engineer and in civil employ in Bengal. He lost an eye at racquets, and never, I think, recovered from that. There was a charm about him too that few men possess. The last of the brothers was Charlie, also in the Calcutta firm of Thomas's, as great as Bobby at polo, whom I do not hesitate to describe as the most popular man of his day in Calcutta. I must not omit to add, on the authority of the ladies, that every member of the Hills family danced divinely. The daughters were, if possible, even more charming and attractive than the sons. All Calcutta residents during the last three decades of the century will recall the spell which was thrown on Society by Mrs. Cubitt, Mrs. Lewis Pugh, and Lady Evans. The youngest of these, then unmarried, the delight of her father's eye, did the honours at Neech in our Chooadanga days, and all the young bachelor sprigs of the Civil Service were attracted thither by her grace and beauty ; but it was the desire of a moth for a star, for the happy winner of the prize was a rising barrister of Calcutta, Sir Griffith Evans, who afterwards attained the highest success in his profession.

So far I have dwelt upon indigo associations of the most agreeable character. But of course every planter was not an Archie Hills. Their life was on the whole a hard one with laborious days, and if there were amenities such as many a young man craves for, there were also temptations. In the saddle before daybreak with many a wide expanse of country to visit, a planter would often ride out three horses under a blazing sun and in the teeth of a fiery wind, and not get back to his factory before mid-day. After a bath there came breakfast and a quenching of thirst. It is said by Kipling that only those who have lived east of Suez know what thirst means, and of all men east of Suez I should say that these indigo planters had reason to know best. Whisky had not yet established any footing in India ; a peg meant brandy *pawnee* in a long glass, and I do not deny that plenty of brandy was consumed, but at the time of which I write Bass's bottled beer reigned supreme. Hodgson's Pale Ale had had its day, and Pilsener was yet unbrewed. These young planters as a body were as hard as nails, and they could stand with impunity an amount which would astonish the more temperate habits of the present generation. But not always ! I can remember the twelve-bottle men, as they were called, who could get through twelve quart bottles of Bass at a sitting. There were very few of them, and they were relics of a day that was dying out ; none, I think, lived to the age of forty.

The relations of a Magistrate with the indigo planters were as delicate then as they are and always have been, say, with the tea planters of Assam. They were even more delicate in the case of indigo, as the indigo planter was ordinarily a landlord exercising almost patriarchal influence over his tenantry —who grew the plant for him under contract and a system of advances—as well as a manufacturer of the dye. Such a system is obviously unsound, and it led from time immemorial to frequent disputes between the planter and the ryot which had culminated in a crisis before I came to Chooadanga. The fate of the industry in Lower Bengal was then doomed, but indigo cultivation struggled on for many years, and there were few signs of the total collapse which ensued after I left the district. Within ten years of my leaving Chooadanga nearly all the indigo factories had been dismantled, the palatial residences of the planters had been pulled down and their sites were unrecognisable amid the ordinary cultivation of the country. I imagine that even the oldest inhabitant would now have some difficulty in pointing out the exact location where the great piles of buildings representing Katchikatta, Peerpore, Kanhaidanga, and Lokenathpore once stood. Even in my time the system was in rapid decline, and I knew it was decaying, though I did not anticipate such early collapse. It was the more important, therefore, that I should have been strictly on my guard in my personal relations with the planting community. But I acted as others did and had always done, and I am free to admit that I was on a degree of intimacy with the planters of the district which must inevitably and insensibly have impaired that attitude of absolute impartiality which it is the first duty of judicial officers to maintain.

It would have been impossible for a young man in my position to have deliberately isolated himself and shut himself off from communication with his fellow-countrymen. Such an idea is unthinkable. But it was to have been expected that I should display circumspection and exercise discrimination. I claim to have done something in this direction, but I do not claim to have been always successful. A case occurred in which there was a dispute between the ryots of the large village of Joyrampore and the neighbouring factory of Lokenathpore, of which a Mr. Glascott was manager. Glascott was said to have been once a seaman before the mast, and it was believed that a deeply sunk scar on his right temple had been caused by a blow from a marline-spike. Whether this was so or not, it may be fairly assumed that he was not the type of man for whom I could have any special liking. The fact remains that I decided this dispute in favour of the factory, and that when the case came before Government, as it did on a petition from the villagers, I was censured for partiality, and I remember that the Indian newspapers of the time—the *Amrita Bazar Patrika*, then published as a biglot in Jessore, and the *Hindoo Patriot*, then an English weekly in Calcutta—got hold of the Government letter and rubbed in the P's and Q's with characteristic emphasis. I was aggrieved at this, for really I was not very much to blame, and the case did not call for all the pother it excited ; but when I look back at all the circumstances I have no doubt that on this occasion, and probably on others which never came to notice, I did not exercise the strict impartiality which is due from a Magistrate. That the censure did me good I am certain, for it made me more careful, and I have never ceased to realise the difficulty and responsibility which rest on English Magistrates in disposing of cases between their own fellow-countrymen and Indian litigants.

CHAPTER VIII

ALL IN THE DAY'S WORK

THE tenure of my office at Chooadanga coincided with the heaviest flood ever known in that part of the country. This was in August, 1871. There was one vast sheet of water over hundreds of square miles. The villages and sparse tracts of high land appeared like islands in the deluge. The villagers were driven to seek refuge on the thatched roofs of their houses. In many places they were confined to a diet of rotten fish and rice almost as rotten. The peepul-trees were denuded of their boughs and leaves in order to procure fodder for cattle. The flood poured into our own compound, and I remember the feeble effort I made to keep it back by attempting to raise protective earthworks.

There were six feet of water over the little road which led from our house to the railway station. The main roads were flooded. An unfortunate man who was trying to gain access to our bungalow was drowned in the compound—he must have stepped from the path into the ditch at its side—and his dead body was found floating at our doorstep. I lost no time in sending away my wife and little children by boat to the friendly shelter of Neechindipore, which was always high and dry even during the worst period of the flood. Our bungalow was well raised, the water never came more than an inch or two over the floor, and I continued to sleep at home, but all my days were passed in a little boat with two or three stout oarsmen, who would take me at a rapid pace from village to village. Men as I approached them would swim out to me—*rari nantes in gurgite vasto*—and I would give them such comfort as I could.

Early in September the rivers receded about two feet from the height of their highest flood and then again rose rapidly. By the middle of September the inundation was only imperceptibly less than it had been on the 30th of August. The effect of this recurrence of flood was most disastrous, for the seeds of the cold-weather crops, which had been scattered by hand all over the country as the waters subsided and had sprouted up in twenty-four hours, were submerged and lost. If anything could have discouraged the wretched peasantry, this would. But they showed wonderful self-reliance and self-help, and their courage and patience were admirable beyond description.

The embankment of the Eastern Bengal Railway, which then provided altogether insufficient waterway, was breached by these floods in several places. For some time the level of the inundation stood much higher on one side of the line than on the other. At last the water, slowly rising, trickled over the embankment, and by a force almost imperceptible at first, but after two or three days with irresistible pressure, swept away the earthwork and in a rushing torrent scoured out wide channels, one of which made a breach of a quarter of a mile in length, and was measured to be eighty feet in depth. Railway communication was, of course, interrupted, and it was no small difficulty to organise an efficient service of boats to convey passengers, mails, baggage, and goods from one point of the line to another where the train service could be continued.

At this crisis the Lieutenant-Governor, Sir George Campbell, came along the line, returning to Calcutta from Darjiling, and saw the state of the country for himself. I was in attendance on him, as in duty bound, and only too willing to give every possible information which even his inquisitive spirit could demand. I take this opportunity of saying that there never was a Governor in India equal to Sir George Campbell in his insatiable capacity for asking questions on every conceivable subject from his subordinates. A story runs that on this occasion when Sir George turned from me and put a question to an Inspector of Police who was with us, I interrupted by saying: "If you please, sir, I will answer that; I am the boss of this show." That is the story as it was repeated to me twenty years later by one who was present, but I content myself with saying that I do not remember the incident, and neither vouch for nor deny its truth.

An amazing invasion of snakes accompanied this inundation. Driven out of their holes, they sought refuge wherever they could find it. No one who has not witnessed a similar spectacle would credit the enormous number of snakes which these floods unearthed. They are strong swimmers and were to be seen swimming in all directions. I have seen scores of them twisted around the boughs of trees; all cobras, mostly of the black and yellow variety—*gokhura*—but also the still more poisonous *keute*, or black cobra, and I have let fly into them with my shotgun with deadly destruction. They crowded on the railway line, on which trollies were continually running between the breaches, and it is a fact that the line stank with the dead bodies which the trollies had run over. They were a terror in our bungalow. At every opportunity I would take a long bamboo and prod with it into every conceivable corner and under every place, such as a wardrobe or bed, where a cobra might lurk; and never without execution. I often found them in the bathroom. On the day before my wife left for Neechindipore she was looking after my clothes in a chest of drawers, and had hardly finished before I was round with my bamboo, and out slipped a hissing cobra just where she had stood.

I was adroit enough in dispatch, though it does not need much skill to kill a cobra; a smart tap or two on the body and the thing is done, its back is broken; but it is worse than useless to try and batter it over the head. It is also well to realise that a cobra's power to attack is limited; when it is poised, in venomous and graceful motion, with its hood extended, and darting its head this way and that in the act to strike, it can strike at no greater distance—eighteen inches or so—than its head is raised from the ground, and to strike effectively it must first gather itself into this attitude of offence. I used to wear riding-boots, not for riding, for there was none, but simply for protection from snakes, and it was as well that I did so. I went over one day to Mr. Hills's house, where my family were, and was playing whist with three young planters in the hall, when, as I rose from my seat to change partners, I trod on a cobra which had been coiled under my chair. The feeling was not a pleasant one, and there was no delay on our part in polishing it off. The brute was a measured five feet long, which is big for a cobra, the usual length not being more than four feet.

There were more serious tragedies in our own bungalow. A man of the police guard who was sleeping on a cot in my verandah must have unconsciously disturbed a cobra, which bit him in the hand, and the unfortunate fellow was dead in a couple of hours.

I was out in my boat when this occurred, and when I returned the man was stark and cold. The faithful old Bulaki—this was the name of my bearer or body-servant—was one afternoon getting some grain for my horse from an earthenware jar, in which it appears that a snake was curled up, and, as he roused it, it bit him not once only but twice on the first finger of his right hand. "*Ham ko samp mara, ham ko samp mara khudawand,*" he cried as he came splashing into the house, "*ham margaya*"—"O master, I am bitten by a snake, I am a dead man." It was a case for heroic measures, and I lost no time. I seized an ordinary table knife and with it gashed his finger, hard and deep, two or three times so as to make the blood flow freely. Then I twisted my own handkerchief, as a tourniquet, round his wrist, and bound it firmly by the aid of the first implement I could lay hold of, I hope in approved fashion. In this way all the blood flowed away from his hand. Then I gave him as much brandy as he could stand and more, and marched him sharply up and down the verandah. Anything to prevent the fatal torpor which follows so quickly in cases of snakebite. The poor fellow was moaning piteously from the pain of the tourniquet, but I dared not remove it, as I knew I could not stop the bleeding which would ensue if I did. In the meantime I had sent for the local native doctor, who came at last and took charge of the case. Bulaki recovered, but he never could use his finger properly. In this instance I am sorry to say we never caught the snake. A few months later I gave the good man leave to go on a visit to his country and loaded him with presents, clothes, and money. He was a most grateful, devoted servant, and we were very fond of him. In an evil moment I permitted a groom who lived in the same locality as he did to accompany him, and poor Bulaki was brutally murdered on the journey for the sake of the presents. Although the groom was prosecuted, no conviction resulted, and of course I never saw him again. Bulaki's son remained with us as the children's bearer, and was most attached to them till they left for England.

The inundation was followed by severe sickness among the people. We had cholera in our own camp, and a groom and an orderly died from smallpox. It was but small compensation that the cold-weather crops were the finest ever known. The inundation had left behind it such a fertilising silt that it was enough to scatter seed broadcast by hand, and no cultivation was needed. In this way I sowed with my own hands the whole of our own and of the Court compound with pulses.

There was an extraordinary epidemic among cattle. In their half-starved condition they were poisoned by eating the rank herbage which was their only fodder after the subsidence of the floods. In ordinary times a dying bullock is sighted from afar by the natural scavengers of the country, adjutant birds and vultures, dogs and jackals, who swarm on the carcass and make short shrift of the remains. I have counted one hundred and twenty-three of these gorging on one carcass. I have ridden out in the early morning and noticed a dying bullock by the wayside ; I have returned two hours later, and no trace of it was left other than a clean-picked skull and bones. But during this epidemic of cattle plague the virtue of these natural scavengers was exhausted. Dead cattle lay everywhere, and an intolerable stench spread over the land. In vain did I try to induce the villagers to bury the bodies, and it was with the utmost difficulty I managed to get those buried which tainted the air in the proximity of our own house. In order to gain some idea of the mortality I inquired into the number of cattle-hides which were exported from the four railway stations of my Subdivision to Calcutta during a period of two months. The number was eighty thousand, and this must represent only a fraction of the mortality, for the greater number of carcasses were never skinned at all. In ordinary years the number of hides exported during the same period was found to be ten thousand. It so happened that at this time the Government of India had appointed a Commission to investigate the whole question of cattle plague in India. They came to Chooadanga after the severity of the epidemic had passed, but they examined me at some length, and their presence was found by us to be a very pleasant interlude in the monotony of Subdivisional life.

I think I may say that as a young Magistrate I was not wanting in activity. We were encouraged then to exercise considerable executive interference with the ordinary course of justice, and very often have I mounted my horse and ridden off to seize and sequestrate the fraudulent papers of a pound-keeper or even of a Sub-Inspector, or to inquire into a riot case on the spot, and I have afterwards in these cases given evidence before myself in court. I do not remember that this procedure was ever challenged successfully, and once at least, when it was objected to in the High Court, the learned Chief Justice accorded his approval to it. I once rode out to the scene of a murder, where the dead body, covered with wounds, was still lying, and recorded with my own hands in the vernacular the confession of the murderer, who gloried in the deed before his fellow-villagers, and claimed to be hanged on the nearest tree for it. On one occasion I scored a distinct personal triumph. I had private information that on a certain day it was the intention of a factory to sow indigo forcibly on village lands, and that there would be resistance from the villagers. So I was up in the saddle before sunrise and in the village, ten miles away, at early dawn, just in time to find the whole population turned out, with *lathis* already whistling ominously through the air, and two or three planters on horseback with a whole *posse comitatus* at their heels, spoiling for the fray. The moment I approached the contending forces collapsed, the *lathis* disappeared like magic, every sign of friction vanished, and the planters laughed and rode away. There was never any further trouble there.

Another experience of my official life in those days I recall with no satisfaction. Passing three or four months of every year in camp, there was no village in the Subdivision which I had not visited more than once, and the local knowledge thus acquired was utilised in the assessment of the Income Tax, which was then a fresh impost, and greatly to our disgust imposed on the shoulders of Subdivisional officers. Sub-deputies did not exist, and we had no assistants to help us in this duty. There was no old registers and nothing to guide us in making a first assessment but general knowledge, and this was only to be acquired by most vexatious personal inquiries. No occupation could have been more calculated to disseminate mistrust between a Subdivisional officer and the people. The annual advent of my winter tour came to be anticipated with dread, the presence of my camp in the village to be watched with terror, and the pleasure of camp life was blighted.

The good old times had vanished when, in all the flush of enthusiasm of work, the day's toil ended, the last paper signed, and the troubles of the court at rest, I could break into familiar conversation with the grey-bearded householders of the village, garrulous old men, gossiping of many things—the quarrels with their landlord, the dacoity in a neighbouring dwelling, the rice crop gathered in the garner, the dry-rot in the ripening chillies, the pestilence in April, the cattle plague in March, the rates of rent and labour when they were young, the rise of the river during the late rains and the crumbling of its banks, and the loss of all the spring indigo that grew below them as far as you could see. Those times had gone; and in their stead there was the same old householder, with three ploughs, asseverating by all he held most sacred that he had but one; his flocks and ample herds, that were the pride of his caste-fellows, had dwindled down to a few wretched bullocks, the rent-roll that was eighty rupees had become twenty, the barn that had been well stored with paddy was empty, sometimes was wholly removed and the foundations razed; not one word of information, no look of sympathy, no expression of confidence, and no friendly voice.

A single incident will serve to illustrate the demoralising effect which my visit to a village was destined to produce. On arrival I inquired after the leading grain-dealer, who met me in person and, after assuring me that he had lost all his business, called me to witness with my own eyes his empty barns. They were empty, no doubt of that, so I condoled with him and left. The same evening I happened to be riding out to the same village and was struck by the sight of a long string of coolies carrying covered baskets along the village track. I stopped and asked them what they were carrying, and it turned out that they were returning to the owner's storehouse the quantities of grain which he had deliberately sent away to a distant place in anticipation of my visit as soon as he knew I was to camp in the neighbourhood.

I must not omit some mention of the Census of

1872, the first ever taken in India, in which I took immense interest. It was done without any cost in my Subdivision. The services of every literate man were in a sense impressed, and it was marvellous what pains they took and how willingly they worked. I was not content with mere enumeration, and, before sending away the returns to be tabulated at the Head Office, I organised a huge local agency and brought up my totals complete within a week. I extended the official tables on my own account so as to include an educational census. The proportion of those who could read and write to the total population was 2·4 per cent.; the proportion to the total adult male population was 7·4 per cent. Only five women—four of whom were Brahmans and one a Mussulman—were reported as having any education. Only two Mussulmans were to be found who were acquainted with the Persian character, and only 3·5 per cent. among adult males were able to read and write in the Bengalee language. The proportion among the adult male Hindoo population was 13 per cent. Among male adult Brahmans 70·1 per cent.; among Kyasthas or members of the writer caste 69·7 per cent.; among the higher commercial and mercantile castes 38·8 per cent.; among petty shopkeepers and artisans 6 per cent.; among Hindoo agriculturists 6·2 per cent.; and among fishermen 2·3 per cent. could read and write. The whole of these results were elaborately tabulated, caste by caste, and must still be on record in the Bengal Secretariat. The effort was a unique one at the time, and Sir George Campbell congratulated me heartily on it. I wonder how these statistics would compare with figures from the same area if they were now compiled after an interval of forty years!

Lord Mayo, who at this time was Governor-General, was a first-class sportsman and passionately fond of pig-sticking, which he could get nowhere better than under the auspices of Archie Hills. So he would come through Chooadanga for the purpose. He brought his own Irish hunters with him, and once as we were crossing the river there in the ferry-boat of the period, which was adequate for planters' horses and my own, who were accustomed to the job, but not for a Viceroy's stud, one or both of the hunters got frightened and jumped overboard, and there was some delay and trouble in swimming them to the other bank. To say that I was annoyed does not do justice to the situation. I could see that Lord Mayo was vexed, though he did not say much. But about six weeks later there came down a circular letter from the Government of India, addressed to all local governments and administrations, calling attention to the general inadequacy of ferry-boats on Indian rivers, and insisting on their improvement.

Those were the only occasions when I saw that noble-looking and excellent man. It was a profound shock in our quiet provincial life when the news came of his murder in the Andamans on the 8th of February, 1872. The official telegram announcing that sad event was received by me when I was in camp, and every official in my court, from the lawyers in attendance down to the humblest orderly, assumed a garb of mourning, which they wore for several days. Everywhere the social grief and feeling of public loss at his death were overwhelming. This national calamity had been preceded by the tragic assassination of the Officiating Chief Justice Norman on the 20th of September, 1871. No one was more beloved than Chief Justice Norman, and he could not have had an enemy. He was struck down on the steps of the Town Hall in Calcutta, where his court was being held. In both cases the murderers were Pathans from beyond our frontier, and in both the closest inquiry failed to show any grounds for the rumours and suspicions of political conspiracy.

I conclude this record of our Chooadanga life with the following extract from a household memorandum made by my wife, which I am sure will be read with the most lively interest, I am afraid not unmingled with envy, by every young housewife in Bengal who, forty years after, is battling with her household accounts and trying her best to make two ends meet :—

5th of March, 1872.

Paid to Khansaman for fowls as follows :—

53 large-sized fowls	... ...	12 rupees 2 annas
66 middle-sized fowls	... ...	6 rupees 3 annas
51 small-sized fowls	... ...	3 rupees 3 annas
4 ducks	... ...	1 rupee 4 annas

At that time the value of a rupee was, broadly speaking, two shillings, and an anna was the equivalent of a penny-halfpenny.

On the 16th of March, 1872, I was transferred on promotion to Calcutta. It was in accordance with the genius of those days, and I do not think that there is very much change in this respect, to hold that a member of the Civil Service was fully competent to discharge the duties of any office to which he might be appointed. I accepted, therefore, with alacrity and without the smallest misgiving the offer of an appointment as Judge of the Small Cause Court in the first grade. There was a tangible improvement in salary. I had always been keen to get a Calcutta billet, and I felt that my foot was now planted on the rung of the ladder of promotion. It would not be my fault if I did not mount it.

CHAPTER IX

IN CALCUTTA

WE found Calcutta a very agreeable change after our up-country life. Society was much smaller and on the whole more select than it is now. There was more hospitality. Hill stations were comparatively inaccessible, and ladies were not in the habit of running away to the hills at the beginning of each spell of hot weather. Opera companies were imported from Italy, and maintained by public subscription during the winter months. Assembly dances in the Town Hall were organised under the control of a committee. All the beauty and fashion of Calcutta were to be found after the evening drive listening to the strains of the Town Band in the Eden Gardens. Madame Bodelio, in Dalhousie Square, was the fashionable *modiste*.

The Saturday Club was started at this time by Louis Jackson, a civilian Judge of the High Court. Its home was in Theatre Road, and its principal object was to provide "small and earlies" for the *élite* of Society who found the assemblies too common. Then it became a centre of croquet and badminton, and, in later years, of lawn tennis. Life in Calcutta was certainly as gay and enjoyable as it has ever been. Some of the amenities of the present time were wanting. Electric fans are, of course, a very modern invention. But Wenham Lake ice was procurable on terms which, under the agreement between Government and the Ice Company, could not be raised above threepence for two pounds, and I remember how acutely we seemed to suffer when the ice supply failed, as it occasionally did, from delay in the arrival of a ship or other cause.

There was no tramway system, and it was not till tramlines were laid down some five or six years later that palanquins received their quietus. Bad as the *ticca 'gari*, or cab, supply may be now, it was infinitely worse then, and the spectacle of miserable ponies falling down dead in the shafts was not uncommon. The Maidan was still full of jackals, which made night hideous with their howlings. I remember the killing of a jackal on the ground floor of the old Bengal Secretariat in Sudder Street. I never saw a snake in Calcutta, though I once found the sloughed skin of a cobra on a bookshelf in my study. Jackals and adjutant birds—which, owing to improved sanitation, have long since disappeared, and are not now to be found nearer Calcutta than the municipal slaughter-houses at Palmer's Bridge—were the nocturnal scavengers of the city.

The adjutant bird was to be seen all day long during the winter months perched on one leg on the heads of the stone lions on the top of the gateway to Government House, or on roofs and pinnacles, or on one or other of the many statues which beautified the landscape. I do not know whether it is true, but I used to hear that these great birds migrated from Tibet and, when the hot weather came on, flew back over the snow-capped mountains to their home. Certain it is that they are wonderful fliers. A gruesome story was told of how an adjutant bird, alighting as it does on the ground with a whirr and a rush, came flopping along the Chowringhee Road and, running into a palanquin coming in the opposite direction, impaled with its sharp huge beak and killed on the spot the foremost of the unfortunate palanquin-bearers. No sportsman ever shot an adjutant bird or a vulture. The latter are filthy-looking creatures, though from a distance they have a superficial resemblance to a turkey and may be found in flocks with a solitary adjutant or two among them. And this reminds me of another story, how poor dear Mike Finucane, then a Griffin fresh from home, excited shrieks of laughter when, seeing a collection of vultures near the Magistrate's bungalow, he burst out with the remark, "I say, what a lot of turkeys you keep!"

The Tent Club was a great institution in Calcutta in the seventies, and under its auspices many a famous pig-sticking meet was organised. Most young fellows belonged to it. There was Franklin Prestage, the general manager of the Eastern Bengal Railway. He was an excellent sportsman and a good fellow to boot, but he could not boast an *h* in his composition. When it was rumoured that he was about to be made "Sir Prestage"—which he never was—"Suppressed H" promptly went the round of malicious Calcutta, and his house at Darjiling, which he imprudently named "The Rock," was known as "The Rock of Aitches." There were Bobby and Charley Hills, of whom I have already spoken, Willie and Long John Thomas, keen as mustard both of them, and, among members of the Civil Service, Willie Oldham and Luttman-Johnson. Like nearly all good riders, they were first-rate officers. There was also Alfred Croft of the Education Service. To these three men I am linked by the devoted friendship of more than forty years. There were W. G. Willson and Meyrick Beebee of the same Service. No more brilliant man ever came out into the Education Department of the Government of India than Beebee.

He had pulled bow in the Cambridge boat in '66, and in the same year had graduated as a very high Wrangler and with a First Class in Classics. He threw himself with ardour into every field sport, but physical exertion and exposure told on him, and he died after only two or three years in the country, to our infinite sorrow. There were Griffith Evans, of whom I have made mention, and Harry Marindin, another very promising young barrister whose premature death, due to the climate and a peculiarly malignant attack of what was known as dengue fever, was also a great loss. To the best of my recollection Colonel James was at this time the president of the Tent Club. He was a beautiful horseman, and his graceful seat was the envy and admiration of us all. It was on Christmas Day in 1874 that he met his death out pig-sticking with Archie Hills. His horse put its foot into a hole and came down with its rider, who broke his neck and never moved again. I had been invited to this party myself. I bade James a hearty farewell on the morning he left us, and with a troop of other mourning friends I followed his bier to the grave.

There never could have been better players in the Calcutta Cricket Club than there were at this time. Denzil Onslow had just gone home, but among veterans there were Harry Aitken, always bright and cheery—and bright and cheery still in a green old age—who had in his day been captain of the Eton and Oxford elevens and played in Gentlemen and Players, and Bobby Hills, of Rugby, and Colonel Cubitt, V.C., who were both first-rate bowlers. Among younger men there were F. J. Crooke and Alexis Apcar. The former was from Winchester and the latter from Harrow. Crooke had a wonderful faculty for knocking up centuries, and Apcar had patented a leg hit like a kicking horse. Crooke did well in business and retired early, but Apcar still remains in Calcutta, the *doyen* of the merchant princes as his father was before him. There was no more hospitable house in Calcutta in the seventies, and no more charming and gracious hostess than dear old Mrs. Apcar of Russell Street.

But it was mainly on the cricketers of the Civil Service that our reputation must rest. Rivers Thompson, Secretary to Government, and afterwards Lieutenant-Governor, had given up playing except occasionally to keep wicket, where he excelled. He was an old Eton blue and had also rowed in the Eton boat. Among players were Warren Hastings D'Oyly, who succeeded to the baronetcy in later years, and Willie Ward, who afterwards went to Assam and preceded me in the Chief Commissionership of that province. Sir William Ward was a sort of Admirable Crichton, being the best billiard player and one of the best dancers and cricketers in the Service. He was our chief bowler. Then there was Henry Harrison, of whom I shall have much to say later on in these pages, of Westminster and Christ Church, a very sound bat and safe field. Alfred Wace and Charley Buckland, both Etonians, and Cecil Wilkins, who retired from the Service as a High Court Judge, were more than useful members of the eleven.

I have reserved to the last the two who were best of all, Lennie Abbott and James Austin Bourdillon. These two young friends came out together in the Civil Service,

> "Animae quales neque candidiores
> Terra tulit, neque queis me sit devinctior alter."

The one had been captain of Cheltenham and the other of Marlborough. Lennie Abbott, after a brief Indian career which opened brilliantly, was compelled to retire, when still a young man, with shattered health, the result of a carriage accident in England. Sir James Bourdillon, who served for his full time, rose to great distinction, and retired as Resident of Mysore, after having acted for a year as Lieutenant-Governor of Bengal. If Abbott was the more graceful bat, Bourdillon also made big scores, and was a good bowler as well as bat. Both were beautiful fields. They came down together on the Calcutta cricket-ground in the early seventies in the vigour of their youth, and it is small wonder that the Indian Civil Service in those days succeeded in holding its own triumphantly against the full strength of the Calcutta Club.

There was no Golf Club then in Calcutta. The first germs of the present prosperous institution are due to Mr. Morriss, who was manager of the local branch of the Shanghai and Hongkong Bank. I forget his Christian name, but he was known as "Nosey" Morriss for an obvious reason, and he and his wife were among the most popular of Calcutta citizens. He really founded the Golf Club with J. H. Mudie, a famous player, and one or two others about the middle of the seventies. They trudged round the Maidan in the early morning with their caddies and clubs just where their successors still play—if they have not all removed themselves to Tollygunge—but it was not until the beginning of the eighties that the game caught on and the Club House was built, with its subsequent attractions of lawn tennis and one of the most perfect bowling-greens on which any enthusiastic skip ever sent down the jack.

Paullo majora canamus. The curtain of the past was dropping on old Calcutta in 1872. The labours of our predecessors were already bearing fruit. The Calcutta of the twentieth century is the product of a sanitary revolution which to sight and sense was slowly unfolding itself during all the closing years of the nineteenth. I can remember the day when thousands of human corpses and many thousand tons of night-soil were annually shot into the Hooghly, when the whole of the shipping and the greater part of the inhabitants of the city supplied themselves with water from this polluted source, and abominable open drains or elongated cesspools formed the only drainage of the town. The average annual mortality from cholera during the decade from 1860 to 1869 was 4,747. In 1872 the obliteration of the open drains had begun, and an elaborate system of underground drainage was making its way, though many years were to elapse before its completion. At the same time, the beginnings of a pure water supply, conveyed by pipes from above Barrackpore, were being brought into the city. The average annual mortality from cholera during the seventies fell to 1,327. May we not inscribe the names of William Clark and "Waterworks" Smith in the roll of public benefactors for their share in these results? In the north of the town new main streets, called after the names of Lieutenant-Governors Beadon and Grey, were being opened out, and a new and first-class market had been constructed in the European quarter. All these good works were undertaken by the Corporation of the Justices, which expired in 1876 to make way for the Calcutta Municipality which rose like a phœnix from its ashes.

At the same time commercial Calcutta was in the early stages of an equally dramatic transformation. The Calcutta Port Commission was established in 1870. Sailing vessels had not yet given way to steamers, and the present generation can hardly realise what the condition of the port then was. We are officially informed that the Port of Calcutta "had the reputation of being the dearest and at the same time, as regards the provision of modern appliances to facilitate shipping, the most backward port in the world." There were no docks, no jetties, and no hydraulic crane power. The construction of a raised embankment along the Strand Road did not come till a much later period. But it was in the early seventies that the Port Trust Commissioners, under the guidance of their energetic engineer, Duff Bruce, laid the foundation of the splendid scheme of jetties and docks which are now as much the pride of Calcutta as their absence was formerly her disgrace.

I am not writing a Gazetteer, but I cannot omit to say that at this time was constructed the floating pontoon bridge which is still the only connecting link between Calcutta and Howrah on the opposite side of the river. This bridge, designed and carried out by Sir Bradford Leslie, son of one Royal Academician and elder brother of another, was opened for traffic in October, 1874.

My duties as Judge of a Small Cause Court, corresponding to those of a County Court Judge at home, were, unlike his, not onerous. My jurisdiction extended up to cases of one thousand rupees in value, and over an area comprising the Suburbs of Calcutta, inclusive of Howrah. I used to dispose of about forty cases a day, but most of them were uncontested. On the whole this was the easiest office I ever held in India, and I found myself with plenty of leisure on my hands for other pursuits. I wrote largely to the newspapers. I had been in the habit of doing this for a long time past at Chooadanga. I wrote several articles in the *Calcutta Review*, then edited by my old friend Lethbridge of the Education Service, now Sir Roper Lethbridge. I was rather proud of them at the time, but they were really very crude both in substance and style, and I think I should be sorry to hold myself responsible for them now. Nevertheless that old-established Review maintained then, and for some years afterwards, the high reputation for the character of its contents which it had justly won in the palmy days of Sir John Kaye, Sir Henry Lawrence, and Walter Scott Seton-Kerr.

Great laxity was allowed to members of the Civil Service in writing to the Press—more than I think was wise—but it was characteristic of the tolerance of a Government which could afford to be indifferent to criticism. For instance, Sir William Hunter, then a junior civilian, who far surpassed all other members of the Service in ease and brilliancy of style, was practically on the permanent staff of the *Englishman.* There was an unworthy jealousy of his abilities in many quarters, but I do not remember that there was ever any interference with his literary independence. I wrote myself frequently to the *Englishman*, to the *Pioneer*, and to the *Bengalee*, which was then a weekly paper. The proprietor of the *Englishman* was J. O'B. Saunders, a big, heavy man than whom there was never a more genial and kindly soul in Calcutta society. His editor at the time of which I write was James Furrell, who had been in the Civil Service but resigned in consequence of some disagreement with the Government regarding the commercial character of some private business on which he had embarked. The editor of the *Pioneer* was A. P. Sinnett, who in later life was identified with theosophy and physical research. From both these sources I received many a liberal cheque which helped materially to eke out my means of subsistence. At one time I was in negotiation with the *Pioneer* to become a permanent member of the staff, writing so many articles a month on a fixed salary, but nothing came of it owing to my transfer to the Secretariat, when of course I stopped all Press writing. The editor of the *Bengalee* was Girish Chunder Ghose, a name I am afraid now forgotten even among his own countrymen, but whom I remember as a most able publicist and a worthy forerunner of Surendro Nath Banerjea, his more famous successor.

I was closely associated with the *Indian Observer* during its brief and meteoric existence. The first issue of that weekly organ appeared on the 4th of February, 1870, and the last on the 28th of December, 1872. It was organised in Calcutta by a very clever group of young writers, all of whom, I think without exception, were in Government service. Foremost among them were Charles Tawney of the Education Department, who had been Senior Classic of his year at Cambridge ; Alfred Croft, afterwards for twenty years Director of Public Instruction ; R. H. Wilson of the Civil Service, and Lieutenant-Colonel Robert Durie Osborn, who acted as editor. The paper was run on strikingly independent lines, and very quickly proved a remarkable success. Every one took in the *Observer*, and contributions poured in from all parts of Upper India. There were few young men of ambition or promise who did not air their hobbies in its columns. Little real secrecy was maintained in regard to the staff, though the authorship of one or two particularly stinging leaders was never betrayed. In 1872 it passed into the proprietorship of Thomas Dunbar Ingram, a member of the Calcutta Bar, who many years later, after he had retired, crossed swords with Mr. Gladstone on the question of Home Rule. He was the younger brother of John Kells Ingram of Trinity College, Dublin, the immortal author of "Who Fears to Speak of '98?" It was during this year, at a time when, I am bound to add, Croft and I were practically acting as editors, that a particularly clever and offensive attack on the Lieutenant-Governor appeared. Sir George Campbell was then goaded into some form of action, but with characteristic generosity he did not seek out the author, but took the more subtle step of breaking up the paper altogether by promoting and transferring the best known Calcutta contributors to other stations, and as for myself, he spirited me away to his own Secretariat.

At this time there was a great agitation in the Civil Service in connection with the slowness of promotion, which had been blocked by the large batches that had been imported into India for three or four years after the Mutiny, to fill the vacancies then created. Thirty-three civilians were killed by the mutineers, and nine others died during the Mutiny from sickness and exposure. The number of officers recruited into the Service during each of the three years 1861, 1862, and 1863 was eighty, or about double the average of ordinary years. I had myself nothing to complain of in the matter of promotion, but I joined heartily in the campaign and contributed as my share a Bengal Civil Service List for 1882, illustrating the hopeless position in which members of the Service would find themselves in ten years' time. This was, of course, the merest skit, but there was in it some element of ingenuity and humour, and it caught on like wildfire, and I believe that every member of the Service must have bought a copy. The agitation was continued, and resulted in special concessions by the Secretary of State, which enabled a number of senior officers to retire before completing their full service. In 1877 there was the unprecedented number of thirty-six retirements, and the block was thus practically removed.

These reminiscences of 1872 would be incomplete without some reference to what I can only describe as the massacre at Maler Kotla—generally known as the Cowan Case—an incident now forgotten by all but a few. The facts may be summarised in a small space. On the 14th of January a band of about a hundred Kukas, a sect of Sikh dissenters known to be disaffected to British rule, broke out into open violence, and, after making a raid on Malodh, attacked the town of Maler Kotla, the capital of the small Cis-Sutlej State of that name. They were repelled after a bloody and obstinate fight, with heavy loss on both sides. The survivors, sixty-six in number, including twenty-two who were wounded, some severely, fled into the Patiala State. There they surrendered on the 15th of January, and were lodged for the night in the Fort of Sherpore. With their surrender the Kuka rising came to an end.

On the 16th of January Mr. Cowan, who was then Deputy Commissioner of the adjoining British District of Loodhiana, ordered the prisoners to be sent in to Kotla, where he himself arrived during the day. That evening he wrote to his official superior, the Commissioner, a letter reporting that tranquillity had been completely restored, and adding: "The entire gang has thus been nearly destroyed. I purpose blowing away from guns or hanging the prisoners to-morrow morning at daybreak." About noon of the following day (the 17th) he received a note from Mr. Forsyth, the Commissioner, desiring him to keep the prisoners at Sherpore till a guard could be sent from Loodhiana. This note he says he put in his pocket "and thought no more about it." It was not until 4 p.m. on the afternoon of the 17th that the captured Kukas were marched into Kotla, and then and there, without delay or the semblance of a trial, Mr. Cowan caused forty-nine of them to be blown away from guns. Close on 7 p.m., when the last batch of six men had been lashed to the guns, there came an official order from Mr. Forsyth to send the prisoners to him for trial. In his explanation to Government, Mr. Cowan wrote of that order: "After reading Mr. Forsyth's letter, I handed it to Colonel Perkins with the remark that it would be impossible to stay the execution of the men already tied to the guns; that such a proceeding would have the worst effect on the people around us"; and so the last six rebels were blown away as had been the forty-three others before them. One man, who would have made the fiftieth, broke from the guard, rushed at Mr. Cowan and caught him by the beard, but was promptly cut down by the sabres of the native officers who were in attendance.

Such was Mr. Cowan's share in this transaction. The Commissioner, Mr. Forsyth, had repeatedly enjoined on him to proceed with legal formalities, and on the 17th he telegraphed to the Government: "I am on the spot, and can dispose of the cases according to form and without delay. Exceptional action not necessary and would increase excitement better allayed." On the 18th, however, having been informed by Mr. Cowan of the ghastly tragedy which had been enacted, he wrote to him in the following terms: "My dear Cowan, I fully approve and confirm all you have done. You have acted admirably. I am coming out." He did come out, and sanctioned within the terms of the law the execution of the sixteen remaining prisoners. They were hanged.

The Government of India recorded an elaborate Resolution on these proceedings. It was understood to have been drafted by Mr. (afterwards Justice) Fitzjames Stephen, whose tenure of the Legal Membership of Council was then drawing to a close. "His Excellency in Council is under the painful necessity of affirming that the course followed by Mr. Cowan was illegal, that it was not palliated by any public necessity, and that it was characterised by incidents which give it a complexion of barbarity." And so his Excellency was compelled "with deep regret" to direct that "Mr. Cowan be removed from the Service." As for Mr. Forsyth, he was severely censured and transferred to another province in a corresponding office with the same emoluments. He subsequently became Sir Douglas Forsyth, having been decorated for service beyond the frontier at Yarkand.

The circumstances of this case and of the orders passed divided public opinion in India into two camps, in much the same way as Governor Eyre's case had shortly before convulsed public opinion in England. The sympathy of officials generally and of the Anglo-Indian Press was with Messrs. Cowan and Forsyth. The Indian Press at this time exercised but a feeble influence, but it raised its voice, such as it was, in horror of what had occurred. For my part, I can recall nothing during my service in India more revolting and shocking than these executions, and there were many who thought, as I did and still think, that the final orders of the Government of India were lamentably inadequate. The Viceroy of the time was Lord Napier and Ettrick, who was temporarily in charge between the death of Lord Mayo and the arrival of Lord Northbrook on the 3rd of May.

CHAPTER X

ON THE LADDER

ON the 20th of January, 1873, I was appointed by Sir George Campbell to be Assistant Secretary to the Bengal Government.

In his early days Sir George Campbell had served in the Punjab under Sir John Lawrence, and he carried with him to the close of his service a lively appreciation of Punjab methods; as Civil Commissioner he had taken part in the events of the Mutiny, and after a career in Oudh he was, by one of the freaks of promotion which are only possible in India, brought down in 1863 as a High Court Judge to Calcutta. He was then made President of the Orissa Famine Commission, and for two years was Chief Commissioner of the Central Provinces. The Lieutenant-Governorship was conferred on him when he was on furlough, meditating retirement in favour of a political life at home. He was well equipped for the duties both by careful training and natural qualifications, and was not unacquainted, like many of his successors have been, with the conditions and personnel of Bengal. His tenure of the Lieutenant-Governorship lasted for only three years, but he put into that time an amount of energy and masterfulness which revolutionised the administration of the province. My opinion will be taken for what it is worth, but I unhesitatingly place

Sir George Campbell in the highest rank of all the Lieutenant-Governors under whom I have served for the possession of qualities which go to make a ruler of men.

On his retirement he was made a Member of Council of the Secretary of State, but he very soon threw up that office for a seat in Parliament for the Kirkcaldy Burghs, which he represented till his death in 1892. There he was not a success. By training and temperament he was not fitted to take part in a deliberative assembly. He was deficient in tact and deference to the environment of the House. He was afflicted with a voice like a file, which would have been fatal to his career in any case, but he was also prone to the unwise habit of addressing the House on any and every subject, and it cannot be denied that he fell into the category of parliamentary bores. But he always held high before him the flag of Liberalism, and was respected for his wide knowledge and experience not less than for the honesty and earnestness of his convictions.

In Bengal he was not popular; reform was the principal feature of his government, and there was no department of the administration which was not called on to justify its method of working. He infused life and vigour everywhere and ran counter to all the cherished ideas of a conservative province. It is small wonder that he enjoyed very little of the goodwill of the English residents and was slow to gain the confidence of the Civil Service; nor is it surprising, perhaps, that the people of the country did not appreciate his value until long after he had left them. But the excellence of his work was vindicated by time, and Bengal never relapsed into the *non possumus* condition from which he effectually roused her somewhat slumbrous mechanism.

"I abhor the *non possumus* policy," said Sir

George on one occasion, and he imported into Bengal as his Secretary a man who above all others was qualified to give effect to his views. Sir Charles Bernard was a splendid specimen of the resourceful civilian. A nephew of the Lawrences and educated at Rugby, he also began his service in the Punjab, but quickly gravitated to the Central Provinces, where he made his mark above all the young men of his time. He was a small man but extremely strong and active, with a great football reputation, and one year in Calcutta managed to pull off the Silver Racquet from such doughty champions as Apcar and Crooke. His power of work was enormous, and he never shirked responsibility. He was withal the most modest and unassuming of men. No man was ever more loved by his subordinates and those who had the privilege of working with him. In the minds of all he was destined to be a future Lieutenant-Governor, but that hope was not fulfilled. He closed his Indian career as Chief Commissioner of Burma, and on his retirement in 1888 was appointed to be Revenue Secretary in the India Office. It must be admitted that Sir Charles Bernard was not always animated by that excess of personal dignity which is supposed to be an essential attribute of authority in the East, and it is said that his arrival in Rangoon on his appointment there was signalised by his leaping in full-dress uniform, cocked hat, and sword, from the steamer deck—without waiting for the lowering of the gangway—into the midst of the officials and crowd who had assembled to welcome him on the jetty.

Sir George Campbell, like all hard workers, expected other men to work hard also. This led to an amusing incident on the part of a young civilian who dared to play a practical joke on his Lieutenant-Governor. I was not present, but I tell the story as it was told me at the time. Sir George was on tour and, attended by his staff and the leading officials of the place, entered a certain Magistrate's *Cutcherry*, or Court. That officer never looked up, but continued writing. After waiting some little time without any recognition of his presence his Honour thought he had better intervene. He accordingly intimated his surprise that his subordinate did not show him proper respect when he came to visit his Cutcherry. "Gracious Heaven, sir! " exclaimed the Magistrate, "I have been considering for the past week the proper mode of receiving your Honour, and I thought I could not please you better than by steady attention to my work."

I always found Sir George Campbell kindness itself as well as a strict taskmaster. It was a pleasure to work under him, for he always acknowledged and appreciated a man who did his best. This was a virtue shared by Sir Richard Temple, who knew as well as his predecessor how much you can get out of a willing worker by judicious encouragement. I was rapidly promoted during the course of six months to be Under-Secretary and then Junior Secretary. It was my duty to organise the new Financial, Statistical, and Agricultural Departments under Bernard's supervision. At Campbell's request, I wrote two portentous articles which appeared in the *Calcutta Review* under my own signature, one entitled "The Rice Trade of Bengal" and the other "The Rice Trade of the World." As soon as I became Junior Secretary I worked with the Lieutenant-Governor direct, and used to draft the Government Resolutions on the Commissioners' and Departmental Reports as well as the Annual Administration Reports of the Government itself. For several years I did this, and, if credit be any test of efficiency, I proved an expert at this kind of employment. Both

Campbell and Temple wrote the Introductions to their Annual Reports with their own hand, but the high-water mark was attained by Campbell, of one of whose summaries Bishop Milman declared that it was "as clear as crystal, as complete as a circle, and as amusing as a novel."

Sir George Campbell was an autocrat—quite as much so as any civilian of his day. But he was also a large-hearted and large-minded man, and did not share that prejudice against Bengalis which is usual among those Governors who have been transplanted, late in their service, from another province. He did not like the criticism of the Press, but he did not resent it. Following in the footsteps of many of the sagacious rulers of India in the past, he was not blinded by the contemplation of a permanent benevolent despotism in the country, but believed in the education of the people onwards and towards a time when a nation capable of self-government would be built up. I myself heard him declare to a large Bengali audience that he looked forward to the day when a Bengali House of Commons would be sitting within the walls of the building in which he was speaking. That was a splendid and attractive rôle to take up in 1873, but now, nearly forty years later, I am afraid it will hardly be found to raise a responsive echo among his successors.

The Bengal Office was, when I joined it, located in two houses, one in Sudder Street and the other in Chowringhee, on the site of the present School of Art. It was not until 1880 that a permanent home was found for it in the historic range of Writers Buildings, which was then occupied by the East Indian Railway Company. At this period there was great activity in Calcutta in the construction of public offices. The present High Court was completed in 1872, when the old Sudder Buildings on the road to

Alipore were abandoned to the Military Department. The present Small Cause Court was opened in 1874. The General Post Office had been opened to the public as far back as 1868, but the present Telegraph Office was not commenced before 1873. The Indian Museum, several years under construction, was completed in 1875. I remember the large cracks which were visible in its walls, wide enough it seemed for a slim man to pass through, but the result has justified the verdict of the engineers that there was no real danger involved by them.

The separation of Assam from Bengal was definitely settled in 1873, and the first Chief Commissioner, Colonel R. H. Keatinge, V.C., arrived in Calcutta at the close of the year. He had to decide upon the selection of a Secretary, and it was a toss-up whether my old friend Henry Luttman-Johnson, who was then Private Secretary to the Lieutenant-Governor, or myself should be chosen. At the same time the Registrarship of the High Court fell vacant, and it was at first proposed that I should go to Assam and Luttman-Johnson to the High Court. But there are always secret influences at work on these occasions, and I was nothing loath when I found myself appointed to the Registrarship, and Luttman began his long and distinguished service in the Assam Province.

By this time I had gone a long way to shed many of my old prejudices. I had been no more fond of the High Court than any other Magistrate, but I had the luck as a Magistrate to escape the animadversion of the Honourable Judges, and for a long time I treasured a copy of a judgment by Chief Justice Norman which gave me, I am sure, more kudos than I deserved. The High Court and barristers are always in about an equal degree the *bête noire* of every "strong Magistrate." In the early seventies the composition of the High Court reflected a special lustre on the administration of justice, and it was therefore more than usually disliked by the members of an Executive Service.

The Chief Justice was Sir Richard Couch, who for many years after his retirement was a leading Judge on the Judicial Committee of the Privy Council. He lived in the big house in Russell Street which had been occupied by Sir Barnes Peacock, his predecessor, and is now, I believe, tenanted by the Calcutta Club. Among the Puisne Judges were Sir John Budd Phear, Sir Arthur Macpherson, Sir William Markby, and Sir Charles Pontifex. I do not remember that at any time a stronger galaxy of barrister Judges ever adorned the Calcutta Bench. Sir John Phear had been a high Wrangler at Cambridge and a Fellow of his college ; he afterwards became Chief Justice of Ceylon, and on his retirement settled down in Devonshire, where he contested both the Honiton and Tiverton Divisions in the Liberal interest, but without success. A man of the highest rectitude and with an inflexible sense of justice, he excited stronger feelings of dislike on the part of the Magistracy than any other Judge. Sir Arthur Macpherson became Legal Adviser to the Secretary of State, and was for many years Judicial Secretary in the India Office. Sir William and Lady Markby lived at this time in No. 1, Theatre Road, and their hospitable house was then as well known to Calcutta residents as their home at Headington has been to many generations of Oxford men. Sir Charles Pontifex had been an old Cambridge cricket blue and was one of the foremost of amateur tennis players in the fifties. He enjoyed the highest reputation as a good Judge, and was also one of the most delightful social companions I have ever met. These eminent Judges were always most kind to me, and my close association with them was of inestimable advantage in influencing the bent of my disposition and character.

Among the civilian Judges of the time I need only mention Mr. Kemp and Sir Louis Jackson. Old Mr. Justice Kemp had joined the Civil Service as long ago as 1831; he had married an Indian wife, and did not retire till after her death, when he had completed a service of nearly fifty years. He was a most conscientious Judge. Sir Louis Jackson was a man of very brilliant parts who arrived in India in 1843 and did not retire till 1880. He was in charge of what was called the English Department of the High Court, and I served more particularly under his orders. Like other brilliant men, he had many weaknesses, and he entertained not only an undue sense of his own importance, but also of the dignity and rank of others. Woe betide any subordinate who did not treat him with the deference he exacted from them! Every Indian civil judge who went to see him came cringing in and out of his presence. *Per contra*, I remember his coming into my room one day in the profoundest perturbation because, in driving down to the court, his coachman had dared to pass by and outstrip the carriage of the Chief Justice on the way. I remember, too, how gravely he lectured another Judge (who had been newly appointed) because he ventured to drive to the court in a one-horse brougham. He regarded me as far too independent in my demeanour, and once or twice it was lucky for me that I had a very staunch friend in Sir Richard Couch.

There was then only one Indian on the Bench, and he was a very remarkable man, Mr. Justice Dwarka Nath Mitter. I did not know him very well, for he was in ill-health and died in February, 1874, being then only in his forty-second year. His fame as a pleader reached its zenith when he addressed the court for seven days in the great Rent Case in 1865, a wonderful display of forensic eloquence, and he was raised to the Bench in 1867. He was probably the ablest Indian Judge who has ever sat on the Bench of a High Court in India. He became a Positivist, and taught himself French in order to read the works of Comte in the original, and so acquired a breadth of culture which influenced his whole life. He maintained an active correspondence with Dr. Congreve in London, and visited Mrs. Congreve when she was staying with us in Calcutta, a few days before his lamented death.

If the High Court is rightly regarded by Indian public opinion as the palladium of justice, it is no less true that the members of the Calcutta Bar have from historic times been recognised as the champions of liberty and the freedom of the subject. The names of Longueville Clarke and Theodore Dickens must be accorded the foremost place in the agitation for the freedom of the Press, which was granted by Lord Metcalfe in 1835, and at a later period it was Lewis Pugh who led the resistance to any interference with the right of trial by jury. The Bar at the time of my connection with the High Court was still a British Bar, and very few Indian barristers had been admitted as advocates. The Father of the Bar, though he was not then practising, was old John Cochrane, who had been admitted as long ago as 1827. He was famous as a chess player, and had played in his youth with Labourdonnais and Macdonnell. He gave his name to a brilliant variation on the Salvio form of the King's Gambit. Cochrane's games with a Brahmin coruscated in the old *Illustrated London News*, and many of them will be found in Staunton's classical works on chess. The Brahmin's name is never given in Staunton, but I record it here as Mohesh Chunder Banerjea. In his old age Cochrane played with Sir Henry Harrison in Calcutta with very even results.

The senior practising barrister was W. A. Montriou, who came out in 1842. He was the last of the members of the Calcutta Bar who regularly smoked his hookah in chambers. Another veteran was Charles Piffard, of whom it was said that he drank a bottle of champagne every day for lunch. At this time Tom Cowie had just given up the Advocate-Generalship. He was succeeded by Joseph Graham, who left India abruptly, having partaken of some poisonous stuff which by deplorable accident was served round at a private dinner party in place of liqueurs, but who lived for many years after at home, and was Chairman of the Assam Company. When I was Registrar the Advocate-General was Sir Charles Paul, who held the office for nearly thirty years until his death in 1900. Among other senior barristers were A. T. T. Peterson, who made his fortune out of the Bengal Coal Company, and John David Bell. But already younger men were forcing themselves into the largest practice. There were James T. Woodroffe, "Tiger" Jackson, Pitt Kennedy, Charlie Macrae, S. G. Sale, Arthur Phillips, C. P. Hill, C. J. Wilkinson, W. F. Agnew, Ernest Trevelyan, Griffith Evans, Gilbert Henderson, W. C. Bonnerjee, and Monomohun Ghose. Many of these became Judges, others acted as Advocate-General, and all have left behind them names well remembered in Calcutta. "Tiger" Jackson alone still lingers on the scene of his former triumphs. Ananda Mohun Bose and Ameer Ali were, I think, admitted as Advocates in 1874. Lewis Pugh was at this time a Welsh Liberal Member of Parliament and did not resume his practice in Calcutta till some years later. On the whole it was an exceptionally strong Bar and worthy of the Judges before whom it practised.

I have only to add that if the tone of the Civil Service was antipathetic to the Bar as a body—certainly never to individual members of the profession—there was a corresponding feeling of antagonism on the part of some of the members of the Bar to the Civil Service, and I recall the indignation with which I heard C. J. Wilkinson—when we were guests together one Durga Pujah vacation at Neech—declare that he wished the whole of the Civil Service had but one neck and that he could wring it. Wilkinson got out of it by saying he did not know I was present, but it required all old Mr. Hills's pacifying influence to quiet the irritation which that remark had, I think not unnaturally, provoked.

I place on record here the circumstances of a criminal trial which occurred in 1874, because while it created the highest degree of local excitement in Calcutta, it is also typical of similar cases which inevitably recur from time to time, in which the elements of race antagonism are vigorously reflected and the most dangerous passions are roused. Gerald Meares was a stalwart young planter whom I knew very well, as his factory was in the Chooadanga Subdivision. For some reason or other he had mercilessly thrashed the Government postman who was bringing his letters. The scene of the offence was across the border in the Jessore District, and Meares, after a careful trial by the Magistrate of Jessore, was convicted and sentenced to two months' imprisonment. The usual result followed: no stone was left unturned by Anglo-Indian agitation to obtain a reversal of the sentence. The whole volume of English opinion found expression in denouncing the verdict; Calcutta Society talked of little else, the Anglo-Indian newspapers added fuel to the flames, public subscriptions were raised to pay the expenses of an appeal, and influentially signed memorials were addressed to the Government praying for Meares's release. The High Court appeal was heard by Justices Kemp and Morris, both civilian Judges, and the verdict of the Magistrate was upheld. The memorial to Government was rejected, and so the case ended. But in the meantime great harm had been done ; all the floodgates of passion and prejudice had been let loose, and a corresponding feeling of resentment and anger had been excited among the members of the Indian community.

On the 19th of April, 1874, my wife and children left Calcutta for England. There comes a time in the career of the Anglo-Indian when he must face the alternative of separation from both wife and children or from children alone. His children cannot be reared in India, and it may be that all the duty of their management and education is thrown off by both parents. Or it may be that the mother in a conflict of duties is torn from her husband and devotes herself to the children. In either case there must be a laceration of domestic ties and the family bond is broken. It is this family dissolution and the domestic anxiety following from it that are the most painful accompaniments of an Indian life. The crisis had now arrived in our case. My wife's health was delicate, and she was now entering on her seventh consecutive hot weather in the Bengal plains. The boys had grown too old to remain any longer in India with safety. And so it was decided that they should go home together. A third and last son was born to us in the September of this year in England. To the care and education of these three boys my wife bestowed for many years the most exemplary devotion, and to her is due the whole of the credit of any successful career to which in after life they may justly lay claim.

CHAPTER XI

CONSULE TEMPLO

DURING the last six months of Sir George Campbell's administration Bengal was under the shadow of a great famine. Lord Northbrook was then Viceroy, and remained at the helm in Bengal during the whole of the year 1874. This is the only occasion during the past fifty years in which the annual migration of the Government of India to Simla for the hot weather months has been suspended. His Private Secretary was Captain Evelyn Baring, now Lord Cromer, whom I then knew pretty well, and never has any Private Secretary, before or since, exercised a more powerful influence over questions of State policy. The famine of 1874 will always be memorable for the definite and practical assertion of the principle that it is the first duty of the Administration to save life. This clear note was sounded from the first by Lord Northbrook; and his able lieutenants, Sir George Campbell and Sir Richard Temple, gave the fullest effect to it. They in their turn were well backed up by the local officers. Foremost among these was Sir Steuart Bayley, then Commissioner of Patna. It was at this time that Lord MacDonnell won his spurs, and the reputation of many a young official was worthily made. The lesson of Orissa had been learnt, and it was not forgotten. It is indubitable that much unnecessary expenditure was incurred, but the humane object for which all were set to strive was attained.

In my official capacity I had nothing to do with the famine, though during some period of the year, when I combined the duties of Junior Secretary to Government with those of High Court Registrar, I acted as a sort of under-study to Bernard in famine affairs when he was away with the Lieutenant-Governor on tour. I may now confess that I wrote a weekly series of letters on the famine to a London daily newspaper. This was the ill-fated *Hour*, a Tory organ, owned by a syndicate to which Mr. Eardley Norton, the well-known Anglo-Indian barrister, was secretary. Their representatives in India were Colonel Nassau Lees, an eminent Orientalist, and Lord Ulick Browne, now the Marquess of Sligo. The *Hour* shut down after a fleeting existence, but it paid its contributors.

Sir George Campbell, spent and exhausted in combating this famine, was compelled by declining health to resign the Lieutenant-Governorship, and he made over his charge on the 9th of April to Sir Richard Temple, who had already been associated with him on famine work. No Lieutenant-Governor was ever appointed to Bengal with a more distinguished record of service than Sir Richard Temple. He also came from the Punjab, and had been Chief Commissioner of the Central Provinces. He had been Resident at Hyderabad, he had been Foreign Secretary, and he had been for more than five years Financial Member of Council. Nor was he ignorant of Bengal affairs, for he had served on both the Indigo and Police Commissions. Of his experience, ability, and energy there is no need to speak. What I think impressed me more than anything else about him was his untiring endurance on horseback, though he was by no means a graceful rider, and his capacity for extracting the last ounce of work out of his subordinates. After leaving Bengal he became Governor of Bombay, and resigned that office to stand as a Conservative candidate for Parliament in 1880, when he was defeated. He was, however, elected for Evesham in 1885 and sat for that Division till 1892, when he was elected for Kingston. He retired from Parliament at the General Election of 1895. It cannot be said that he added to his reputation in the House of Commons, though, of course, he was a recognised authority on Indian affairs, but in one if not two or more Sessions he could boast of having attended every division, and it may confidently be affirmed that no other private member was so often caricatured in *Punch*. Oxford and Cambridge conferred on him their honorary degrees, he was made a Grand Cross and a Baronet, and was appointed a Member of the Privy Council.

There never was a public man in India around whom clustered more stories, good, bad, and indifferent, and some, I am sorry to say, spiteful. His whole career lent itself to anecdote no less than his appearance did to caricature. He was always in the limelight. His manners were ungainly, though he did not lack, when occasion called for it, a dignity of his own ; he enjoyed an absolutely unique physiognomy, grotesque and grisly, and there simmered over his features a perpetual summer of self-content. He was the vital spark to an ephemeral comic newspaper started at this time, the *Indian Charivari*, of which of all men George A. Grierson, probably the greatest of our modern Orientalists, was the leading spirit.

Sir Richard Temple never made a wiser appointment than when he unearthed Herbert Reynolds from the jungles of Mymensingh and brought him down into the Secretariat. He placed the greatest reliance, amply justified by experience, on Reynolds' sagacity and judgment. Of all the Secretaries I have known I consider that Reynolds was the most helpful and accurate, and, when needed, the most brilliant. Yet even Reynolds had his trials, and here is an instance of a cryptic dilemma with which he was once confronted by his Chief. He had recorded in his beautiful handwriting an elaborate note on some complex question, in which there was a great deal to be said on both sides, and concluded with the remark: "It will be for the Lieutenant-Governor to decide which of these alternative courses he will adopt." The file came back to him with the following order in pencil: "I entirely concur with Secretary.—R.T."

Sir Richard revelled in camp life. He could outride all his staff, and write in a railway train with the same facility as in his study. His temper was imperturbable and his nerve of iron. It was said that when driving with a devil-may-care young planter in Behar, he observed that he had never met with a trap accident. "Oh, indeed!" said the other, and they were over the berm of the embankment in a twinkling, but both alighted on their feet none the worse. Only once do I remember that he came off second best, and then who could have helped it? It was on occasion of the presentation of the usual complimentary addresses at a certain District Headquarters, and Sir Richard rose to make a gracious reply. But among the local magnates present was an old Indian gentleman with an imperfect education who had yet been a sufficiently diligent student of public speeches to be aware of the expressions which are interpolated in every newspaper report. He was not content with throwing in an occasional "Hear, hear" during the Lieutenant-Governor's speech, but continued with the whole gamut of "Cheers," "Applause," "Loud Cheers," "Laughter," "Loud Laughter," "Prolonged Applause," until he was incontinently suppressed. Even Temple's assurance was ruffled, and surely the interruptions of a Suffragette could not have been so embarrassing as this well-meaning old gentleman's interjections of "Loud Laughter" and "Prolonged Applause."

I accompanied Sir Richard on a very interesting trip along the line of the Northern Bengal State Railway, which was then under construction. By boat, engine, trolley, and elephants we got along as far as Dinagepore, where it was proposed to hold a Durbar, to which the local dignitaries and authorities were invited. We were attired in full uniform, and Temple had emerged from his tent to mount the gaily caparisoned elephant which was to convey him to the Durbar Hall. He was standing on a ladder and holding with both hands to the howdah, when there was a blare of trumpets, an explosion of triumphal bombs, and the frightened beast, regardless of the mahout, rushed off with the Lieutenant-Governor clinging to its trappings. We were in consternation, but when the elephant was stopped Temple, cool as a cucumber, dropped off into the arms of a tall policeman, quietly remounted, and completed the Durbar function as though nothing had happened. It is well known that once when Sir Richard was riding an Australian mare in Darjiling, she shied at something, fell over the precipice by the side of the road, and was killed, but Temple with great presence of mind threw himself off and escaped unhurt. His worst enemy could never say of him that he suffered from lack of nerve.

My reversion to the Bengal Office was in this way. I received simultaneously two offers, one of an Under-Secretaryship to the Government of India, which if I had accepted would probably have changed the whole course of my career, and the other from Temple, inviting me to return to my old appointment as Junior Secretary to the Government of Bengal. I had no hesitation in sticking to the local Government, and never regretted my choice. Sir Richard Temple was always very partial to me, and entrusted me with a large share of his confidential correspondence. I worked with him direct, and was again in charge of the Financial and Statistical Departments. One of my duties was the editing and compiling of the long since defunct *Statistical Reporter*, and I look with amazement on the prodigious amount of information which was accumulated and published month by month in that official organ. Much of it was superfluous, and should not have been printed at all, but a vast quantity of valuable material lies buried in its pages. No one contributed a good paper without the special thanks of the Lieutenant-Governor being communicated to him through me, and I remember to have been touched in later years when men have recalled to me these acknowledgments as the only direct recognition they had ever received from Government. The surest secret of success in an administrator is to applaud good work wherever he can find it ; and a little encouragement to hard workers, toiling away in depression, and often in ill-health, far away from the immediate eye of Government, is always seed sown on good ground which returns its harvest a hundredfold.

Apart from the famine, Sir Richard Temple is now, I think, best remembered in Bengal for the institution of a Municipality in Calcutta on a representative basis and for the establishment of the Zoological Gardens. These gardens were formally inaugurated by the Prince of Wales during his visit in December, 1875, and have always been much appreciated as a popular resort by all classes of society. It was during their early days that the keeper one afternoon left the door of the tigers' den open after feeding them, and two tigers stepped out and prowled among the affrighted sightseers. But they did no harm to any one, and jumped of their own accord into the rhinoceros enclosure, where they remained for the night. Early the next morning they were shot by the Commissioner of Police, somewhat to the disgust of the public, who thought they might have been caught alive. By an extraordinary coincidence there was a similar tiger escape a little later from the menagerie of the King of Oudh, at Garden Reach, on the bank of the Hooghly. In this case the tiger made straight for the river and swam across to the Botanic Gardens at Sibpore. The Curator, Sir George King, a man of peace and eminent in science, returning alone to his house in the gloaming, met this tiger on the path. There is no record of their interview, but next day the tiger was shot. There was a third case at Lahore in the Punjab, where a tiger walked out of its den in an exactly similar fashion. But here the story runs that the keeper himself sought out the tiger in the gardens and, prostrating himself before it, laid his turban at its feet and with every symbol of abasement professed himself the tiger's slave. So mollified, the tiger gently allowed itself to be led back to the apartment from which it had escaped, and the tiger and the keeper lived together happily ever after.

In the spring of 1875 I paid a short visit to England on three months' leave. There were no special mail trains and no *wagons-lits*, and these flying trips were not as common or comfortable as they are now. But the first return home always seems the most delightful hour of one's life. Happy was I to be again with my wife and children and to catch glimpses of old friends, from whom I had been separated for nearly eight years. My father had died in December, 1867, and the old home at Clifton was broken up. My brothers and sisters were married and settled down ; my mother devoted herself to her little grandchildren. The Camerons had left Freshwater, but I revisited the old haunts, to be welcomed affectionately by dear old Mrs. Prinsep, and renewed my acquaintance with the Poet Laureate, by whom I was pleased to find I was not forgotten. But five or six weeks flew by like a flash, and I was back again in India for two years more of strenuous Secretarial life.

In 1876 I saw Simla for the first time, having been deputed to represent Bengal on a Statistical Conference at which our president was Allan Hume, then Secretary to the Government of India. (Sir) William Mackworth Young, afterwards Lieutenant-Governor of the Punjab, and (Sir) Edward Buck represented the Punjab and North-Western Provinces respectively. It was a frightfully hot journey up in May, and poor Lamouroux, the Consul-General for Italy, died of heat apoplexy in the train. I stayed with my old friend Charles Lyall, then married, and thoroughly enjoyed my visit. As Buck and I came back together, we had a narrow escape of being thrown down the *Khud,* for the tonga capsized when going at full speed and we were all shot out, but we experienced no other inconvenience than having to walk the stage to Solon. And here I desire to record my grateful thanks to John Hill Twigg, a North-West civilian, whom I never saw before or since, but who heard that I was coming down by the train, and like a Good Samaritan on this grilling day turned up at the railway station at Saharunpore with as big a supply of ice as he could carry.

The visit of the Prince of Wales during the cold weather of 1875-6 was a notable event. I went down with Sir Richard Temple and Ross Mangles, who was then Political Secretary, to meet the *Serapis* at Diamond Harbour. It was my duty during the

Prince's stay in Calcutta to take charge of the Bengal Rajas who had come down to pay their respects, and I was present and acted as interpreter when they were introduced to his Royal Highness. I remember one Raja from the Chota Nagpore Hill Tracts, a fine-looking fellow of the old type, without money or modern education, who was the possessor of a jewelled tulwar which had come to him from his ancestors. The Prince's attention was attracted to it, and immediately the old nobleman unbuckled his sword-belt and presented the scimitar as a tribute to Royalty. It would have been accepted, if I had not ventured to intervene and represent that the Raja was a poor man and could not afford to part with what was really the very apple of his eye and the only treasure of his House.

It was at this time that the Prince unveiled the statue to Lord Lawrence which faces the south entrance to Government House, and I stood by as a spectator alongside of Charles Mathews. That distinguished actor had come out to Calcutta for the cold weather, and I saw him playing in many parts such as Puff in "The Critic," in which he was still incomparable, "My Awful Dad," and "Patter and Clatter." The Prince of Wales attended his performances whenever he could, and also showed him marked attention in society, more marked than some of the neglected Calcutta bigwigs altogether appreciated.

Lord Northbrook retired soon after, in April, 1876, being opposed to both the frontier and fiscal policies of Lord Salisbury. He was a wise and sound though not a brilliant Viceroy. He was very fond of whist, and gave pleasant little dinners at Government House, to which I was occasionally invited to take a hand in the Viceregal rubber. With the new Pro-Consul a great change in India's history began. I heard Lord Lytton make a most admirable speech in the Council Chamber in inaugurating his reign. I was still young enough to be filled with high hopes of the promise thus held out, and I left the Chamber in bright expectation of a performance very different from the reality we were destined to witness.

CHAPTER XII

ARMS AND THE MAN

MY most intimate friends at this period were James Cruickshank Geddes, Dr. Henry Elmsley Busteed, and Colonel Mowbray Thomson.

Geddes was a member of the Civil Service who had come out to India at the top of his year in 1861. He was an uncompromising Positivist and a devoted disciple of Dr. Congreve, the Director of Positivism, whose sister-in-law he married. Well versed in classical literature, mathematics, and astronomy, he was a political economist and financial thinker, and there were few who knew the requirements of Bengal and its people better than he did. He had given remarkable evidence before the Royal Commission on Indian finance, he had written a history of Indian famines, and he was now a Judge. He had run a tilt at Sir George Campbell. But it is not for these things that he is remembered. Such was the personal charm of his manner, the honesty and independence of his character, the general simplicity and unselfishness of his life, that he won all who knew him to be his friends. There were not a few who, after taking umbrage at the written record of his advanced and outspoken opinions, found on making his acquaintance that their aversion changed into admiration and admiration grew into a warm regard. His mind was of the religious type, and in the expression of his countenance there seemed at times to light up something of an apostolic fire. One who had been the foremost of his literary antagonists wrote to me at his death: "I have always looked on Geddes as hewn from the same rock as the apostles and martyrs of Holy Church." He lived in open sympathy with the people of the country—high and low, rich and poor. "We are unpopular here," he said, "because we isolate ourselves from the Indians by whose industry we are maintained." And so he invariably set himself in dealing with them to furnish a strong personal example of tolerance, courtesy, and goodwill. With Geddes I lived on terms of the warmest affection, and to no man have I owed more for ready advice and friendly support. He died on the 9th of March, 1880, at Mozufferpore:—

> "Multis ille bonis flebilis occidit,
> Nulli flebilior quam mihi."

Dr. Busteed and Mowbray Thomson are veterans who still survive. Dr. Busteed, who was a member of the Madras Medical Service, served through the Mutiny, being one of the relieving force who marched into Cawnpore. He was appointed Assay Master of the Calcutta Mint in the early seventies, and paid his respects to Sir Richard Temple, who was then Finance Minister, to thank him for having selected him, though a Madras man, for such a prize Bengal billet. "Not at all, not at all," replied Temple, with the peculiar lisp which never left him, and in his happiest vein, "*Tros Tyriusve mihi nullo discrimine agetur*."

Busteed was now meditating on the preparation of the best book ever written about old Anglo-India, his charming "Echoes from Old Calcutta." No man ever qualified himself more laboriously for the task he had undertaken, and his facts were drawn from original sources, old and musty and forgotten. No man out of such material ever evolved a brighter, more delightful and readable narrative. He possessed in an equal degree the gift of industry, accuracy, literary judgment, and Irish humour. During many a pleasant hour did we discuss together the tragedy of the Black Hole, the trial of Nuncomar, the romantic story of Madam Grand, and the duel between Francis and Hastings. Together we sought out the site of the Black Hole, then not so scientifically determined as it has been since, and located the exact spot where the famous duel was fought. With common tastes and interests, we gossiped of the past and lived over again old days in the present. One virtue my old friend always ascribed to me : he said that I gave him the title of his book, and I am proud to think that I must have done so. Dr. Busteed retired in 1886, and during the whole of our residence in Calcutta together we were inseparable companions.

Mowbray Thomson is the last survivor of Cawnpore. I chummed with him for over two years after my family had left for England. We lived from motives of economy in an unhealthy little one-storied house in the corner of what was then called Jora Talao where it joined on to Chowringhee Lane, and very near to the old United Service Club. Mowbray Thomson, at this time forty-two years of age, was gifted with a fine presence, a noble beard, a clear and honest eye, and bronzed features. When he was playing tennis, and often in privacy, he would tie his beard into a knot under his chin or behind his ears, after the manner of Sikhs who never cut their hair. He had a good tenor voice, though quite untrained, and it was always a pleasure to listen to his hearty singing. His exploits have been recorded ; he wrote a little book himself after the Mutiny, which

From a photograph by Messrs. Bourne and Shepheard, Calcutta, 1876.

is now out of print and forgotten ; the newspapers from time to time with more or less inaccuracy have chronicled his deeds, and they are admirably set down, so far as they go, in Sir George Trevelyan's "Story of Cawnpore." But I, who have a key to their narration which others do not possess, and who lived with him so long, at a time when his memory was distinct and fresh, may be allowed to tell my version of the crisis of his life as I learnt it from his own lips.

Before he joined the Army he had come out to Calcutta as a boy in the Merchant Service. He then displayed his skill and courage, not to say rashness, by a feat which, so far as I know, stands alone. He swam across the Hooghly, a river of most evil reputation for its fatal currents. In his early service he was stationed in Orissa, and used to say that the closest shave he ever had in his life was when he was nearly shot by a brother officer while bear-shooting. When the Mutiny broke out he was with his regiment at Cawnpore. The siege was brief and the trials of the garrison were great. Every Tommy who would run out under fire and bring back a bucket of water from the well got one rupee reward. Once when a soldier was shot down Thomson sprang forward to save him, but was himself knocked over by a spent bullet in the back, and a dozen willing men rushed to the rescue and dragged them into safety. When he was then lying in the infirmary a cannon-ball came crashing through its walls within a few inches of his head, and he fainted for the first and only time in his life.

After the fatal capitulation the boat on which he had embarked was sunk by a treacherous bombardment from the river-bank. Its occupants were thrown into the water, and but few saved themselves by swimming. Among these was Mowbray Thomson, who, as he was striking out for another and larger boat in mid-stream, was struck on the top of the head by a bullet. From that terrible wound he always suffered, and there was room to lay your finger, as I have done, along the deep ridge in the skull which the bullet had torn open. The brain was exposed. How he was ever got into the other boat is a marvel. There he lay and was thought to be dead. "Poor Mowbray! I fear we must pitch him overboard." That is what he heard, and it galvanised him into life.

There were two crowded large boats which floated down the stream that afternoon. At night Mowbray's boat, which was commanded by Captain Vibart, grounded on a sandbank. In the morning nothing of the other boat was seen. The enemy were on the bank, and Vibart was being subjected to a galling fire. So he ordered a detachment of men with two officers to get on shore and drive them off. The senior officer selected for this duty had his wife with him and Mowbray volunteered in his place. The detachment did their work: they drove off the enemy and followed them for some distance along the bank. When they returned they found no trace of their boat and never saw it again. There can be no doubt that, like the other boat, it had been captured by the mutineers and taken back to Cawnpore. None lived to tell the tale.

The small detachment on the bank were now attacked in their turn and were forced along, stubbornly fighting, until they sought refuge in an old Hindoo temple. At this time there were only fourteen of them, with Lieutenants Mowbray Thomson and Delafosse in command. The enemy surrounded the temple and tried to burn them out. Stifled with smoke, a voice was heard, "Better to die in the open than like rats in a hole," and they charged with the bayonet. Madly they rushed to the river-bank; one stalwart fellow who had run his bayonet right through a sepoy fell over on the top of him and was at once cut to pieces; the bayonets "passed through men's bodies like butter"; it was a charge for life; but all perished except six, who cut their way through and plunged into the river. Two of these were struck and sank, and four swam into mid-stream out of gunshot—Mowbray Thomson, Delafosse, Murphy, and Sullivan. These swam bravely on with the current away from the scene of the fateful massacre in all the heat of a June afternoon sun, and one of their number with a gaping wound in his skull.

They threw off all their clothes in the water, and Mowbray alone stuck to his red Thresher and Glennie shirt, for which Madame Tussaud's afterwards offered him a price in vain. For miles they swam; the sepoys had at last left them, and villagers on the bank invited them to come on shore. But they dared not trust them, and only Murphy, who was exhausted, obeyed the siren's voice. No sooner had he approached the shore than they rushed at him with their bamboo clubs, and Murphy sprang back into the river just in time. One blow fell on the sole of his foot. "Och! The dhirty spalpeens!" he cried, and made a long nose at them as he regained his companions in their weary swim. For six long miles they swam, and then, utterly worn out, as darkness was coming on landed on the opposite bank naked and defenceless. They thought their fate was sealed when they saw a band of armed men approaching and staggered down to the river to make a last attempt to escape. But it was a kindly shout they heard: they had met friends at last. Their protector was Raja Drigbejoy Singh, an influential landholder, who succoured them and showered on them kindnesses and hospitality for several weeks. Thrice ordered by the then powerful Nana to surrender them, he thrice refused. Only poor Murphy, who was wearing a belt into which he had sewn the rupees he had won for carrying buckets from the well, was relieved of his hardly earned treasure. In due course they were enabled to rejoin a British force. The Raja's son, Raja Sheopal Singh, who was in command of the armed band that rescued them, did not die until January, 1911, after he had enjoyed for more than forty years the greatly augmented possessions with which his father had been endowed by a grateful Government.

The gallant Murphy did not live long. Sad to say, he ruined himself by drink. His comrade Sullivan was in due course placed in charge of the Memorial Well at Cawnpore, but it must be nearly forty years since he died. General Delafosse remained in the Army and passed away comparatively recently full of years and honours, but without, I believe, seeing any further service. Mowbray Thomson was soon again in the thick of it, and I could fill pages if I dared with more anecdotes of enterprise and hairbreadth 'scapes. The honourable scars he bears are a tribute to his personal valour. He was put on special duty to catch the Nana, whom he knew well, but he never could catch him.

Those were the days when men's passions were bitterly roused and strange things were done and scenes unutterably horrible were enacted. "I 'eard 'im say Cawnpore, and I called Bill, and 'e 'eard 'im say Cawnpore, so we polished 'im off." That is a story Trevelyan tells, and it is typical of the horrors which accompanied the suppression of the Mutiny. Mowbray Thomson was once in close pursuit of the Nana with a detachment of Sikhs, and they captured some Pathan sepoys who had been with the Nana as part of his escort. Late in the evening a Sikh orderly came to his tent and, saluting, said: "I think, sir, you would like to see what we have done to the prisoners." Suspecting the worst, he sprang up and rushed to the guard-room, and there witnessed the spectacle of these wretched Mohammedans at their last gasp, tied to the ground stripped of their clothing, and deeply branded over every part of their bodies from head to foot with red-hot coppers. With his own hand he put an end to their agony by blowing out their brains. "Good God!" said I, when I heard the story, "and what happened?" "Nothing," was the reply.

Before he came to Calcutta Mowbray Thomson had been for two years Political Agent at Manipur, and he was at the time I lived with him holding the post of Governor-General's Agent with the ex-King of Oudh. Of all the Indian gentlemen I have ever known the pink of courtesy was old Nawab Ameer Ali, who was also holding high office at the Court of the ex-King. He used to come and see Colonel Thomson very often on business and then he would come over and talk to me. He did not know English, but his Hindustani was based on the model of the Delhi Court. He had rendered conspicuous service to the Government during the Mutiny at Patna. Of the same age was old Baboo Juggudanondo Mukherjea, who was equally full of talk and gossip, and told stories, even of a *risqué* character, from the time of Lord William Bentinck. He made a bold departure, which rather electrified Indian society, by inviting the Prince of Wales to visit his zenana.

An incident in our domestic life at this time was the arrival of the Manipuri polo players, who came down to play the Calcutta Polo Club before the Prince. The Agent, Dr. Brown, a very quaint old type of official as extinct as the dodo, was staying with us, and the Manipuris when they crowded into our compound with their ponies made a very animated sight. Dr. Brown had entirely relapsed into what were called "native ways," and it was said of him that he had registered on the Medical Civil Fund the birth of two of his children by separate women on the same day.

It was during this period that lawn tennis dawned on Calcutta. It was established in the United Service Club by Mowbray Thomson and myself, but in those days we played with uncovered balls in a court 120 feet long, which narrowed in the middle like an hour-glass. However, it was a first-rate game, and lent itself to furious hitting and rallies. The first name down on the list of members was that of poor Pomeroy Colley, who was then Military Secretary at Government House. Every one joined, and we had four courts in the compound of 3, Kyd Street. The new Chief Justice, Sir Richard Garth, was as keen as any one, and it was asserted that he used to don his flannels in his brougham as he drove down from the High Court. Sir Richard enjoyed unbounded popularity. He was an old Etonian and Oxford cricket blue, and could then jump his own height. Though his hair was white he was very vigorous, and he delighted to tell the story of his conversation with an Indian gentleman when they were guessing one another's ages, and his friend gravely said, "*Malum ki Huzoor ka ek sau baras se kam nahin hoga*"—"I think your Honour cannot be less than a hundred years old."

The year 1877 began with a blaze by Lord Lytton's Durbar at Delhi on the 1st of January, when there was announced the assumption of the Imperial title by Her Majesty the Queen. On the 8th of January Sir Richard Temple proceeded on famine duty to Madras and Bombay before taking up the Governorship of Bombay, and made over charge of the Lieutenant-Governorship of Bengal to Sir Ashley Eden. There was a nervous feeling in the Service that it had been proposed to appoint a Madras civilian, Sir Alexander Arbuthnot, to the office, and much satisfaction followed when the choice ultimately fell on a member of our own body.

I am not going to indulge in a character sketch of Sir Ashley Eden. He made an able Lieutenant-Governor, the seasons were favourable, and Bengal prospered under his rule. But I may freely confess that he was not the type of man for whom I could personally feel much admiration. I served for a little more than six months under him in the Secretariat. I do not remember that on any occasion we did not get on well together, but there was no prejudice on his part in favour of either Campbell's or Temple's men, and he was animated with a very natural desire to surround himself with Secretaries of his own choice. So Ross Mangles was gazetted to be a Commissioner, and I availed myself as soon as I could of the furlough I had always intended to take. But this was not until July, as it was necessary to complete a special report I had in hand on the trade of Bengal, in which Eden took no interest, but for which I was very pleased to receive in due course the special thanks of the Secretary of State. It was not, therefore, until I had put in nearly ten years' service that I took my first furlough for a period of sixteen months.

CHAPTER XIII

ON FURLOUGH

I THINK I have enjoyed myself in my own way on furlough as much as any man. It is delightful in any case to be back in the Old Country after long exile. Moreover, I have always enjoyed the special felicity not only of rejoining my family, but of going straight into a comfortable home. As long ago as 1875 my wife had taken a charming and quiet *pied-à-terre* in St. John's Wood, which was always my children's home, and where we still live. For a time, at least, I became a man at mine ease,

> "who having wherewithal
> And in the fallow leisure of my life
> Did what I would."

But it has never been my idiosyncrasy to cultivate idleness. I plunged at once into some kind or other of literary work. I made the acquaintance of Professor Minto and wrote on Indian subjects for the *Examiner*, and also for the *Academy*, which was then edited by my brother James. I co-operated with Sir William Hunter in his great work, the "Gazetteer of India," and stayed a week with him in Edinburgh for the purpose. Hunter was a first-rate whip, and drove me out with him in his tandem every day. His principal coadjutors were my brother and Grant Allen, whose brilliant talents had not yet dazzled the public. My brother remained working with Hunter until the end, and so acquired that remarkable knowledge of India which he turned to such good account when he became Editor in Chief of the new "Imperial Gazetteer," which has recently superseded Hunter's work.

I wrote an article entitled "Has India Food for its People?" which to my delight was at once accepted by Mr. John Morley, and appeared in the *Fortnightly* for December, 1877. I followed this up with another paper which was published in September, 1878, entitled "The Prospects of Moral Progress in India." The little courtesies and attentions which were then bestowed by Mr. Morley on a humble and unknown contributor were a source of much pleasure at the time, and remain a grateful remembrance.

There was perhaps more implied in the publication of an article in the *Fortnightly* in those days than there is now, for I soon found myself on the fringe, as it were, of literary circles where I met such eminent writers as Browning and Goldwin Smith. I had been for some time past a member of the Savile Club, and there made many friends. It would be easy now to get up an afternoon rubber there between those who played whist together nearly forty years ago. Among the friends of my youth who have passed away were Baxter and Corfield, Byrne and John Nettleship, and Clifford. I will not mention those who are happily still living, but among my new friends of this period were Carlton Massey, son of the Indian Finance Minister, a man of very sweet and lovable disposition; the Rev. E. C. Hawkins, who had been my form master at Brighton College; H. E. Watts, rugged, good-natured, cynical, and famous for his researches into Spanish and "Don Quixote"; and Charles Kegan Paul, with whom I was on terms of close intimacy. Wrapped up in a clerical and Etonian atmosphere, from which he could never emerge, of genial manners, gracious presence, and an admirable conversationalist, Kegan Paul was a general favourite. It was personal regard and admiration for the saintly character of Dr. Congreve that attracted him to the ranks of Positivism, in which he remained for several years. On many a Sunday afternoon have I tramped Oxford Street with him as far as the Marble Arch discussing the sermon we had just heard, with an appreciation and sympathy we shared alike. But it never came on me as a surprise when, as he grew old and his life was tinged with trouble, he gradually fell back into the arms of the old Roman Church, and he died a sincere and devout Catholic.

I had myself been admitted into the inner circle of Positivism, and with my friend Geddes, who was also at home on furlough, played a not inactive part in those discussions which rent our body at this time and divided the small number of Positivists in England into separate groups of thought. The lapse of years has obliterated the bitterness that was once felt, and friendly feelings have long been as cordial on both sides as though there had never been a break. Geddes and I stood staunchly by the side of Dr. Congreve. But my friendship with Frederic Harrison and Beesly and Bridges and the Lushingtons, who were the leaders in opposition, never waned. Dr. Bridges and Godfrey Lushington, Henry and Albert Crompton have died. Dr. Congreve himself has now been lost to us for many years, all who took a leading part in the controversy of the seventies and are still living have grown old, and all will feel that it would do no service now to rake up old memories. But all will also share in the respectful and affectionate commemoration of our old Master, who, endowed with learning, abilities, and character of the highest order, abandoned all worldly prospects and ambition and devoted a long life of self-sacrifice to the service of his fellow-men.

Lieutenant-Colonel Osborn, whom I have mentioned as at one time editor of the *Indian Observer* in Calcutta, was now settled in a little house very near to us in Marlborough Road. I had known him well in India; he now became one of my closest and dearest friends. He had entered the Army in 1853—the same year as Mowbray Thomson—and had served, not without credit, in a cavalry regiment during the Mutiny. But I do him no justice when I say that he was never intended for a military career. He was not happy doing duty with his regiment. He had found some civil employment in Calcutta, but nothing worthy of his powers. He was a man of such eminent gifts that if his lot had fallen on more congenial lines he could not have failed to rise to distinction. He was a writer of beautiful English—I have hardly known any one his superior—and was now reduced to adding to a very modest income by writing to the Press in India and in America as well as in this country. But he was living a happy life, if ever any man did, in the enjoyment of the society of his friends, by whom he was honoured and loved in a measure that falls to the lot of few.

These friends mostly belonged to the little world of artists in St. John's Wood. Foremost among them were Briton Riviere and Philip Calderon. Following close upon these were John Evan Hodgson, William Frederick Yeames, John Pettie, David Wilkie Wynfield, H. W. B. Davis, and many others. Through Osborn I came into contact with his friends, and the golden days I lived in close communion with the members of this charmed circle are among the happiest of my life.

We were linked together in the first instance by the bond of lawn tennis, and during the autumn and winter months met together to play at the Portsdown Road disused Skating Rink. When we first joined this club it was very select and our numbers were but slowly increased by the adhesion of Pepys Cockerell, another artist, Quintin Twiss, and William Yardley; but later on it became the rendezvous of the best lawn-tennis players in London. Twiss and Yardley were famous members of the Amateur Dramatic Club. Twiss was a senior clerk at the Treasury and one of the most amusing and genial of companions. I remember him and "Dolly" Storey to our delight, in Calderon's drawing-room, playing and singing nearly all the airs of "Pinafore," which was then coming out at the Savoy. Yardley was quite young, but his hair was already turning grey. He wrote plays, and was the best of amateur clowns. He had been a great cricketer, and scored his century for Cambridge in the 'Varsity match. Then Harry Aitken my old Calcutta friend, Albert Schlotel, W. C. Taylor, who played in high collars and immaculate cuffs, and Herbert Chipp, ambidextrous, with a vicious left-handed service, joined our ranks, and presently Lestocq Erskine and H. B. Lawford. In his day Erskine was probably the best lawn-tennis player in England, though he never won the championship. He would give the odds of half-fifteen to Lawford with ease and affluence. I remember that, at Hawkins's request, I gave a game or two to Anthony Hope, then a young lad, which I am sure he enjoyed. A regular player was "Cavendish" Jones, all for twist and screw and with no power in his stroke. At last two boys, who were just leaving school, the brothers Renshaw, burst like a meteor into our troubled vision, and the history of lawn tennis as it is now played began.

Philip Calderon was the life and soul, the centre and acknowledged head of the group of St. John's Wood artists. Never was there a man more dignified and courtly in manner, more sweet and affectionate in character, more charming to children, more liberal-minded and sympathetic in disposition, and more beloved by his friends. Two or three days a week all through the summer did we gather in his garden at Weston Lodge playing lawn tennis together, till the sun went down, in unrestrained enjoyment. I seem to see Calderon now, hovering at the net, Yeames with his fair beard flying in the air, active as a cat at the back of the court, Osborn with his left-hand deadly drives, and Hodgson concentrating with wrinkled brows all his energy into his service. I see Mrs. Calderon at the tea-table, the sons and daughters of the house with strawberries and claret cup and cigarettes, and wise old Wynfield, who did not play himself, perched on a chair and recording with pencil in hand the winning strokes and misses of every player, to be read out publicly after each set to their glory or their shame.

Once a week there was a more formal function to which the artistic world far and near would be invited. The old President, Sir Francis Grant, would often come, and his son, Colonel Grant, sometimes joined us in our games. There were few more popular garden parties in London and nowhere a more courteous host. When we did not play at Calderon's we were entertained at Hodgson's, where there was just room for a lawn tennis court, or in the spacious garden of H. W. B. Davis, who lived in a house in St. John's Wood Road which had been the residence of Landseer but has long since passed into the merciless hands of the Great Central Railway. I recall with peculiar pleasure the afternoons at Davis's. We went there on business bent and played on till we were tired. His sons were as bright and winsome as young men could be, and Davis was another of those ideal hosts whose courtesies linger for ever in one's memory. We met Linley Sambourne there, but he was no performer with the racquet. In later years when Calderon had migrated to Burlington House, where he lived as Keeper of the Academy, and Hodgson and Davis had left us for their country homes, we found another haven of bliss in Circus Road, where the *doyen* of British sculptors, Henry Hugh Armstead, with his wife and charming daughters, revived for a younger generation the hospitality of Weston Lodge.

After our games were over we used to turn into the studio and gossip, and I remember the delightful versatility with which Hodgson would snatch up a chalk and sketch upon the floor any grotesque or ingenious fantasy that had entered into his mind. Moorish subjects were his *specialité*, and there was a picture on his easel called "Loot," on which he invited criticism with engaging frankness. That, indeed, was a feature of all the artists I have known, for they seemed to value the opinion of a hopeless Philistine like myself—partly I think from utter courtesy, but perhaps as typical of the hydra-headed monster, the British Public, to whose verdict all had to submit. Calderon was the most perfect colourist of his day. His pictures found their way largely into the galleries of Mr. Schwabe and Sir John Aird, who were often knocking about his studio. He did not disdain portraits, and I cherish as a particular treasure his picture of my wife and children which was hung on the walls of the Academy in 1879. Little sketches from his brush which I greatly valued were lost for ever in the wreck of the Assam earthquake many years later. Of Yeames I still possess an association in a photograph of one of his best

LADY COTTON AND HER CHILDREN.

From a painting by Philip H. Calderon, R.A., 1879.

[To face p. 152.

pictures, "When did you last see your Father?" on which he has written a very pleasant inscription. Pettie's portraits always reminded me in their pose of Mrs. Cameron's work. Hodgson painted a life-like portrait of Osborn, which passed into the possession of the Colonel's family. If Calderon was the life and soul of the St. John's Wood artists, Osborn was the member of the group whom, though not an artist, all welcomed and loved. And none more than Briton Riviere, towards whom our combined movement gravitated for billiards, for Riviere never joined our tennis orgies, and it was Osborn who was always the centre of attraction on the Saturday evenings at his house in Finchley Road.

Osborn died in the spring of 1889, dropping down dead in court while playing lawn tennis with Ernest Renshaw. It was a great shock to his friends, but I would fain think it was a happy death, in the full flush of pleasurable excitement; and it may be that he himself might have chosen to end thus. More than a year after his death, on the 11th of June, 1890, Philip Calderon wrote to me in India:—

"It was a genuine pleasure to receive a letter from you; a rare boon, the scarcity of which one did not note in the days when fresh news of you filtered through from Osborn. As you know, besides his frequent calls, I met him continually at Riviere's, where we used to engage in rare battles at billiards, and there he used to tell us about you and your doings. For some years now the dear old fellow used to spend his autumn holidays near us, and we saw him when out of town even oftener than when in London. So accustomed had we become to this that now my holiday seems shorn of half its pleasure and lawn tennis afternoons of all their interest. As for the billiard evenings, I never go to them; I have tried to do so, and the whole evening long have been looking for Osborn and turned to the door expectant of him at each fresh arrival."

But our little group had broken up before Osborn's death. Wynfield died; Calderon moved to Burlington House; Yeames to Hanwell, of all places; and Hodgson retired, like Cincinnatus, into country life. "Hodgson," wrote Calderon to me in one of his sunny letters, "has gone to live in the country on the borders of Buckinghamshire, near Amersham, in pretty scenery and in a pretty country house. He seems so far to revel in young peas, and his talk is of asparagus and strawberries. Rain has become to him a matter of importance, and the sun which blesses others seems to him a curse which shrivels young broccoli and plays the deuce generally with the kitchen garden."

The memory of the old days of our unbroken companionship is not dim, but it is distant. Not only is Osborn gone but Calderon and Hodgson have themselves long since passed away. If a group of St. John's Wood artists still survives, it is the group of another and a younger generation. But the memory lingers; no charm can be more sweet and tender than the joyous concert of friends which old times recall, and it is this charm that hallows the memory of my first furlough, now more than thirty-three years ago.

CHAPTER XIV

OLD CHITTAGONG

I WENT back to India in October, 1878, by Venice and Ancona, and heard at Aden that I had been posted to be Magistrate and Collector of the important district of Chittagong. Thus was I to resume executive work which had been interrupted since I left Chooadanga six and a half years before. I had changed in the interval ; I had gained experience and knowledge, and I sometimes think that my short tenure of office in Chittagong was the best period of work I ever put in during my Indian service. Certainly at no other time did I work harder. I plunged almost at once into camp life. The District consists of a long and narrow strip of coast valleys and low ranges of hills on the north-east corner of the Bay of Bengal. Its length is about one hundred and sixty-five miles and its average breadth about twenty miles. It is altogether unlike any other Bengal District, and possesses a variety of infinitely interesting features of its own. During two cold weathers I visited every part of it, and thoroughly enjoyed the life, though my experiences were often somewhat rough and the climate is by no means a healthy one.

A great portion of the District is intersected by innumerable tidal creeks containing not much water but any quantity of soft mud. The only bridges are bamboos, sometimes not more than two or three tightly tied together, with another very shaky bamboo as a handrail. They are awkward things to cross, especially when slippery and wet in the early morning dew, and men who have lost their nerve dare not face them. When out of repair they are occasionally impassable, and for this reason I generally had an elephant with me on which I could fall back in need. But once I found this elephant a source of more danger than any bamboo bridge, however rickety. The unfortunate brute sank into the mud up to its belly and made the most frantic efforts to extricate itself in vain. The mahout shouted to me to jump off, tail end, and away I went. Fortunately, as the creek was a narrow one, I alighted on decent landing ground. The mahout followed me double quick, and then we collected bamboos and boughs and whatever solid material we could pick up and flung them before the elephant, which kneaded them with the greatest skill under its feet, and eventually, with the aid of this friendly purchase, struggled its way out. The alarm of the mahout, of course, was that the elephant would use us as its footstool for this kneading process, and my observation showed me that it was quite intelligent enough to have done so. Elephants are wonderful swimmers, and old Roostum—that was his name—on one occasion swam behind my boat for miles when I was crossing from the mainland to an island in the south of the District.

An attraction to my office was the possession of a little schooner, which, in the fine weather that always prevailed during December and January, I could utilise in sailing along the coast. It was extremely small, and could be propelled by oars when necessary as well as sail ; and it was most enjoyable to glide along on the limpid waters in the moonlight by the beautiful island of Moiscal while the rowers chanted their boating songs to the rhythm of their stroke. I was always fond of swimming and indulged in this exercise, leaping into the sea from the schooner's deck, but it annoyed me when I found that two or three men always followed as closely as they could in a little boat. At last, when I remonstrated, they replied, "Well, sir, we thought it better as the sea here swarms with sharks"; and I refrained from any more sea bathing.

In Chittagong I gained my first experience of tea planters. There were only a handful of them, and a few were of the best; but, taken as a whole, they were not up to the standard of those with whom I came in contact afterwards in Assam. A peculiarly abominable outrage had been perpetrated on a coolie woman just before I joined the District—the flogging of a woman under most revolting conditions—and I was on my guard. But some of these planters were quite out of hand. When I was trying one for common assault he calmly came and seated himself on the Bench by my side, and was much surprised when I ordered him to stand down and take his place in court. There was an old fellow, a man of ungovernable temper, who, when my predecessor came to inspect his garden, not only threatened violence, but actually fired his gun at the Magistrate, without, however, interfering with the inspection, which duly took place. Yet the Magistrate took no other action. I wrote to the same man, intimating that I intended to inspect his garden, and he replied that he would shoot me if I did. I went to inspect, and sure enough he turned up gun in hand, but this time did not fire, and raised no further objection to the discharge of my duty. There was another queer old Scotsman in charge of a garden in the south of the District in an inaccessible corner which was rarely visited, and when I went to see him I found a man gone over entirely to "native ways," clothed in an Indian shawl and loin cloth, but speaking in a rasping Glasgow accent. Such were extreme cases, no doubt. The life these men led did not tend to soften their manners. But there remained some who were of the best type of English gentlemen, with whom, I am glad to say, I was always on very friendly terms. Indentured labour in the District had ceased, and practically no complaints of a serious nature were made in my time.

My working hours were chiefly devoted to revenue administration. A revision of the land revenue was in progress, and I found myself involved in a controversy which was prolonged for years. For more than a century an invariable custom had been followed in the assessment of waste lands brought under cultivation, and during this long period the Government had concluded more than fifty thousand settlements with individual tenure-holders on one consistent principle. That principle was now being completely reversed, and I protested against the change. I allude to this only to explain how it was that my interest was aroused by an examination of the musty and worm-eaten old papers in the Record Room into the compilation of a volume of considerable dimensions, which was published by the Government in April, 1880, under the name of a "Memorandum on the Revenue History of Chittagong." This was a work of infinite labour, and night after night I sat up into the small hours absorbed in the task. It is not for me to judge of the merits of this book, but I may be allowed to suggest that it was not altogether so prosaic as its title would invite the reader to expect. It was an official production, but I ventured to transfer to its pages something of the humour and something perhaps of the pathos which unconsciously enliven the record of every forgotten past. Here, for instance, is a letter which I reproduce as a fine specimen reprimand of the olden times :—

" *To* HENRY GOODWIN, Esqre., *Chief of Chittagong.*

" We have received your letter dated the 12th of last month, enclosing copy of one addressed to you by Mr. Barton.

" As that gentleman had received a severe reprimand from the Board for his misconduct in a late instance, we are the more astonished at the very unbecoming style and contents of the letter you have referred to us. The insinuation contained in the beginning of it, 'that a respectful demeanour towards you is what he pays merely to your superior station and the immediate control in which you are placed over him and which to an equal he should have dispensed with,' may be considered equally as a mark of presumption and folly, and as we are determined effectually to check a behaviour so entirely subversive of all authority and so repugnant to the common rules of good manners, we must insist on Mr. Barton's immediately making to you in writing a suitable apology for so contumacious a behaviour. This you will accordingly require by furnishing him with a copy of this paragraph, which will at the same time show the sense we entertain of his conduct.

" We are, sir, your most obedient servants,

WARREN HASTINGS,
W. ALDERSEY,
P. M. DACRES,
JAMES LAWRELL,
J. GRAHAM,
N. GRUEBER.

" FORT WILLIAM.
" *The 4th August,* 1774."

Here, again, is a letter from poor Charles Croftes, "died Chief of Chittagong 1786, aged 42 years," which is remarkable even in an age when official self-abnegation and abasement were more marked than they are in the correspondence of modern times :—

"I hope, gentlemen, when you have been pleased to read what I have taken the liberty to submit that you will not deem me deserving of the censure which you have been pleased to pass upon me ; and that while I am using every exertion that a worn-out decrepit constitution is capable of, merely for the purpose of obtaining your good opinion and acquiring some reputation in the service of my employers, you will not suffer a censure so injurious to me to stand upon your records, and especially if, upon a reconsideration, you shall be pleased to think I have not deserved it."

Another Chief, Mr. Sumner, records in 1779 how he found it "very grating to communicate" that the collection of revenue had fallen into arrears.

The following is a pompous and punctilious letter addressed to Captain Ellerker, commanding at Chittagong, on the 24th of August, 1775, by the Pooh Bah of the station at that period :—

"SIR,—I yesterday received a letter from you directed to me as Chief, in which capacity I cannot comprehend its meaning, not having made the request of a return from you. I therefore imagine you have made a mistake, which, on referring to a letter sent you yesterday from the Collector of the Government Customs, you can easily rectify by addressing me in that capacity."

In 1776 the Government took the extraordinary

step of dissociating itself from the Post Office and leaving the local residents of Chittagong to make the best arrangement for themselves they could. A "Dawk Committee" was at once established, and its proceedings are of the most entertaining character. Here is one entry :—

"The Bearers having assembled at the time of the Board's sitting and interrupted their proceedings by making a confounded noise in order to obtain an increase of wages of four annas a month, it was resolved that each man laid hold of should receive twelve strokes with a rattan, which was accordingly put into execution, and it is agreed that on every future insurrection of the kind they shall receive the same encouragement."

Other extracts are :—

"Mr. Leeke to regulate the price of provisions."

"The proprietors and ladies of the Settlement dine with Mr. Law on the first day of each month."

"Any member showing the book of these proceedings to a non-member to be fined Rs. 20."

"Cotes, Calvert, and Shardon fined Rs. 5 each for late attendance. Bright fined Rs. 20 for non-attendance."

Bright, however, refuses to be bound by the regulations as "unworthy of freemen," and asks to be excused from attending the meetings as "for private reasons I cannot have the honour of meeting you at Mr. Law's." The Committee refused to alter the regulations and called upon him to resign, whereupon Mr. Bright replies : "As your sentiments and mine differ as wide as slavery and freedom, I decline being a member of your meeting." It was then resolved by the Committee that "as Mr. Bright declines to continue a member of our meeting, we will no longer permit him to be a subscriber to our Dawk."

But perhaps the most remarkable extracts from the early correspondence are those that illustrate the punishment of criminals, and especially the practice of impaling dacoits which prevailed at the close of the eighteenth century. An order runs to the military authorities: "You are directed to attend the body of Tunnoo until the sentence is executed, which will not be complete until three days after the body is impaled." These sentences were carried out on the spot where the crime was committed. Among other punishments I find in 1773, "Man Ghazy and Yakoob for decoyting, their right hand and left foot to be cut off," and there is a special letter from Warren Hastings directing this warrant to be carried into immediate execution. Another sentence is "25 to 50 stripes every seven days for six months for theft"; and on the 24th of July, 1774, I find Mr. Goodwin mildly protesting against the orders he had received in regard to one Soognee Dye, these orders being "to leave her to her own reflections."

After all, these are digressions, and the "Revenue History of Chittagong," was what it pretended to be—a Revenue History. Sir Henry Ricketts was at this time living at Surbiton in his old age. He had come out to India in 1821, and had from 1841 to 1848 been employed on revenue settlement operations in Chittagong. When he retired, in 1860, he had refused a Lieutenant-Governorship. He was the greatest revenue authority ever known in Bengal. I do not think that any letter ever gave me more pleasure than one from Sir Henry Ricketts which he wrote to me after reading my book, and declared that if he were forty years younger he would go out again to India, pitch his tent in my compound, and serve as my Assistant as long as I would retain his services. That is the highest tribute I have received in respect of any work I have done.

This book was not the only literary work on which I was engaged in Chittagong. I wrote an unsigned article which was published in the *New Quarterly Review* of October, 1879, entitled "India's Need and England's Duty," in which I sketched in outline and foreshadowed the principles afterwards enunciated in "New India."

In September of this year the Commissionership of the Chittagong Division fell temporarily vacant and I was promoted to act in it. A Commissioner is the supervising authority over the District officers posted within the area of his Division, and is the link of communication between them and the Board of Revenue for revenue matters and with the Government for all other purposes. It is a high office to which a civilian could not ordinarily aspire until after twenty years' service. So I was deemed to be, and actually was, uncommonly lucky to get the acting appointment. By a very objectionable arrangement, which was shortly afterwards set aside, the Commissioner of Chittagong exercised also the functions of District and Sessions Judge. But as there was an Assistant Judge who had full powers this did not greatly matter, and it was only in occasional appellate and very special business that the Judge ever interfered.

I had hardly taken charge of my new duties before there occurred one of those frightful cyclones to which this part of the Bay of Bengal seems peculiarly liable. I was off immediately in a Government steamer to inspect the damage done. It was not very great in comparison with that which had been caused three years before in the neighbouring Districts of Noacolly and Backergunge, when it was estimated that a hundred thousand persons were drowned by a tidal wave. But in itself it was a frightful calamity. It was a strange sight to see the mangrove swamps all along the coast, no longer green, but brown, and looking as though they had been burnt with fire. The rice crops, ripening to the harvest, were everywhere levelled to the ground, and the ears of grain blown away. There was a little fishing village I had known. The sea had risen and swept it from the face of the earth so that not a trace remained. Every inhabitant of this village perished except one, and he was only saved by his absence on the mainland. On all sides trees and huts were blown down. There was great distress and suffering; and again I had occasion to admire the marvellous resourcefulness and patience of the Bengal peasantry.

The south of the Chittagong District borders on Burma, and parts of it are inhabited by Burmese, locally known as Muggs. There are settlements there of Buddhist monasteries from one of which I obtained by purchase a very curious manuscript, known as the "Golden Book," the *Kamma Vacha*, or Buddhist ritual, in beautiful "tamarind seed" letters of the old Pali character, painted with a black, resinous gum on thick, gilt lacquer leaves, each leaf containing six lines on either side. The *Kamma Vacha* is the basis of Buddhist monkhood. It is held in unlimited veneration by the Buddhist clergy of Burma, Siam, and Ceylon, and contains the entire history of the order of Buddhist monks from its foundation to its maturity. I was on the most friendly terms, which lasted for many years, with the Buddhist High Priest of Harbung, and through his kind offices afterwards obtained another copy, which passed into the possession of Sir Charles Elliott.

It is perhaps needless to say that Chittagong at the close of the seventies was a very different station from what it is now. There was then no talk of any railway. The post came round *viâ* Dacca and Comilla, and took three or four days to arrive from Calcutta. I remember one occasion when the postal runner was carried off by a tiger. The runners ran in couples with a great shouting and ringing of bells in order to scare away wild animals. Once a week a small coasting steamer from Calcutta would bring the mails direct, and the incoming of that steamer was always an event. No large steamers could then navigate the Chittagong River. There was no Port Trust, and the river bar, which needs such constant attention, was never cleared. But a brisk trade was still done by native brigs, which were built and owned in Chittagong itself.

I was stationed in Chittagong only for a very short time, and though my hard work there was emphatically a labour of love, and I have always taken the most lively interest and concern in Chittagong men and Chittagong affairs, I confess that I was very glad to get back to Calcutta, and I received with a full measure of delight a telegram in January, 1880, announcing that I was posted to the appointment of Senior Secretary to the Board of Revenue.

CHAPTER XV

LORD LYTTON

I HAD no part or lot in any of the measures which marked the individuality of Lord Lytton's Government; but every department of the administration was indirectly affected by them. The life of every Magistrate and of every British resident in India was stirred to its depth by the incidents which signalised his tenure of office, and I deem it no diversion from the current of my story to record the impressions created and memories left on my mind by the Lytton period.

Lord Lytton began well, and it would be an injustice not to place to his credit the episode of the "Fuller Case," which occurred in 1876 and has not been forgotten in India to this day. The facts of the case are typical of a hundred similar cases before and since. One Sunday morning Mr. Fuller, an English pleader at Agra, was about to drive to church with his family. When the carriage was brought to the door the groom failed to be in attendance, but made his appearance when sent for. For this fault Mr. Fuller struck the groom with his open hand on the head and face and pulled him by the hair so as to cause him to fall down. Mr. Fuller and his family drove on to church; the groom got up, went into an adjoining compound, and there died almost immediately. The medical evidence was to the effect that the man had died from rupture of the spleen, which very slight violence would be sufficient to cause in consequence of the morbid enlargement of that organ. The Joint Magistrate of the Station found Mr. Fuller guilty of "voluntarily causing what distinctly amounts to hurt," and sentenced him to pay a fine of Rs. 30 (or £2), which was to be paid over as compensation to the widow of the deceased.

At the request of the Local Government, the High Court of Allahabad expressed an opinion on the case, which was to the effect that the sentence, though perhaps lighter than the High Court would have been disposed to inflict under the circumstances, was not specially open to objection. It was then that Lord Lytton rose in his wrath :—

"The Governor-General in Council cannot but regret that the High Court should have considered that its duties and responsibilities in this matter were adequately fulfilled by the expression of such an opinion. He also regrets that the Local Government should have made no inquiry, until directed to do so by the Government of India, into the circumstances of a case so injurious to the honour of British rule and so damaging to the reputation of British justice in this country.

* * * * * *

"The class of misconduct out of which this crime has arisen is believed to be dying out ; but the Governor-General in Council would take this opportunity of expressing his abhorrence of the practice, instances of which occasionally come to light, of European masters treating their native servants in a manner in which they would not treat men of their own race. This practice is all the more cowardly because those who are least able to retaliate injury or insult have the strongest claim upon the forbearance and protection of their employers. But, bad as it is from every point of view, it is made worse by the fact, known to all residents in India, that Asiatics are subject to internal disease which often renders fatal to life even a slight external shock. The Governor-General in Council considers that the habit of resorting to blows on every trifling provocation should be visited by adequate legal penalties, and that those who indulge in it should reflect that they may be put in jeopardy for a serious crime."

The whole of this letter, which was addressed to the Government of the North-Western, now called the United, Provinces, was a scathing condemnation of what had taken place. Its publication evoked, as was to have been expected, a storm of Anglo-Indian and official indignation; while in the Indian Press there was, of course, a chorus of approbation. It is to be feared that the effect of utterances of this nature is too often to kindle the embers of racial antagonism which are ever smouldering. Be it so; but there are occasions when it seems to be better to run any risk. There is borne on my mind the famous order passed by Lord Dalhousie on a case in which he had successfully insisted on justice being done at the risk of a tumult. "I circulate these papers," wrote that Governor-General; "they are an instance of the principle that we should do what is right without fear of the consequences." The passions excited by the Fuller controversy have faded into the past; but Lord Lytton's attitude will always stand to his indelible credit.

I would that I could continue to write of Lord Lytton's administration in this flattering strain. But I am confronted by facts, and, while I do not wish to dip my pen in gall, veracity will compel me to confine my record to unfavourable comment. I must affirm at once that the personal habits of the Viceroy were so Bohemian that they jarred on the proprieties of those who had been accustomed to the decorum of a Northbrook. It struck one as odd at least when the official Levée was interrupted while the Viceroy indulged in a cigarette, and the practice of smoking a cigarette between the courses at dinner did not commend itself to the ladies or, indeed, to any of the guests at Government House. The incessant indulgence in liqueurs, the turning of night into day and transacting business after midnight, and the Viceroy's personal demeanour on occasion of public functions—these things became matter of common gossip, and sometimes gave ground for offence. I remember Mowbray Thomson coming home one night from a full-dress function at Government House in a towering rage. It seems that Lord Lytton, without rhyme or reason, when addressing himself to him during the evening had plucked him by the beard with the remark, "A virgin beard, I'll swear!" Such manners could not elevate the ethical standard of society about Government House or the Viceregal Lodge, and one of the gravest charges brought against Lord Lytton relates to the laxity of his entourage. At least one very scandalous case occurred which was not only the talk of Simla but of every regimental mess throughout India. From such causes any moral influence the Viceroy might have exercised in the country, or on the Services in particular, was completely lost.

Lord Lytton had been appointed by Mr. Disraeli to carry out a policy in Afghanistan, and to that task he devoted his energies. Neither the Delhi Durbar nor the terrible famine in Madras, a calamity unprecedented in its intensity within memory, from which five millions of people perished, could divert him from the object he had placed before him. Russophobia was at the bottom of this policy. We know now of Lord Salisbury's telegram to Lord Lytton in October, 1876, which said that Great Britain was on the verge of a war with Russia, which might be declared in three weeks' time, and inquired "whether in that case we can undertake to strike a rapid blow on Central Asia and raise the population against her." The pigeon-holes of the Military Secretariat at Simla were full of programmes and schemes for striking a deadly blow on Russia in Asia. A hostile Afghanistan was looked on as a matter of small importance. The kingdom of Cabul was described by Lord Lytton in a letter to the Ameer as an earthen pipkin between two iron pots. Sir George Pomeroy Colley, the Military, and afterwards Private, Secretary, who exercised an undue and dangerous influence with the Viceroy, believed that a thousand men armed with Martinis could march anywhere in Afghanistan. It is known that Lord Lytton actually proposed the invasion of Central Asia through Afghanistan by the dispatch of a small force to seize Tashkend. The misconceptions and delusions of the late seventies, both in England and in India, in respect of the Afghan frontier were astonishing.

The declaration of war with the Ameer was a foregone conclusion. The long-established policy of previous Viceroys was upset, and the peace which had been maintained for a generation was disturbed. The war was declared after peace with Russia had been secured by the Treaty of Berlin. It was not undertaken, said Lord Beaconsfield on the 9th of November, 1878, in a speech at the Lord Mayor's Banquet, to punish Shere Ali for his reception of the

Russian Mission, or for his refusal to receive an English Mission, but for the rectification of boundaries and for securing a scientific frontier. Was ever greater mockery implied than in these words? On the advance of British troops Shere Ali fled to Turkestan, and there died. On the 26th of May, 1879, his son Yakub Khan signed the Treaty of Gundamak. "We have secured a scientific and adequate frontier," wrote Lord Beaconsfield to the Viceroy in August. "It will always be a source of real satisfaction to me that I had the opportunity of placing you on the throne of the Great Mogul." Was ever congratulation more premature? Soon, indeed, were there stirring events on foot, and bloody war was raging on the North-West Frontier. Blunder after blunder was committed, and India was racked with suspense and anxiety which can only be paralleled by the feeling that prevailed in England during the sensational episodes of the Boer War.

The summer of 1879 was darkened by the Mission of Sir Louis Cavagnari to Cabul and its tragic sequel. Lord Lawrence greeted the news of his departure with the prophetic cry, "They will be murdered, every one of them," but none was then found to listen to the warnings of that sagacious statesman. It was enough that Lord Lytton and Lord Salisbury expressed implicit confidence in the stability of the situation. But Cavagnari himself was under no illusions. He knew that he was going to his doom, and when he bade farewell to his friends he told them that the chances were four to one that he would never return. "If my death," he said, "places the red line on the Hindu Kush, I don't mind." On the 6th of July Cavagnari left Simla, on the 24th of July the Mission arrived at Cabul, and on the 3rd of September every member of the Mission and the whole of the escort, excepting three or four men of the Guides who escaped, were massacred at the Residency.

In an incredibly short space of time the "avenging" army, as it was called, was in occupation of Cabul. Martial law was established, men were hanged in batches, the Ameer, Yakub Khan, was deported to India, the country was ravaged for supplies, and village-burning was the order of the day. There was no more gallant officer engaged in this campaign than Sir Charles Macgregor, the Chief of Lord Roberts' Staff, and it is pathetic to read in that distinguished soldier's diary the doubts and anxieties which tormented him as to the justice and wisdom of these summary executions. "I do not believe," he wrote, "that it ever does good to kill men indiscriminately, and I will not lend myself to it." Macgregor did his best, and the responsibility for the executions, which, when they were known, created a storm of indignation in England, rests solely on Lord Roberts. It is to the credit of Sir Donald Stewart that he never tolerated such savage reprisals.

What happened? The exasperated tribesmen rose in their thousands; disasters followed in quick succession, redeemed by incidents of splendid courage and devotion; and Lord Roberts found himself besieged under most perilous conditions at Sherpore in the vicinity of Cabul. The courage and resource displayed by Lord Roberts at all stages of the war, and emphatically when placed in the most trying and critical positions, bring but into bolder relief the serious errors of judgment and tactical blunders which led him into more than one grave reverse, from which he was only rescued by his own fortitude and the unvarying gallantry of the officers and men under his command. The heroism of Herbert

Macpherson, White, Hammond, and Baker, the timely advent of Charles Gough's Brigade, the memorable march of Donald Stewart from Candahar to Cabul, the consequent relief of Sherpore, the negotiations with Abdur Rahman and his enthronement as Ameer, the hundred and one kaleidoscopic movements which shook India with excitement—these are the echoes from Afghanistan which were wafted to anxious dwellers in the plains by Howard Hensman through the pages of the *Pioneer*, and are now chronicled with icy impartiality in a classic history of the war by my friend Colonel Hanna, who was himself serving on the Staff and took an honourable part in the campaign.

When the record of battle closed at Cabul it reopened at Candahar. Ayub Khan, the brother of the Ameer Yakub Khan, was advancing rapidly from Herat with a large and growing army. The British forces sent out to meet him under General Burrows were totally defeated at Maiwand, and fled in hopeless confusion to the shelter of the Candahar fort. So complete a rout was unprecedented in the annals of the British Army in India. Candahar was besieged. The general officer commanding was incompetent, but he had an excellent Staff, among whom John Hills and E. P. Leach, both of the Royal Engineers, were pre-eminent. The immediate relief of Candahar at all hazards was demanded, and Sir Donald Stewart, with an abnegation which recalls the memory of Outram, deputed General Roberts to command the relieving force and so afforded him the opportunity of his life, the march from Cabul to Candahar. That march was a triumphal procession : Candahar was relieved, Ayub Khan's troops were decisively defeated and dispersed, and Ayub himself ultimately surrendered.

The war was over, and nothing remained but

retirement and the evacuation of Afghanistan. In spite of strenuous protests this was done: a wise decision directly due to the change of Government in England.

CHAPTER XVI

LORD RIPON

WHEN Mr. Gladstone succeeded Mr. Disraeli after the General Election in the spring of 1880, there was a change of Viceroy in India. Lord Lytton retired, and the Marquess of Ripon assumed charge on the 8th of June, 1880. With Lord Ripon's arrival a new era in the history of India was inaugurated, and I refrain a little longer from personal narrative to indulge in some reflections on the character and incidents of this period, which, though I was not directly concerned with them, yet vitally affected the whole course of my subsequent career. I may admit, perhaps I should claim, that I am identified as much as any man with the development and interpretation of Lord Ripon's policy in its practical application to Indian affairs. But I had no share, however humble, in the inception of that policy. I did not come in contact with Lord Ripon, and he had not heard of me until his administration was drawing to a close. He then sent for me and expressed his regret that he had only come to know me when it was too late. So that whatever part I may have taken in the fray afterwards, I wish to make it plain that while Lord Ripon was in India I was a witness and spectator only.

What was Lord Ripon's policy? I know how it

was described in the House of Lords by his predecessor, an acute and bitterly hostile critic. "It is the policy of gradually transferring political power in India from European to native hands." "Does it not mean," asked Lord Lytton, "nay, ought it not to be taken as meaning, we, the English Government in India, have put ourselves in a false position from which we wish to extricate ourselves as quickly as possible? We must, no doubt, hold office for a certain time in order to train up you natives to take our places; but this is our only object. As soon as it is accomplished, and the sooner the better, we shall retire and leave India to be governed by whatever body the native representative assemblies may see fit to entrust with the task of government."

This is Lord Lytton's gloss on Lord Ripon's policy. It goes without saying that such language was at once repudiated by the Ministers of a Liberal Government, who are always ready to deprecate the conclusions which logically follow from the conscientious application of their professed principles. The friends and supporters of Lord Ripon were eager to offer the excuse that the measures which excited so much violent and bitter opposition were really isolated in character and individually of small importance. It is not impossible that Lord Ripon himself was in the first instance as unconscious of the inevitable tendency of his own measures as he was admittedly unprepared for the tremendous antagonism they provoked. And yet all can now see that the policy he espoused was but the logical development of principles which had long been ripening to maturity. He was the instrument at whose hands a slow and elaborate preparation at last received its fulfilment.

There are no Governor-Generals in the past, not even Lord Lytton himself, who have not taken their part in the united and continuous efforts which are the prelude to all great measures of reform. If there have been some temporary spasms of reaction, these are but vexatious aberrations from the path of progress, and the current of advance has never been really stemmed. Lord Ripon struck while the iron was hot, and availed himself of all the impetus his predecessors had accumulated. He was, of course, more than a mere instrument. By his personal enthusiasm he infused life into the dry bones of the administrative machine, and by the vigour of his example he stimulated the subordinate Governments to give practical expression to his views.

There was no change in the constitution of the Government, which remained supreme as that of the Tsar of Russia. But in the spirit and disposition of the exercise of supreme power a change became visible. The Vernacular Press Act of Lord Lytton was repealed. In Afghanistan there was a complete reversal of an erroneous policy, an unreserved withdrawal from an unjust aggression. The Province of Mysore, after having been for nearly fifty years under British rule, was restored to its hereditary prince, and, for the first time in the history of India, the red line of British possessions receded. A vigorous attempt was made to scale the last barriers of civil inequality, and the local authorities were set to busy themselves in organising a scheme of local self-government. The benevolent despotism of an autocratic administration began to merge into a system of free representation and municipal and local independence. There were the signs of the beginning of a new order and a new life. The way was being gradually made straight for the emancipation of the Indian people. The period of Lord Ripon has been well described as the Golden Age of Indian Reformers, when the aspirations of the people were encouraged, education and local self-government were fostered, and the foundations of Indian Nationality were firmly laid.

If I were to venture on any criticism of Lord Ripon, it would be to say that he laboured under the defect, or weakness, of not surrounding himself with those whom he knew to be in sympathy with his own views. This is a voluntary handicap to which Liberal statesmen seem to be constitutionally liable to subject themselves. I confess that, for my part, I have more appreciation of the attitude of a Viceroy like Lord Curzon, who had also a policy to enforce and never hesitated to choose his own agents to carry it out. If the head of a great Government wants to get a thing done as he wishes it, he must employ instruments in whom he has implicit confidence. And yet Lord Ripon was willing to accept, in one of the most difficult positions a Viceroy ever had to face, the unsympathetic and ordinary Simla material he found ready to his hand. There was, if he had cared to seek for them, a little band of senior officers, of capacity and knowledge, who were animated by devotion to his own principles. Such men were Allan Hume, C.B., of Allahabad, Sir William Wedderburn of Bombay, Sir Henry Harrison of Calcutta, and Sir William Hunter. But he did not turn to these men. Nay, more! he conferred the highest promotion at his disposal on a man whom he knew to be his bitterest political opponent. Sir Rivers Thompson as a Member of his Council had strenuously opposed the evacuation of Candahar, and he was known to be hostile to the so-called Ilbert Bill. Yet Lord Ripon made Sir Rivers Thompson Lieutenant-Governor of Bengal, and planted there a thorn in his side who became the recognised and official focus of agitation against the principal measure with which as Viceroy he was identified.

The readers of Trevelyan's biography of Lord

Macaulay will remember how the whole non-official world in India was banded together to resist what it conceived to be the monstrous injustice of Macaulay's "Black Act," which authorised Indian Judges to exercise Civil jurisdiction over British-born subjects. But this crisis was as nothing in comparison with that which occurred in Lord Ripon's time when Sir Ashley Eden, shortly before his retirement, proposed an amendment in the Criminal Law to give Indian Magistrates jurisdiction to try European offenders. This is the measure known as the Ilbert Bill, because it was introduced into the Legislative Council by Sir Courtenay Ilbert, who was then Legal Member. A public meeting of protest by the European community was held at the Town Hall in Calcutta ; members of the Bar abandoned the noble traditions of their profession, and speakers and audience, frenzied with excitement, were lost to all sense of moderation and propriety. The Viceroy was personally insulted at the gates of Government House. A gathering of tea planters assembled and hooted him at a railway station as he was returning from Darjiling, when "Bill" Beresford, then an A.D.C., was with difficulty restrained from leaping from the railway carriage into their midst to avenge the insult to his Chief. The non-official European community almost to a man boycotted the entertainments at Government House. Matters had reached such a pitch that a conspiracy was formed by a number of men in Calcutta, who bound themselves, in the event of Government adhering to the proposed legislation, to overpower the sentries at Government House, put the Viceroy on board a steamer at Chandpal Ghat, and deport him to England round the Cape. I heard this story at the time, and it would seem to be incredible, but the facts are understood to have been within the knowledge of the Lieutenant-Governor and the Commissioner of Police.

It is with a feeling of shame that I am bound to add that the opposition to the Ilbert Bill was headed by members of my own Service, and that the practical unanimity of opposition to that measure was as complete among civilian Magistrates and Judges as it was among planters, merchants, and members of the legal profession. Lord Ripon was thus harassed and hampered in an inconceivable degree by the bigotry and race feeling of his own fellow-countrymen. He was paralysed from want of support, and neither he nor any man in his position, single-handed, could have overcome the dead wall of antagonism by which he was confronted. The result was a sort of compromise which, according to Sir John Strachey—no mean authority—was "the virtual though not avowed abandonment of the measure proposed by the Government."

That was the immediate result. The ultimate effect of the insane agitation was to give rise to a movement of the widest reaching character and scope which few at that time were able to foresee. It is one of the ironies of history that the very object which agitations are intended to serve or to suppress should so often be lost or gained by the counter-irritation which agitation sets up in a community. The great Indian movement, of which we now hear so much and are assuredly destined to hear much more, is due to causes intended to produce a very different effect. The germ of a national organisation on the basis of English education had long existed, but it only sprang to life in the eighties. The Anglo-Indian agitation against Lord Ripon's government, the protests which asserted that "the only people who have any right to India are the British," the whole attitude of Englishmen in regard to Indian interests—these things have succeeded far more in advancing the cause of Indian unity than any action or legislation on the lines contemplated by that Viceroy could have accomplished.

The Ilbert Bill, if it had been allowed to pass without opposition, would have proved innocuous and comparatively ineffective in any direction. But the unreasonable clamour and rancour of its opponents and the unexpected success which attended their efforts suggested reprisals. Indignation found its voice ; clamour was met by clamour ; and a national agitation was carried on throughout the length and breadth of India. The very object was attained which, if the Anglo-Indian leaders had been wise in their generation, they would have spared no labour to prevent. The people of India were not slow to follow the example set to them by Englishmen ; they learned their strength, the power of combination, the force of numbers ; and there was quickly kindled in all the provinces a national movement which is destined to develop and increase until it receives its fulfilment in the systematic regeneration of the whole country.

It is literally true that Lord Ripon was able to accomplish little, and that the political revolution which is now taking place in India is far more largely attributable to the blind fanaticism of those who opposed him than to his own exertions. The actual results of his government as shown upon the Statute Book are not very great. But one thing he did. He made a humble beginning in extending the elective system and in giving the people some share in the administration of local affairs. Nothing is more calculated to minimise the inherent dislike of a people to alien rule than the invitation to partake in the duties and responsibilities of government. It was in this way that Munro and Elphinstone succeeded in consolidating the Indian Empire in the early years of the last century, and it was the adoption of this policy that made the government of Lord Ripon so popular among the people. He caused to be published a series of Resolutions, which were drafted by his own hand, on the principles of local self-government.

"Freedom from official tutelage is essential to healthy and independent growth."

"To officials, zealous for improvement, it is trying to see important schemes, calculated to confer great benefit on a large community, postponed or marred from ignorance or apathy or indifference. But patience is necessary in the conduct of all public affairs, and those whose favourite projects are thwarted and opposed should remember that the establishment, development, and practical working of self-government are not only an end to be pursued but a great object of political education to be attained."

"It is better that even useful reforms should be postponed for a time and ultimately carried out with the consent of local bodies and in the form most acceptable to them, than that they should be enforced at once with a disregard of the feelings of the local body. We should respect the independence of such bodies ; we should retain sufficient control over them to see that they do not permanently, obstinately, or slothfully neglect their duties towards their fellow-citizens ; but having planted this small tree of self-government, we ought not always to be pulling it up to look at its roots in order to see how far they have got down into the ground."

"It is hopeless to expect any real development of local self-government if local bodies are subjected to check and interference in matters of detail."

The enunciation of such principles, not in Resolutions only but also in public addresses to local bodies, had never before been heard in India. They lay down a policy not very pleasing or acceptable to the bureaucratic mind ; but they electrified the educated classes of the community and sank deep into the hearts of a grateful people. It is a tribute to their wisdom as well as a reflection on the slowness of the adoption of Liberal principles in our Indian administration that Lord Morley, in the most important of the published dispatches issued to the Government of India during the tenure of his office as Secretary of State, should have fallen back on the very words of Lord Ripon in his exhortation to the authorities in India a quarter of a century after they had been uttered.

Lord Ripon may not have been a great orator. He was not gifted with the commanding presence of a Mayo or the rhetoric of a Curzon. But he was dominated by sincerity and zeal, and above all things by moral earnestness without which no man was ever truly great. On the 7th of January, 1884, I sat side by side with Dr. Busteed listening to a long debate on the Ilbert Bill, which was held not in the Council Chamber but, in order to meet the demand of the public for more room, in the large Banqueting Hall of Government House. The official Member for Madras—Mr. Henry Sullivan Thomas, remembered now only for this incident and a book on fishing entitled "The Rod in India"—had just delivered, with wagging beard and all the emphasis he could command, a violent philippic not only on the measure before the Council but on the principles of the Indian Magna Charta, the Queen's Proclamation of 1858. To him replied Lord Ripon, in a voice rich with emotion, in the following memorable words which are familiar to every educated Indian from that day to this :—

"To me it seems a very serious thing to put forth to the people of India a doctrine which renders worthless the solemn words of their Sovereign, and which converts her gracious promises, which her Indian subjects have cherished for a quarter of a century, into a hollow mockery, as meaningless as the compliments which form the invariable opening of an Oriental letter. It seems to me to be inconsistent with the character of my Sovereign and with the honour of my country, and, if it were once to be received and acted upon by the Government of England, it would do more than anything else could possibly do to strike at the root of our power and to destroy our just influence, because that power and that influence rest upon the conviction of our good faith more than upon any other foundation, aye, more than upon the valour of our soldiers and the reputation of our arms. I have heard to-day with no little surprise a very different argument. The Honourable Mr. Thomas, in a speech in which he did his utmost to stir up the bitterness of a controversy which was approaching settlement and to fan again the dying embers of race animosity, has asked, 'Was there ever a nation which retained her supremacy by the righteousness of her laws?' I have read in a book, the authority of which the Honourable Mr. Thomas will admit, that 'righteousness exalteth a nation,' and my study of history has led me to the conclusion that it is not by the force of her armies or by the might of her soldiery that a great Empire is permanently maintained, but that it is by the righteousness of her laws and by her respect for the principles of justice. To believe otherwise appears to me to assume that there is not a God in heaven who rules over the affairs of men, and who can punish injustice and iniquity in nations as surely as in the individuals of whom they are composed. It is against doctrines like this that I desire to protest, and it is against principles of this description that the gracious Proclamation of our Queen was directed. So long, then, as I hold the office which I now fill I shall conduct the administration of this country in strict accordance with the policy which has been enjoined upon me by my Queen and by Parliament."

The Marquess of Ripon left India in December, 1884, and the first Indian National Congress met in 1885. The date of his departure is the natal day of a New India. "His journey from Simla to Bombay," writes Meredith Townsend, "was a triumphal march, such as India has never witnessed —a long procession in which seventy millions of people sang hosannas to their friend." The homage that was tendered to Lord Ripon by all classes and creeds was never before tendered to any foreign ruler. The spectacle of a whole nation stirred by one common impulse of gratitude was never before beheld in Indian history. I took my share in the great demonstration in Calcutta. No public movement could have been more characterised by unanimity and spontaneity. No sign could have shown more clearly that the germ of a nationality had already sprung into life.

CHAPTER XVII

HIC ET UBIQUE

I OWED my appointment in the Board of Revenue to Henry Lucius Dampier, then senior member of the Board, who has always been one of my kindest friends. His father had served in the Civil Service before him for forty years, and Mr. Dampier himself was a fine type of the Haileybury civilian. I had known him very well in the past while he was Revenue Secretary to Government; we thoroughly understood one another, and it was a great pleasure to me to work under such admirable revenue officers as Dampier and my other old friend Reynolds who succeeded him. But I admit that when I joined the Board as its Secretary I never expected to remain in that office for as long as seven years. My promotion had gone on up to that point by leaps and bounds: there now ensued a check.

Early in 1882, just before Sir Ashley Eden's retirement, I was offered the Revenue Secretaryship to Government, but the offer was accompanied by a condition that the pay of the office should be reduced to the amount I was then drawing in the Board. My pride was touched, and I declined the offer. It was accepted by my friend Antony (now Lord) MacDonnell, who thus got his first step on the rung of that brilliant career of success after success which it has delighted no one more than myself to applaud and admire. MacDonnell and I were not always in accord in our views, but we had a real regard for one another, and never has there been an interruption in our friendship from the early days of our service to the present time.

It was my own doing that I did not get back into the Bengal Secretariat in 1882. After that I had no chance for many years, and was passed over by more than one of my juniors on various occasions. The reason of this calls for explanation. I never made any concealment of my opinions, every one knew that I identified myself with Lord Ripon's policy, and I was already described as a white Baboo. Sir Rivers Thompson, who was Lieutenant-Governor for five years from the spring of 1882, was the principal opponent of Lord Ripon's policy. I could not expect promotion in his time.

I had left Chittagong with some malaria in my system. For the first time in my service I got brief but sharp attacks of ague, followed by high fever and nausea. Sometimes these would recur every afternoon, but they never affected me so seriously as to prevent my going to work next morning. The peculiarity of the form of ague was the suddenness of the attack and its severity while it lasted. I was at this time a manager of the Bengal Civil Fund, then under the control of the Civil Service, and once while I was actually addressing a meeting of subscribers in the Town Hall I collapsed and had to be carried out of the room. A couple of years later, in England, when I was feeling poorly, but had no anticipation of an attack, I was suddenly taken ill with ague in the same way while having my hair cut at Douglas's, and would have fallen without assistance. It was an unpleasant type of malarial fever which clung to me for years, and for the sake of my health as well as on private grounds I was glad to be able to get three months' privilege leave home in 1882, to be followed by eight months' furlough in 1883.

In 1882 I came home with a return railway ticket between Suez and Alexandria. On July the 7th I left London for Brindisi, expecting to travel through Egypt again by the railway route. On arrival at Brindisi we heard of the British ultimatum that, if the Egyptians continued their work on the fortifications of Alexandria, the British fleet would open fire on them. I never dreamed that this threat would become a reality—for was not Mr. Gladstone Prime Minister?—but nevertheless I was on deck at night as we neared Alexandria and, on gazing towards the city, saw the whole of the horizon lit up with a great blaze of flame. The bombardment had taken place on the 11th; incendiaries had set fire to the town that night, and we arrived a little after midnight of the 12th. We were directed to anchor outside the fleet, and await orders. There we remained for two or three days, when the excitement and suspense were at last relieved by a cable from London, and the old *Pekin* was the first steamer to proceed through the Canal after hostilities had been declared.

One thing I remember very well, and that is that I was the only passenger who expressed indignation at the bombardment. There was a general uneasiness lest Arabi should take steps to block the passage of the Canal, or possibly attack the steamer. A supply of arms was served out among some of the passengers, who patrolled the deck for the two nights we were at anchor in the Canal. Occasional caravans of camels were a source of more than ordinary interest, for might they not denote the flanking attack of an avenging army? But we got through to Suez without incident. There one or two men-of-war were at anchor, and burning with anxiety for news. A smart lieutenant put out in a steam-launch and came up in fine style to the *Pekin's* ladder, but he jumped too soon and fell into the sea, from which he was fished out by a quartermaster. I am bound to say that no young fellow in this humiliating predicament could have stepped on deck with a better grace. The next year when I went home we travelled again by the railway from Suez to Alexandria, and I witnessed the terrible damage which had been done to the great square by the bombardment and the fire ; but two years after that, in 1885, when I again traversed the same route, no trace remained.

It was during my furlough in 1883 that I became entangled in the attractive meshes of chess. There was an International Tournament then going on in London, of which my uncle, James Innes Minchin, was the principal promoter. My uncle was a remarkable man. After retirement from the Madras Civil Service, in which he had served with distinction, he devoted himself in an extraordinary degree to the study of classical and Italian literature, and he would read any Greek or Latin or Italian book with the same facility and pleasure as an English one. He translated Dante into *terza rima*. With no pretensions to scholarship, he had acquired a profound knowledge of the classics. His leisure he devoted to chess, and was for many years honorary secretary of the St. George's Chess Club, of which I was a member. Under his auspices I attended the tournament almost every day, and made the acquaintance of the leading players, among whom Steinitz and Zukertort were the chief. It was a certainty from the beginning that one or other of these would win the first prize, and as a matter of fact in the final result Zukertort was first and Steinitz second.

How well I remember Steinitz !—short, squat, and stout, with thick red hair and beard, and rejoicing in a nose unusually small for one of the Semitic race.

He smoked and sipped claret and water, or gin and water—scrupulously iced notwithstanding the coldness of the weather—all the time he played. He rarely rose from his seat during a game, in this respect being a contrast to most of the other players, and especially to Zukertort, whose excitable nature induced him to walk about and follow more or less all the other games in progress in addition to his own. He thought out his moves with his arms folded on the table before him, and did not stroke his beard or twirl his moustache. Nor is there any failure in my memory of Zukertort, whose figure was the very opposite to that of Steinitz. He was short and thin, with a brown beard, over which, while thinking, his fingers were perpetually moving ; the nervous twitch that he gave his head was peculiar to himself ; his countenance indicated great intelligence and determination.

Tchigorin and Noa were young and sallow, with black beards. Rosenthal, the French champion, and Winawer, from Poland, were seedy-looking little men. Mackenzie was a fine, manly fellow who would have been distinguished in almost any company. Sellman was stone deaf. I recall how Zukertort once confided to me that dominoes was the game at which he really played best, and not chess ; that he considered himself to be the best player in the world at dominoes, and that Rosenthal came next ; and also how Bird assured me that the quality of chess play was steadily improving, and that he himself played a far stronger game than he had done when he met Morphy twenty-five years before

It was in this year also that I became a member of the M.C.C. I know not how many delectable hours I have spent in watching cricket from the pavilion at Lord's and tennis from the *dedans*. I took a few lessons at tennis from that grand player

George Lambert, who was, I am convinced, as good as Peter Latham at his best. Tennis, be it said, is a game for the immortals; and my ideal of a young Greek god at play will always be Alfred Lyttelton, whose "superb groan" alone betrayed the signs of human frailty when he forgot himself so far as to fail at an easy stroke.

From 1883 and for many years onwards I was associated with my friends Sir Henry Harrison and Robert Steel in the organisation and encouragement of chess matches in Calcutta. We used to get up a Christmas tournament every year, at which the best players in Upper India would compete; and Harrison and I would have a chess symposium on Sunday afternoons, at which Calcutta players would drop in all the year round. Steel was a jute merchant, a man of exceptional ability, who was more than once president of the Bengal Chamber of Commerce, and served on the Viceroy's Legislative Council. Robert Steel, George Yule, and James Mackay (now Lord Inchcape) were the ablest men of business whom I knew in India. Steel was quite first-rate at chess and at other games of skill. He was a great patron of Steinitz, who dedicated to him in 1899 his "whole work on chess," of which only one volume, or Part I. of the "Modern Chess Instructor," ever appeared.

The Indian game of chess differs considerably from the game as we are accustomed to play it. The pawn is only allowed to advance one square, and this condition, which practically bars all gambits, tends to lead to a close style of game. The pawn, when it is moved to the eighth square, is converted into the piece to which the square belongs; it becomes a bishop if on bishop's eighth, a rook if on rook's eighth, and so on. The rules of castling are different; and if the king remains alone on the board, with all pieces and pawns taken, he becomes

"Fakeer," and the game is drawn. There are other differences; but as a fact all the good Indian players I have met know and prefer the European game. They are most skilful players, and the greatest master in chess would hesitate about the odds he gave to them. They were the equals of Steel and Harrison, and therefore not below the level of the most accomplished amateurs of the day. I record the names of five: Meera Buksh, a stalwart, grey-bearded Mahomedan from the Punjab; Rughoonundun Chobey and Mahadeb Chobey, up-country Brahmins from the sacred city of Muttra; and Ishwar Chunder Gossain and Dwarkanath Banerjee, Brahmins of Calcutta. Only the last of these was acquainted with English. There were many other players in our chess circle, but they did not attain unto the first five.

I lived on terms of brotherly affection with Sir Henry Harrison for ten years until his death in 1892. He had been a mathematical Student at Christ Church, was president of the Union at Oxford, where he also won for himself a reputation at cricket and rackets, and came out to Bengal in 1860. As District officer of Midnapore he left behind him a great record, and I succeeded him as Secretary to the Board of Revenue. He was then appointed to be Chairman of the Calcutta Corporation and Commissioner of Police, and held those offices for nine years. As Chairman of the Municipality he achieved the distinction, which no one attained before him, of not only advancing important reforms, but of gaining the confidence of the popular representatives of the city, and of thereby carrying out those reforms, not in spite of the opinion of the majority of Municipal Commisioners or in opposition to their wishes, but in cordial co-operation with them and with their active support.

It is an easy matter for the civic administrators of a great metropolis to enforce their schemes of improvement when they are untrammelled by the attitude of the ratepayers and can move this way or that independently of public criticism and prejudice. The possession of this administrative faculty is a common gift. But it involves higher qualifications to take in hand progressive measures and gradually but yet firmly persuade those whom they affect of their wisdom and necessity, and so accomplish the end in view through the instrumentality of the people and with their assistance. Such a gift is rare.

I have seen Sir Henry Harrison during a stormy debate, with the thermometer over 100°, harassed and worried and wearied, bearing almost the whole burden of the attack on his shoulders, but always unruffled in temper, always courteous and kindly, never overbearing, and ultimately leading to victory what seemed almost a forlorn hope by virtue of his earnest persuasiveness and transparent sincerity. His eloquence demands from me more than a passing notice. Of extraordinary readiness and fluency of speech, he possessed debating power in a marked degree, and, as I listened to him with admiration, I could not but regret that he was not afforded the opportunity of displaying his talent in a wider sphere.

Rarely, if ever, have I known a Government official who was more kind and devoted to the people of the country, and more genuinely sympathetic with the aspirations of the educated classes. His mind was cast in the largest and most liberal mould. In due course he was appointed a member of the Board of Revenue. Though his abilities would justly have entitled him to the highest promotion open to the Civil Service, he accepted this appointment as the close of his active career. He continued to take a part in the civic life of the metropolis, and there was naturally no more prominent citizen in Calcutta. But he devoted himself mainly, as he was bound to do, to his revenue work. In the discharge of his duties he proceeded to Chittagong in the sultry month of May, 1892, and there succumbed, with his daughter, to an attack of cholera. The memory of his name is perpetuated by the municipal representatives of Calcutta in more than one memorial of a permanent character. The Harrison Road, which crosses Calcutta from east to west, was called after him, and a bust, which I had the pleasure to unveil, was placed in his honour in the Town Hall.

Early in 1884 I was employed on the preparation of a memorandum on the land tenures of Bengal which was required for the information of members of the Government of India while the Bengal Tenancy Act was on the anvil. I may say that I got credit for this from those who were most competent to judge, but I suppose it was not reprinted, for when I left India eighteen years later I could not get a copy of it for love or money. In the spring of this year I was posted again to Chittagong to act as Commissioner for three months. This was not an eventful time, and I was principally engaged in reporting on the Tenancy Act and on local self-government proposals and on frontier matters. My old friend Colonel Lewin had then retired from frontier work. He was a handsome fellow, black-haired and swarthy, with a genius for dealing with ignorant and savage people, and I found the name of Tom Lewin a talisman for the settlement of their disputes.

On my return to Calcutta I was unexpectedly involved in an embittered controversy affecting the municipal government of the metropolis. Sir Richard Temple's constitution of the municipality on a representative basis had always been distasteful to the European residents of the city, though their dislike had not found formal expression. But now the anti-Ripon organisation diverted its energies in this direction, and a skilfully engineered agitation, ostensibly aimed at the sanitary condition of Calcutta, threatened a vital blow at the very existence of local self-government in the city. The result of more than one memorial, numerously and influentially signed, addressed to a Lieutenant-Governor who had no reluctance to support the movement of his friends, was that Sir Rivers Thompson accepted the opinion of the memorialists that "the Commissioners as a body are not qualified to judge of the special sanitary measures most immediately required or to realise the responsibility under which they lie as regards the present condition of the unhealthy portions of the city; that no good can be expected from further admonitions addressed by the Government to the Commissioners; but that the only hope of real improvement lies in the appointment of a select body of experts outside the municipality who would be capable of forming an opinion, at once scientific and independent, on the requirements of the case and the best practical manner of meeting them, and whose recommendations might be immediately carried out by orders of the Government." He appointed a Sanitary Commission for Calcutta, with an able officer, who was made a High Court Judge at the conclusion of its inquiries, as president, and the Sanitary Commissioner of Bengal as a member. The selection of the third member was vested by law in the Municipal Commissioners, and they appointed me.

I look back with satisfaction to the part I played in this controversy. The work of the Commission was arduous, and the report submitted was a valuable one. But I vindicated very thoroughly and at every opportunity the importance of the principles which were at stake, and the net result was that the statutory powers of the Government to supersede the functions of the members of the corporation were never exercised. I incurred much odium among the promoters of the agitation, and the Anglo-Indian Press denounced me in unmeasured terms for having, among other things, displayed all the qualifications of "a wheezy Old Bailey practitioner." On the other hand, I was on the height of a wave of popularity in the Indian Press, and the Municipal Commissioners of the city went so far as to propose to place my bust in the Town Hall. For obvious reasons the offer was respectfully declined. But I was easily induced to put myself up as a candidate for the Chowringhee Ward of the Corporation, where I was elected without opposition, and I remained an active member of the Town Council for several years. It was at this time also, as far as I remember, that I was appointed by the Government of India to be a Fellow of the Calcutta University. I served on the Syndicate of that body and took as keen a share in university discussion as I did in civic affairs.

The year 1885 was an important landmark in my career. Under the liberal leave rules of the Civil Service I availed myself of another furlough for six months. In 1883 I had already delivered a public address to a London audience, in which I vindicated the policy of Lord Ripon's Government. This was published in the form of a pamphlet entitled "England and India." I devoted my holiday in 1885 to the development of the ideas there foreshadowed, and in November published a book, "New India, or India in Transition," which has since passed through many editions, and has been translated into all the principal vernacular languages of India. This work made a considerable stir at the time of its publication, and was most highly spoken of by such diverse authorities as the *Times* newspaper and Mr. John Bright. It was, if I may be allowed to say so, a bold forecast, singularly justified by the event, of the future that attends the Indian races and of the great Indian movement upon which, after the lapse of a quarter of a century, public attention has been fixed, but to which at that time men's eyes were blind.

The book was dedicated by permission to Lord Ripon, who examined the proof-sheets as they passed through the press. He invited me to stay with him at Studley Royal, and I have the most pleasant recollections of his kindly hospitality and of his delightful relations with the neighbouring peasantry. With what natural pride he descanted on the beauties of the undulating park, on the glories of Fountains Abbey, and on the traditions of Friar Tuck and the gallant Robin Hood! There were children's games in the garden into which he entered with the utmost zest, himself joining in the children's races. One race I remember in which he ran hopping on one leg against a little lass who flew along her best, and his lordship lost. These were associations with a retired Viceroy more precious than any gilded memories of official courtesy. For many years, and indeed until my retirement from India, Lord Ripon maintained a regular correspondence with me, and his active interest in events there, and especially in the progress and development of local self-government, with respect to which I am afraid I could not give him much comfort, was unabated to the last.

CHAPTER XVIII

BACK ON THE LADDER

Of course I was roughly handled in the Anglo-Indian Press on my return to India, but I was used to that by this time and unaffected by it. I had thrown away the scabbard and was a marked man. But this is true, that not even my bitterest opponent was ever found to say that my individual opinions or personal predilections had in any way impaired my sense of official responsibility. Nor do I believe that my official position at the time was sensibly damaged by the publication of "New India." The air had been cleared by that utterance, and my influence in one direction at least, as an interpreter between the official world and the Indian public, had been immensely strengthened by it.

In point of fact I think I was rather a favourite of Lord Dufferin, who had succeeded Lord Ripon as Viceroy. He liked to have me behind his shoulder at public functions or at garden parties, so that I could quietly whisper into his ear who people were and tell him something about them ; and it was sure to follow that every scrap of information would be utilised to the best advantage. There was no one, and he knew it, who had a larger acquaintance or had mingled as freely as I had with members of the Indian community. Lord Dufferin consulted me about various matters in private correspondence, and when he retired he sent me a very nice letter of farewell with his photograph, which, like all other treasures I had with me, was destined to be destroyed in the Assam earthquake. I was appointed to be Honorary Secretary in Bengal to the Countess of Dufferin's Fund for Supplying Female Medical Aid to the Women of India, and in that capacity knew Lady Dufferin very well. She impressed me with her masterful character and business qualities, and the magnificent foundation on which that Fund was established and has since prospered was entirely due to her energies. Her example set a fine spirit among Calcutta ladies, who devoted themselves to carrying out her work and when she left India presented her with a handsome keepsake and an address full of womanly feeling which I had drafted for them.

The second gathering of the Indian National Congress met in the Town Hall of Calcutta at the close of 1886. Mr. Dadabhai Naoroji was its President, and as there was no official ban against attending the Congress at that time, I was present at its meetings as a spectator. Sir Charles Elliott, who was then President of a Committee for inquiring into public expenditure, accompanied me once, and Lord Dufferin, with his customary courtesy, invited the delegates to a garden party at Government House. Never, I suppose, was a more interesting and picturesque assemblage collected there, from all parts of India, from Lahore and Sind to Travancore.

In connection with this Congress I received a letter from Lord Ripon, dated the 20th of May, 1887, from which I make an extract :—

"I read your account of the meeting of the National Congress at Calcutta and of the lessons to be drawn from it with great interest. I fully share your opinion as to the importance of the question of the re-organisation of the Legislative Councils. But to obtain any attention to that or any other Indian question from the people of this country at the present time is simply impossible. Men's thoughts, so much at least of them as they are able to give to politics, are totally absorbed now upon Irish affairs, and they have not five minutes to give to any other matter whatsoever, let alone the affairs of India, about which at the best of times they understand and care so little.

"This is, of course, a very unsatisfactory and in some respects dangerous state of things. Under it Indian discontent will grow, and with that growing discontent the demand for changes will strengthen and enlarge until it may become very difficult to deal with.

"I am not at all insensible to the many difficulties connected with the introduction of a representative element into the Indian Legislative Councils. I recognise them as great, greater perhaps than many persons who have not seen the inside working of the machine of Indian Government would suppose. But they are not at all the dangers which the Anglo-Indian party foretell, and they are much more likely to be satisfactorily overcome by a timely dealing with the question than by its postponement. But the only hope of its being dealt with in time is that the Viceroy may take it up. He might, probably would, be able to settle it; no one else in the present state of things can.

"The condition of affairs here is miserable. The narrow, retrograde, hopeless policy of the Government about Ireland, if policy it deserves to be called at all, can only lead to renewed failure, increased complications, and growing exasperation. It is very disheartening. The very same spirit against which I had to fight in India is rampant here, and, though I firmly believe in the ultimate triumph of Home Rule, the immediate outlook is unpleasant enough."

It so happened that the question of the Legislative Councils was taken up by Lord Dufferin, and this is one of the matters on which I corresponded with him. But the wheels of progress in India always drag heavily; and it was not until five years later, in 1892, that a Bill was passed through Parliament which, thanks to Mr. Gladstone's powerful intervention, made a first small advance in the direction of introducing a representative element into the Councils.

Lord Dufferin took more interest than any other Viceroy has ever done in the affairs of the Calcutta municipality, and I remember his paying a visit to one of our meetings in the Town Hall at a time when, as I happened to be on my legs, he lost, I fear, the impression of eloquence which would certainly have been borne in on him if one of our more practised Indian speakers had been addressing the Council. On another occasion Lord Dufferin arranged with Sir Henry Harrison for a personal and private inspection of the slums of the city. I accompanied them, with his Private Secretary, Sir Donald Mackenzie Wallace, and we perambulated without observation or notice some of the most insanitary slums and alleys. This visit was prolonged to the Nimtollah Burning Ghat, where we witnessed the incineration of a dead body on the funeral pile with all the painful features, even to the bursting of the skull, which mark these ceremonies. Harrison and I were well inured to the worst of Calcutta smells, and the Viceroy did not suffer, but I am afraid that Wallace was not so fortunate, for he was ill and out-of-sorts for some time after this experience.

In January, 1887, I gave evidence before the Indian Public Service Commission. Out of the 442 witnesses examined by the Commission, all, I think, except myself assumed the maintenance of the Covenanted Civil Service as the basis of the Indian polity, and the schemes propounded by them had all more or less reference to the remodelling and recruitment of the Service. I ventured to take upon myself to propose to modify the central position and to formulate a scheme of reconstructive policy. While not slow to accord deserved praise to the able band of administrators who have contributed so much towards the progress of the Indian Empire, I urged that so centralised a system of government was already outworn in the more advanced provinces, and that the time had come for gradually replacing it by some more suitable machinery. To shape into another mould the favoured monopoly of the Civil Service, to utilise all that is wisest and most effective in English guidance while at the same time to develop Indian powers of government, to reduce the cost of administration, to bring justice to the doors of the poor, to kill the anomaly of a prosecutor-judge—these are some of the problems I concerned myself to attempt to solve. I was brushed aside as a visionary. I console myself with the reflection that years before this I had been the first to advocate the enlargement of the Legislative Councils. That too was then a dream, but it has now been slowly realised.

No. 3, Kyd Street, which was the home I shared with Sir Henry Harrison, was the centre, not only of chess symposia but of large social gatherings where all classes, races, and creeds would meet together, and increasing friendliness and good feeling were promoted. Our excellent friend George Yule, a leading Calcutta merchant, had been Sheriff of Calcutta in 1886 and had interested himself actively in the improvement of social relations between Indians and Englishmen. He placed in my hands the proceeds of his earnings as Sheriff, which were considerable, with a request to distribute them as I might think best among deserving Calcutta institutions. He took a prominent part on the Town Council and was one of the most popular of Calcutta citizens. He presided over the Fourth Indian National Congress, which was held at Allahabad in December, 1888. So Harrison and I decided to give a banquet in honour of Yule and his wife, and there were grand illuminations and a large party to follow in the evening.

I am induced to dwell on this, as it illustrates the prevalence of the cordial and friendly relations which it was not impossible to maintain in Calcutta a quarter of a century ago, and which are now, I am glad to hear, being re-established and revived. I have before me the table-plan of this dinner, given on the 19th of February, 1887, and reproduce the names of some of the guests. There were Mr. A. O. Hume, C.B., founder of the Indian National Congress; Sir Charles Elliott, soon to become Lieutenant-Governor of Bengal, and Miss Elliott; Mr. Ameer Ali, now a member of the Judicial Committee of the Privy Council, and Mrs. Ameer Ali; the late Sir James Peile, a Bombay civilian and a Member of Council; Mr. David Yule; the late Sir William Hunter; the late Mr. W. C. Bonnerjee, a leader of the Calcutta Bar and first President of the Congress, and Mrs. Bonnerjee; Surendro Nath Banerjea, the great orator and patriot and twice President of the Congress; Mr. Satyendra Nath Tagore, a Bombay civilian and representative of a great Calcutta family, and Mrs. Tagore; his brothers Robindro Nath, the famous poet, and Jotirendro Nath; the late Prince

Ferokh Shah, great-grandson of Tippoo Sultan; Robert Steel, a well-known merchant whose name I have already mentioned; Miss Chandra Mukhi Bose, Principal of the Bethune College for Girls; the late Nawab Ameer Hussain, Police Magistrate; Sir Comer Petheram, Chief Justice of Bengal; the late Sir Charles Turner, Chief Justice of Madras; the late Mr. Manomohun Ghose, the greatest of Calcutta criminal barristers, than whom no one ever gave his services *gratis* more often to the poor, and Mrs. Ghose; his brother, Lal Mohun, once candidate for Parliament at Deptford and a President of the Congress; the late Mr. A. M. Bose, another distinguished barrister and a President of the Congress, and Mrs. Bose; O. C. Dutt, a member of a gifted family and one of the ablest Indians I have known; Dr. P. K. Roy of the Education Department, and Mrs. Roy; old "Bobby" Turnbull, Secretary to the Municipality, and his sister Miss Turnbull; the late Rev. Father Lafont, S.J., an eminent scientist and educational authority; Sir Edward Buck; Norendro Nath Sen, the late *doyen* of the Indian Press, who was employed at the close of his life in editing a paper subsidised by Government; the late Mr. N. N. Ghose, one of the best of Indian writers and scholars, and many others. This was the most ambitious and successful of our entertainments, but it was typical of the kind that we were able to continue for several years.

On the 2nd of April, 1887, Sir Steuart Bayley succeeded Sir Rivers Thompson as Lieutenant-Governor of Bengal. Sir Steuart belonged to a traditional Anglo-Indian family. His father, William Butterworth Bayley, was one of the most eminent civil servants ever employed under the Company. Arriving in India in 1799, he acted as Governor-General in 1828, and on his retirement was for many years a Director of the Company. Sir Steuart himself possessed every qualification for the Lieutenant-Governorship. He was a man of commanding presence, of scholarly tastes, and of ripe experience in every department of administration. I had known him since the Behar Famine ; he has always been a generous friend, and I have ever been the recipient of kindness at his hands. It happened that Harrison took furlough to England in the middle of April, and Sir Steuart did not hesitate to appoint me to act in his place as Chairman of the Municipality and Commissioner of Police.

In this way I opened a new official career after my long spell at the Board. The Municipal Commissioners showed their appreciation of the Lieutenant-Governor's choice by voting for me the maximum salary attached to the office. But it must not be inferred from this that I found it all plain sailing in the municipality. I had more cause than ever to admire the skill and temper with which Harrison discharged the functions of Chairman. I did my best to follow in his steps, but it was often an arduous duty. There was once a crisis in the conservancy arrangements which I only overcame after a long June day's broiling exposure in the sewage-farm at the Salt Water Lakes. The most important work I accomplished was the passing through the Town Council of all the steps required for the construction of the central road, which, at my suggestion, was called after Harrison's name. That was my scheme, and I have always been proud of it.

The Commissionership of Police, which at a later date was separated from the Chairmanship, was a comparatively easy post, as the principal burden of the duties was borne by a very efficient Deputy. There was a frightful cyclone in the Bay soon after

I took charge, and on the 25th of May no ship left Calcutta except the *Godiva* in tow of the steam-tug *Retriever*, and the *Sir John Lawrence* with 735 passengers, nearly all pilgrims to the shrine of Juggernauth. The *Retriever* and the *Sir John Lawrence* foundered, and all on board were lost except one fireman from the tug, who had a miraculous escape ; the *Godiva* cast off, went ashore, and was ultimately saved. The loss of the pilgrim steamer was a terrible shock to Calcutta. A few English ladies sympathetically subscribed for a memorial tablet which I caused to be put up on a public bathing ghat near the Howrah Bridge, and I trust it is there still.

Another event which occurred during the year was the death of the ex-King of Oudh. He resided in Garden Reach, and many thousands of his fellow-countrymen, a turbulent lot over whom the police were often able to exercise only imperfect control, lived there with and round about him. *Chota* or Little Lucknow was the colloquial name of the locality. The King's death was expected to be the signal for disturbance and looting, and we strained every nerve in taking precautions, with a result that no actual trouble ensued.

In the same year I gained practical experience of the working of Regulation III. of 1818. This is an old enactment of the Company, passed in the time of the Marquess of Hastings, with the object of suspending the operation of *habeas corpus*, and enabling the Governor-General without charge or trial to arrest and deport or detain in imprisonment for an indefinite period any person whom "for reasons of State it may be necessary to place under personal restraint" and "against whom there may not be sufficient grounds to institute any judicial proceedings." The British public are acquainted with these un-English provisions by reason of the wholesale resort which the Government of India have recently made to them. They were once worked through me in 1887. Under a warrant signed by the Foreign Secretary, I caused an Indian to be arrested in Calcutta. He was a Sikh who had been living for some time in England, and a stranger to the city. A Detective-Inspector wormed himself into his confidence, got into a cab with him one evening, and drove him unsuspectingly into the police station in Lal Bazar. The next day he was dispatched by rail to the fortress of Chunar, and I never heard of him again. He was spirited away as quietly as Edmond Dantès. There was not a whisper in the public press, and not a murmur in the bazars. The facts were never heard of by any one until I revealed them twenty years later in the House of Commons.

On Sir Henry Harrison's return to India, I was deputed on special duty as President of a Commission to inquire into the administration and irrigation system of the Sone Canals. There was much discontent, and grave complaints of mismanagement and oppression had been made. One of my colleagues was the Superintending Engineer, Charles W. Odling, an officer of great ability and good temper and a very cheery companion. He was extremely stout, and I remember once that when mounting his horse he rolled over from mere momentum on to the other side. He was appointed to represent departmental interests. The people's representative was an Indian gentleman, Rai Jai Perkash Lal Bahadur, manager of the great Dumraon Raj estate, two hundred thousand acres of which were irrigable by the canals. It was largely due to his unfailing attentions and courtesy that the personal amenities of this inquiry were so pleasant. We made local investigations over the whole of the canal system, recorded the oral evidence of 158 witnesses, and received more than 2,500 written statements. All the cold weather we were on tour in one of the most delightful camping districts in Upper India, with our tents pitched in beautiful mango-groves, and riding and driving with an ample equipage of horses and camels from village to village ; our Christmas was spent in the historic and romantic fortress of Rhotas ; and of no period of my life in India have I a more agreeable remembrance of my direct contact with the people.

I made the friendship of old Walter Thomson and James Mylne of Beheea, and of Mr. Mylne's two sons. The old men—one a septuagenarian and the other nearly eighty years of age—were specimens of the finest type of British settlers in the East ; they had made fortunes in the country, but they were identified with the prosperity of their tenantry, and nowhere have I witnessed a better example of good old patriarchal relations on the one hand and complete trustfulness and confidence on the other. They were in a position to afford, and did afford us, great help in our inquiries.

I cannot say that the preparation of our report was a simple task. My recommendations ran counter to departmental prejudices, and were, therefore, not very well received at headquarters, but they resulted in a permanent amelioration of the conditions we had been sent to remedy. That was the object of the Commission and the justification of its labours, which could never have been attained without the co-operation of my colleagues, who, though they recorded separate minutes of their own from points of view as opposite as the poles, never allowed their differences of opinion to impair their general and loyal assent to the body of my report.

I was now promoted, after a short spell as Revenue Secretary to Government, to be Financial and Municipal Secretary, and, in due course, to be a Member of the Bengal Legislative Council. This was all very congenial work, and the next two years of my service were very happy ones. It was during this period, however, that Sir Henry Harrison and I passed through one of those phases of eclipse of popularity in Indian circles which I do not shrink from recording. Not for the first or last time has the question of the taxation of unearned increment and ground landlords raised a storm. This thorny subject was stirred up by Harrison, and the vials of wrath from the influential classes affected were poured out upon his devoted head. But there was an appeal from Harrison's orders to the Government, and, as I was Municipal Secretary, I had to deal with it. It made no matter that Sir Steuart Bayley was thoroughly satisfied of the wisdom and justice of Harrison's policy. The Government decision was announced, and the papers immediately rang with a denunciation of the "two dear Henries, bound together as an aged oak with a youthful ivy." Perhaps the climax was reached in the *Indian Mirror:* "The Lieutenant-Governor does not speak a word for himself. He leaves the talking to Sir Henry Harrison, the mortal enemy of the Indian ratepayers, and Mr. Secretary Cotton, who hangs on the lips of Sir Henry Harrison as Sir Henry has been known on occasions to hang on the lips of Mr. Cotton. . . . Is it any wonder that the executioner who was afraid of losing his victims should now fall on them with a savage yell of hell and damnation? This is not metaphor, this is the naked truth, and Sir Steuart Bayley knows it. At least he ought to know it." But our withers were unwrung, and in an incredibly short space of time the echo of this bitterness passed away.

Lord Dufferin retired on the 10th of December, 1888, and was succeeded by the Marquess of Lansdowne. It is unfortunate that Lord Dufferin, a month or two before vacating office, should have been persuaded to indulge in a long lecture on the methods of the Indian National Congress, which he delivered to an audience of cheering Scotsmen at the St. Andrew's dinner, when not a single Indian was present to hear his words. This was the speech in which he referred to the Congress as "a microscopic minority." Lord Dufferin had changed his attitude in less than two years, and on this no comment need be made. But his speech was not calculated to make his successor's task an easier one. It may be that some unwise things had been said by some persons connected with the Congress, but both the time and the occasion—particularly the latter—of Lord Dufferin's speech were regrettable, and did not help to make his warnings more effectual with those to whom they were addressed. It is from this date that the policy of alienation from the Congress movement, which all can now recognise as one of the greatest mistakes committed by past Governments, was deliberately laid down, and subsequent troubles, which it would then have been so easy to regulate and obviate, took their rise.

In December, 1890, Sir Steuart Bayley was tempted by the offer of an appointment in the India Office—where he served for five years as Political Secretary and afterwards for ten years as a Member of the Secretary of State's Council—to resign the Lieutenant-Governorship of Bengal. His premature retirement was generally regretted, and on a marble statue which was erected to his memory in Calcutta it is well inscribed: "A just and wise administrator, whose generous sympathies endeared him to the people."

CHAPTER XIX

MEN I HAVE KNOWN

DURING the past twenty-one years no less than three out of five Lieutenant-Governors of Bengal, and one out of the two Lieutenant-Governors of the newly-formed Eastern Province, have been appointed who did not belong to the Lower Bengal branch of the Civil Service. Their early training had been either in the United Provinces or in the Central Provinces. Their experience and knowledge of India had been derived from provinces other than Bengal. They came to Calcutta unacquainted with the language of the people and with little sympathy for the Bengalis, whom they insensibly contrasted in their own minds with the more simple and less educated races among whom they had lived all their best years. They were not in touch with the growing aspirations of the educated classes, the tendencies of popular agitation, the rising influence of the Press and of public opinion, all of which radiate from the metropolis. The nearer they came into contact with these things the more their antipathies and not their sympathies were aroused.

Campbell and Temple, who were also strangers to the province, had not known what it was to be confronted by the expression of an organised opposition. They had never been troubled by popular clamour or the signs of a national movement. But a new generation was now growing up, into which the consciousness of power had been instilled by the reaction and excesses of the anti-Ripon agitation. The breath of unrest was already pervading the atmosphere of public life, and a new spirit and a new temper in the administration were needed to solve the problem of new ideas and changing phases of thought which altered circumstances had brought forth. It was not to have been expected that a solution would come from men who were not in touch and not in sympathy with the sources of the movement. The key of the situation was never in their hands, and, however desirous they may have been to stem the rising flood, it was no more in their power to do so than it was for Canute to withstand the tide. Bengal thus entered under their *régime* into a transitional and unrestful period, from which, with more sympathetic guidance, it might have emerged with peace. In the absence of such guidance it was destined to arrive at the crisis provoked by Lord Curzon's reactionary policy, culminating in the partition of the province.

The first of these Lieutenant-Governors from the Upper Provinces was Sir Charles Elliott. He had informed me that it was his intention to appoint me to be his Chief Secretary when that office would fall vacant in December, 1891, and in order to prepare myself for this duty which I knew would be heavy, I sought and obtained another six months' leave to Europe during the year. This was my last furlough, and is stamped on my memory by reason of the walking tour I undertook in Switzerland, accompanied by my three sons, and of the personal relation into which I was brought with Mr. Gladstone. My two elder boys were at Oxford, and the third was a lad not yet seventeen. Together we traversed the old haunts which had been so familiar to me in my youth, but we ventured on no expeditions of a serious nature. I met again Almer and Anderegg, who were then elderly men but still living on the mountains, and Ulrich Almer, forty years of age, who had climbed, I think, in every mountainous region on the globe, except the Himalayas. It was pleasant to be remembered after five-and-twenty years by such great guides as these.

Mr. Gladstone I had never before met : but I knew his sons—William, who had recently died, with whom I had done some good mountaineering in the Alps ; Henry, who was a merchant in Calcutta ; and Herbert, whom I had also met in that city. So I received a cordial invitation to lunch.

I found Mr. and Mrs. Gladstone quite alone, with the exception of Mrs. Drew, who was not well enough to come to table and remained lying on a couch. There were no servants admitted during the meal, and we helped ourselves from the sideboard, Mr. Gladstone refusing assistance in carving or in any other way. I cannot do justice to the conversation at the luncheon-table. Mr. Gladstone was in high spirits. He had just come from visiting some exhibition which was then on view illustrating early experiments in the direction of gramophone records, and was much interested in it. He spoke of his son William with emotion, and pressed me to tell him of my recollections of him as a young man. After that somehow the conversation drifted on to temperance, and he indulged in reminiscences of his own past. In his youth there had been heavy drinking at table, especially of port, in which he had himself shared, but he had early broken himself of the habit. "By drinking nothing," said he, "you can easily cure yourself from any desire to drink. And so I trained myself until during a long day's tramping on the Scotch moors, I would need to drink nothing at all, not even water. Give me now a glass or two of good sound claret at dinner and I want no more." Then he asked me what I was accustomed to drink in India, and I said two or three long glasses of whisky-and-soda. "Too much," he interposed, "one a day should be enough." And when I ventured to suggest that with the heat and exhaustion of the climate some more stimulus than that was occasionally wanted, "Not at all, not at all," he replied, "you cannot need it. Try, at all events, to do without it." Then I boldly raised the subject of India, and referred to the difficulties and intricacies of the problem we were destined to face in that country. He lifted his hands, and in a tone of pathos cried, "All true! All true! Of that I feel sure. But who is enough for these things? It all comes too late for me. I am too old to take up any big new question now." At last he said he must rest: the heat tried him; it was a sunny day at the end of June. "I am never quite well in this hot weather. I perspire so freely, and need to be continually changing my linen—a good thing, no doubt, but troublesome and exhausting: my health is always best when it is cold." But before he left Mrs. Gladstone came up with a beautiful photograph in her hand, and said, "I am sure you will like to possess this memento of my dear husband." And at her request the Grand Old Man signed his name across it in large, bold letters. That was another treasure destroyed in the earthquake; but I still have the mutilated remains, in which the face and signature are intact.

On my return to India I took up my new appointment under Sir Charles Elliott. There is no one among my old chiefs to whom I am bound by so strong a personal tie of friendship, and with whom I was so intimately associated in the administration.

Sir Charles Elliott possessed great natural abilities which had been cultivated by long training to a high pitch. His mental qualities were supplemented by a powerful physique and exceptional energies. His character was straightforward and guileless to a degree which is very rare among officials who are placed in high position. Himself the soul of honour, there was not in his nature a single spark of suspicion or distrust. A little reserved, and perhaps cold to a stranger, he was beloved by his intimates. Happy in his domestic relations and happy in his friends, I doubt not that the closing years of his official career would have been happier if his lot had been cast to rule in the provinces where he had received his earlier training and which he knew so well.

He was an administrator to his finger-tips. No one was his equal in the grasp of administrative and revenue details. His defect as an administrator was a disposition to concentrate on details, in which he was apt to become so immersed that more important matters were neglected. I remember the hours and hours we spent together on inspection while on tour. We used to divide a district office into sections, and he would take the lion's share, while I played my part conscientiously enough ; and, though I do not say that this time was not profitably employed, it might have been utilised to more advantage. The truth is that Elliott was conscious of his deficiencies as a stranger to the province, and sought by this means to supplement his local knowledge ; but it really was not worth his while, and it would have been better if we had recorded fewer inspection memoranda, done less touring among the districts and subdivisions, and had devoted more thought and attention to the larger questions which were formulating around us in regard to the political and economic tendencies of the time.

There was no falling off in the efficiency of the administration under Sir Charles Elliott. Efficiency was, indeed, as much the keynote of Elliott's life and work in Bengal as it was afterwards of Lord Curzon in the whole of India. Elliott was the forerunner of Curzon. Lord Curzon would have found in Sir Charles Elliott a man after his own heart. One or two serious blunders were made in the early days of his tenure of office. An abortive prosecution was undertaken against a vernacular newspaper, and an attempt which failed was made to modify the classes of offences triable by jury. These measures brought upon the Lieutenant-Governor's shoulders a heavy burden of unpopularity which he was never able to shake off. He made no effort to conceal his contempt for the manner and methods of Bengali agitation, and there were never cordial relations between himself and the leaders of popular opinion. His settlement and survey work, which he not only organised but carried through, supervising every detail himself with magnificent completeness and accuracy, was strongly opposed by the landed interest; his criticism of the judicial proceedings and findings of the criminal courts, and especially of the High Court, was bitterly resented in the Press; and his unvarying loyalty to, and support of, subordinates in a scrape gave offence to the Indian public.

On the other hand, Sir Charles Elliott did far more than any of his predecessors in opening out avenues of employment to educated Indians; at no time had the Provincial Services more ample encouragement; and above all, no Lieutenant-Governor ever identified himself so completely with measures for furthering the welfare of the student classes. He initiated the movement for boarding-houses and hostels. He invited large numbers of students to garden and river parties, and he organised a society among them, subsequently called the University Institute, to which he subscribed liberally out of his own pocket. With the aid of Harry Lee, a very athletic member of the Civil Service, who had succeeded Harrison as Chairman of the Corporation, he did more than any other individual has ever done to encourage English games and athletic exercises among the Calcutta students. He looked forward to great improvement in the physique of Bengalis in the course of one or two generations from this source. It is surely the irony of Fate that, within a period of less than twenty years, the development of *samitis*, or societies, among the student classes and the formation of athletic clubs for drill and gymnastic exercises, which were inaugurated under such favourable auspices and with such high hopes, should have fallen under the ban of the authorities, to be denounced as symptoms and symbols of sedition, and to be stamped out by every means of executive process and special legislation.

Lord Lansdowne was Viceroy from December, 1888, to December, 1893. In 1892 the Indian Councils Act was passed through Parliament, and the Indian people were grateful for the small concessions which this measure gave to them. He was a popular Viceroy ; there was a personal charm about him, and a special grace and charm about Lady Lansdowne, which ingratiated them with everybody. I owe to Lord Lansdowne, on the recommendation of Sir Charles Elliott, the decoration of a Companion of the Star of India, which was accompanied by a handsome letter of appreciation. My personal relations with him were not as close as they had been with Lord Dufferin, but I recall some vigorous doubles at lawn tennis in which he was my partner and which we won hands down. He presented me with his portrait and that of his wife on leaving, but these, too, went their way to limbo at the earthquake. His private secretary was Colonel Sir John Ardagh, R.E., and I have an amusing letter from him, after an invitation to dinner at Government House, warning me that I was to sit next to "Brodrick, a rising young Member of Parliament," in order to coach him on Indian questions, and especially on the jury imbroglio which was then running its course.

Lord William Beresford, V.C., was Military Secretary, as he had been during the Viceroyalties of Lords Ripon and Dufferin. His first appearance in Calcutta was as a gay and debonair subaltern of the 9th Lancers, escorting the Prince of Wales from Prinsep's Ghat to Government House in December, 1875. From that time for eighteen years he was identified with every social and sporting movement in Calcutta. Never was there a man with more magnetic attraction that Bill Beresford. A typical Irishman, with an inexhaustible fund of high spirits, ready sympathy, open-handed generosity, and merry wit, he passed among us like a ray of sunlight. Soldier, sportsman, boon companion, and the best of Military Secretaries, he has left behind him indelible memories among innumerable friends. His gallantry as a soldier, his pluck as a sportsman, his *bonhomie* as a comrade, were equalled by his resource, readiness, and courtesy as an official. It was in the last capacity that I knew him best, but I suppose it is as a sportsman without equal or second in the annals of the Indian turf that his fame and reputation will longest endure. With all my heart I say, *Sit tibi terra levis.*

It was one of the attractions of my appointment in the Secretariat that I accompanied the Lieutenant-

Governor, not only on his tours in all parts of the province, but also to Darjiling, which was the headquarters of the Government for nearly five months every year. I had served in Bengal for twenty years before I saw Darjiling, but in the latter days of my service in the province I think my most pleasant hours were passed in that hill station. It was a great comfort to escape from the stifling heat of the plains to the cool, fresh air, of which the first whiffs would come on the wonderful zigzag railway journey up the mountain-side. My principal friends in Darjiling were the Elliott family, Sir Alfred Croft, Sir Edward Henry, and Alfred Wallis Paul, who had been associated with Darjiling and Sikkim and the Bhutan and Tibet frontiers nearly all his service. Among Sir Charles Elliott's many accomplishments was a rare knowledge and appreciation of English poetry, and very delightful were the evenings when he would collect around him a few kindred spirits for the feast of reason and the flow of soul. With Croft day after day I used to saunter along the paths and through the lovely woods of Birch Hill, Jellapahar, and Ghoom, the while we feasted our eyes on the glorious snow views of Kinchinjunga and the adjoining peaks. I remember a foreign globe-trotter—a professor, I think—who had come up to Darjiling with a determination to scale Kinchinjunga. He consulted me about it, and when I took it on myself to warn him somewhat seriously of the risks involved, quietly met me with the reply, "To break ze neck is not ze objeck." My phlegmatic friend did not break his neck, and, so far as I am aware, never attempted the ascent at all.

In 1890 a Convention was concluded with China in regard to Tibet. The high contracting parties were Lord Lansdowne on the one hand and H. E. Sheng Tai, Amban or Resident at Lhasa on the other. The question of trade regulations was reserved for discussion between Commissioners. Of these A. W. Paul was Commissioner on the British side, while the Chinese representative was James Hart, a member of the Chinese Customs Service, and younger brother of Sir Robert Hart, the head of that Service. After much negotiation these regulations were agreed to, and signed on the 5th of December, 1893, when they were embodied in the Convention itself. Tibet had no part or lot in the discussion. But certain Tibetan Lamas were invited to Darjiling to assist the Chinese Commissioner, and one of them was grossly insulted. For an alleged outrage on an empty rickshaw, with which it was shown he had no concern, he was assaulted at night by a party of Englishmen, pulled from his pony, and dragged along the road by his heels to the police-station. I was then living at the Club and well remember the consternation with which Hart and Paul came to see me the next morning and reported what had been done. The whole of their negotiations, so far as any friendly acceptance by Tibet might be expected, were being shattered at one blow. We got the perpetrators of the outrage together, and it was with the utmost difficulty I managed to extract an apology from them. But the Tibetan Lama retired in dudgeon to his own country. It is not likely that the memory of such an insult would be easily forgotten ; and when Lord Curzon quarrelled with Tibet ten years later he had no cause for annoyance or surprise if he was confronted by the Nemesis of this incident.

For six or seven years I was a member of the Bengal Legislative Council, and among my colleagues were Indian members of the highest ability and debating skill. At one time or another these included Romesh Chunder Dutt, a Bengal civilian of administrative experience, who with equal facility wooed the muse of poetry and applied himself to elaborate studies on the economic and historic aspects of Indian life ; Surendro Nath Banerjea, the greatest of Indian orators, a life-long educationist and publicist, and a devoted patriot, whose labours will never be forgotten by his countrymen ; Lal Mohun Ghose, another brilliant orator whose eloquence excited the admiration of John Bright ; Abdul Jubbar and Serajul Islam, men who were universally respected and the best type of Bengali Mohammedans ; W. C. Bonnerjee, a great lawyer and Congress champion, who contested Barrow-in-Furness in the Liberal interest in 1895 ; Dr. Mohendra Lal Sircar, founder of the Indian Association for the Cultivation of Science ; Syed Fazl Imam of Patna, representative of a family distinguished for eminent public service ; Gonesh Chunder Chunder, a leading Calcutta solicitor ; Rash Behary Ghose, a lawyer of unrivalled reputation, who has also been a President of the Congress ; and noblemen who were rightly brought into the Council to represent the aristocracy of the country, like Prince Mahomed Ferokh Shah and the Maharajas of Durbhungah, Bettiah, Gidhour, and Nattore. With many of these I have crossed swords on the floor of the Council Chamber, and, if I did not come off second best, it is because I was then sitting on the Ministerial Front Bench with a majority I could always command.

The period of my service in Bengal was now drawing to a close, and I cannot leave it without some reference to the troops of Indian friends whom it was my good fortune to make during my residence in the province. Old and young, high and low, I came in contact with all the leaders of thought and of the social and religious movements of my generation. Uma Nath Roy (born 1804), Joy Kissen Mookherjea (1808), Ram Tonu Lahiri (1813), Krishna Mohun Banerjea (1813), and Debendra Nath Tagore (1818), were Brahmans, who were representative of the earlier half of the last century and who carried their influence long into the second half. They were the children of the early renaissance. They belonged to an epoch when men's minds had begun to stir within them in the first dawn of English education under the auspices of David Hare, Captain D. L. Richardson, and Derozio. The gospel of the Christian missionaries was then a revolutionary agency. I knew the Rev. K. M. Banerjea as a man of high public spirit and erudition and a most respected Christian clergyman, but in his youth he had been a firebrand who had scandalised society by throwing beef into a Brahman's *puja bari*, or place of worship. My old friend Ram Tonu, a man of the most exemplary character and saintly life, who had the reputation above all his countrymen for kindliness and piety, had as a young man outraged the feelings of his relatives and friends by renouncing the Brahminical sacred thread.

The venerable Maharshi Debendra Nath Tagore was the successor of Ram Mohun Roy and the teacher and spiritual father of Keshub Chunder Sen. Their names are identified with the Brahmo Samaj, or Theistic Church, in India. The death of Keshub Chunder in January, 1884, was one of the earliest occasions for the manifestation of a truly national sentiment in the country. The residents of all parts of India, irrespective of caste and creed, united with one voice in the expression of sorrow at his loss and pride in him as member of one common nation.

Uma Nath Roy and Joy Kissen Mookherjea were special representatives of the old order of Hindooism. Both were noble specimens of a high-caste Bengali Brahmin. The former was the elder brother of

BABOO UMA NATH ROY: A NOBLE TYPE OF A BENGALI BRAHMIN. 1883.

[To face p. 222.

Juggudish Nath Roy, the first Indian District Superintendent of Police. The latter was a landed proprietor, of exceptional ability and force of character, but old and blind when I knew him, whose son, Raja Peary Mohun, himself now stricken in years, is probably the greatest living authority in Bengal on questions of land management.

Belonging to a somewhat younger generation were my dear friends Maharajas Jotendro Mohun Tagore and Narendro Krishna, the heads of great and historic families, who have lately passed away full of years and honours. Of a humbler station in life was Kristo Das Pal, a great publicist and one of the leading men in his generation. He died as long ago as 1884, and Englishmen and Indians alike vied to do honour to his memory. He was the presiding genius of the transition period into which Bengal at this time was entering, and no other man could have discharged the difficult functions which devolved on him as well and with so much tact. There was Bunkim Chunder Chatterjee, the great Bengali novelist, whom I knew as a member of the Provincial Service. As author of "The Abode of Bliss," in which is enshrined the beautiful poem of "Bande Mataram," the national song of India, his name will be handed down to future generations. And I would not like to omit mention of my very dear friend Jogendro Chunder Ghose of Kidderpore, a profound student and philosopher, who took little or no part in public life, but deeply impressed by his example and teaching the many friends who cherish his memory and mourn his loss. Among Mohammedans I must include the Dacca Nawabs, Abdul Ghunny and his son Ahsanoollah, who were famous for their numerous and munificent acts of public and private charity. And in particular there remains the Nawab Bahadur Abdul Latif of Calcutta, with whom I was very closely associated both in public and private life. I can never forget his dignified appearance and courteous charm, his wise and friendly counsel, and above all his admirable and incomparable zeal in furthering the interests of his own community.

The Maharaja of Durbhunga is the wealthiest and most influential of the noblemen of Bengal. The late Maharaja, Sir Luchmeswar Singh, died in 1898, at the early age of forty-two years. He was a most enlightened man, very charitable, and of high character. I knew him and his brother, who succeeded him in the Raj, from their boyhood, and always enjoyed the confidence of both. He sympathised with the objects and aims of the Indian National Congress, and was known to subscribe to its funds. In spite of his open life and unsullied reputation, his Congress sympathies brought him into the category of suspects, and he complained to me with just indignation that his movements were shadowed by the police. It was not without difficulty that I relieved him of this surveillance. It is impossible for any one to have been more generous and open-handed than he was in the encouragement of sport which he would provide for English visitors. I should not call him a sensitive man, but he once confided to me with no feeling of bitterness the insulting expressions in regard to himself used by English guests in his own house when they thought he heard them not. He was one of Nature's noblemen, and his premature death was a great loss. A marble statue by Onslow Ford perpetuates his memory in Calcutta. His brother, the present Maharaja, Sir Rameshwar Singh, has worthily maintained the family reputation. I have lived with him on most friendly terms. He has been my guest in Assam and I have been his guest in Calcutta. We have many interests in common, including a love for chess. He is very closely

MAHARAJA SIR LUCHMESHWAR SINGH BAHADUR, G.C.I.E., OF DURBHUNGA, AND HIS BROTHER THE PRESENT MAHARAJA SIR RAMESHWAR SINGH BAHADUR, K.C.I.E.

From a photograph by Messrs. Johnston and Hoffman, Calcutta.

[To face p. 224.

associated with my last years in India. There is still a distinguished career before him, in which all my best wishes go for his success and happiness.

Sir Charles Elliott left India in December, 1895, and was succeeded in the Lieutenant-Governorship by a Bengal civilian, Sir Alexander Mackenzie. I served under him for only six months or so, for it was in the summer of 1896 that I was offered by Lord Elgin, who had followed Lord Lansdowne as Viceroy, the post of Home Secretary to the Government of India, which was temporarily vacant. When I accepted this offer and went to Simla, my service in Bengal, extending over nearly twenty-nine years, came to a close.

I confess I found Simla a quite delightful place. My work, though highly important and interesting, was less arduous than that of Chief Secretary in Bengal. The Member of Council under whom I directly worked, Sir John Woodburn, was the most amiable of men. When Mackenzie's health broke down, as it soon did, Woodburn succeeded him in Bengal, and, to the regret of the whole province, died, in harness, in 1902. My most intimate friends in Simla were Colonel Sir Howard Melliss, Inspector General of Imperial Service Troops, with whom I lived, and who was the best of comrades; Colonel Scott Chisholm, a gallant and dashing Lancer and most charming fellow, soon, alas! to be shot dead in a wild charge at the head of his men in one of the earliest engagements in South Africa; Herr von Waldthausen, the German Consul-General, a prince of hospitality and courtesy; and Sir Dennis Fitzpatrick, the Lieutenant-Governor of the Punjab, who has left behind him in every office in which he served an honoured name, not only for his abilities but for justice and sympathy.

Of my personal relations with Lord Elgin I have

the pleasantest memories. A quiet man, deficient in the instinct for ceremonial, he brought a sterling common-sense to bear on every question which came before him, and was head and shoulders—at least, so it seemed to me—above the members of his Government who sat in Council with him. I had not been long at Simla before he conferred on me the appointment of Chief Commissioner of Assam, which was about to fall vacant; and when Sir John Hewett returned from England and relieved me of the Home Secretaryship, I proceeded at once to take charge of my new office. On my way through Calcutta my good friends in the Bengal Civil Service rallied round me and gave me a rousing send-off at a public banquet which they organised in my honour. The principal promoters and secretaries of this dinner were Sir Edward Baker, the present Lieutenant-Governor of Bengal, and Francis Slacke, now senior Member of Council in his Government. At the same time my Indian friends gave me a magnificent entertainment at the Dalhousie Institute, which was converted for the evening into a veritable scene from Fairyland.

I received charge of the Assam Administration from Sir William Ward at Shillong on the 28th of November, 1896, and almost immediately began the first of those prolonged tours, extending over a period of about five months, which were probably the most important and certainly not the least pleasant part of the duties of the head of the Local Government. It was a new country to me, and I passed with the greatest zest from district to district, mingling with all classes, and warmly welcomed by all. The work was not heavy, but the interest of that work could not be surpassed. The Chief Commissioner travelled in a style of dignity and comfort. On the broad face of the Brahmaputra I moved along in a luxurious houseboat, or yacht, the *Sonamukhi*, which had formerly been the viceregal barge, and was made over to the Assam Administration by Lord Northbrook. This yacht was towed along by a powerful and well-equipped Government steamer, the *Brahmakund*. Ample facilities were thus afforded for entertainment and hospitality, and the sight of the yacht illuminated at night was a fascinating spectacle.

The Brahmaputra is one of the grandest rivers in the world ; but during the dry season, when the waters fall, it is a common occurrence to run aground on sandbanks, and I have towed off the mail steamer only to run aground on the same bank myself and remain stuck there until another friendly passing boat came to our rescue. It is wonderful also how the river banks and anchorages will change year after year, and miles will occasionally separate the " ghat," as it is called, of one season from its location in the next. The *Brahmakund* afforded accommodation for my ponies and traps, and I had always, therefore, independent means of locomotion for touring inland. I received a most cordial welcome from the tea-planters of the province, who were very hospitable to me during those tours. As I journeyed from garden to garden and place to place, I made many friends and carried back with me to Shillong after this first camping season a wide experience of the personnel of the province and of the requirements of the country, which stood me in good stead thereafter. During all the six winters I was in Assam I made similar tours, and often during the summer months as well.

CHAPTER XX

A GREAT EARTHQUAKE

On the 12th of June, 1897, occurred one of those terrible calamities which those who lived through it will always speak of with a shudder. I was at our headquarters, the pleasant little station of Shillong, which lies quiet and peaceful amidst some of the most beautiful hill scenery in the world. My wife had just arrived from England and was busy unpacking all her new things and dresses, and the many home treasures we had never before ventured to entrust to India. We were occupied with preparations for celebrating the Diamond Jubilee of Queen Victoria, and no thought of trouble crossed our minds. Invitations had been issued for a State Ball at Government House, and the residents of the station were engrossed with prospective decorations, festivity, and entertainment. The weather had been wet, but on this Saturday afternoon, after two days of rain, the sun shone brightly and all were enjoying themselves in the open air. My wife and I had just taken our seats in the dog-cart and were starting for our usual drive. The reins were in my hand, the groom was adjusting a defect in the harness to which I had called his attention, and other servants and orderlies in their red and gold uniforms were standing by, in accordance with their custom, to see us off.

Without a warning and with no premonitory

GOVERNMENT HOUSE, SHILLONG, BEFORE AND AFTER THE EARTHQUAKE, 1897.

[To face p. 229.

rumble, such as is the ordinary precursor of an earthquake, I heard a clattering on the roof, I felt a swaying of the earth, and the high-spirited pony I was driving dashed off *ventre à terre* like an arrow from a bow. Amid a terrific roar of indescribable elements, we galloped along, missing by a hair's breadth the wooden railing on the winding drive. The road yawned open with cracks beneath our feet, the pine-trees overhead shook and trembled as though under the influence of a mighty storm, and the pine-cones showered an avalanche upon our heads. The Gurkha guard was drawn up for the salute, and we saw the guard-house crumble like a house of cards as we approached it. It was more by luck than skill that we escaped a carriage accident, and I managed to stop the trap about a hundred and fifty yards from where we started. The affrighted pony was then backing over the railings above a crumbling slope. I sprang out, and got my wife out, I know not how. We could scarcely stand. I thought the swaying trees would fall on us and, reeling as we went, rushed with my wife to an open spot before the flag-staff, where we threw ourselves on the ground. As I leaped from the trap, I looked back to where Government House had been, and saw nothing but a great pillar of red dust from earth to heaven.

We were safe. But what a terrible moment! The noises of the earthquake, blended with cries of terror, rose all around us, and the shaking of the surface of the earth continued, like the movement of some titanic piece of machinery. Gradually the crisis passed and comparative silence reigned. My private secretary hurried up from the Club, and others followed in quick succession, men, women, and children. Then the rain began to fall and continued for forty-eight hours without intermission. Darkness was closing in : we had to find some shelter for the night. Government House was a heap of ruins, not one stone standing upon another, and all the masonry houses of Shillong were in a similar plight. My servants and the Gurkha guard tore away the stones from a fallen outhouse in which our camp equipment was stored, and managed to extract therefrom three servants' tents, which were rapidly pitched and afforded a refuge. Kindly Samaritans whose houses had not been so completely wrecked as ours found us food. Ten or twelve persons remained huddled up in each of these small tents that night.

There was little sleep for any : the earth was in constant tremor, and five minutes did not elapse without a specific shock, with its subterranean rumble, and the clattering of the fallen corrugated iron roofs among the adjoining ruins. We kept up a bonfire until the morning, which we fed with the shattered furniture and broken woodwork of the house. Above all was the anxiety for others, for the world outside, which was not relieved until eight days had passed.

I found time to visit many parts of the station. It was a scene of deplorable desolation and distress. Only a very small section of the community had sought a refuge with us in the Government House grounds. Most took shelter as they could find it, in the wooden cricket-ground pavilion, which had not subsided, and in sheds in the bazar : others were in their mat-walled stables or coach-houses. The position of all, and especially of delicate ladies and children exposed to the elements, was a most pitiable one. All had their stories of horror to narrate. Some had been out riding, some bicycling ; some had been walking, and, clinging from tree to tree for protection, had fallen to the ground ; a set had been playing lawn-tennis when the court crumbled away under their feet; others had been golfing and had fallen prone upon the links; a family saved themselves by rushing out of their house and rolling down the steps; the inmates of the Club just escaped by tumbling out of doors. Women were crying out that the Day of Judgment had come. It was no disgrace for the boldest of men to turn pale, or for the nerves of the strongest to be unstrung.

The Government Press was full of compositors, engaged in printing the *Gazette*, when the building fell in on them. Fatigue parties of sepoys were employed all night in endeavouring to extricate those who were entombed and might still be alive. It was a ghastly sight to witness the dead dragged forth, and the pallid, staggering forms of the survivors. The gallant little Gurkhas worked indefatigably amid drenching rain and depressing darkness and earth tremors. Mr. Robert Blair McCabe, Inspector-General of Police and an officer of conspicuous distinction, was found dead, horribly crushed, beneath the ruins of his house. "It had been the Queen's intention to confer a Companionship of the Order of the Star of India on the late Mr. R. B. McCabe, Indian Civil Service, in recognition of his services in Assam, and of his work of exceptional merit among the wild tribes of the north-east frontier of India." Such was the notification which appeared in the *Gazette of India* a short time after his death. I shall never forget his funeral. We laid him in a sheet and carried him, stumbling over the fallen cemetery walls through a tornado of rain, to his grave, which was already half full of water—a tragic close to a career of the most brilliant promise.

There was a simple system of nine seismometric cylinders of varying heights and sizes in Shillong—an arrangement not sensitive enough to record even moderately severe shocks and so of comparatively little use on ordinary occasions ; but in this case it was of no use at all, as all the cylinders were levelled indiscriminately to the ground. The great embankment which closed in the beautiful Shillong Lakes had collapsed with a terrific roar ; the water, pouring down a ravine, rushed up the river below and destroyed an iron bridge, carrying the heavy girders a considerable distance upstream. The native bazar was in ruins. The jail, with all other public buildings, had fallen, and the panic-stricken prisoners spent the night in the open. Such was the fear on them that not one attempted to regain his freedom.

The immediate result of the catastrophe was a houseless population, without any change of raiment for day or night, exposed to the fury of the rains, destitute of food, and many of them wounded, crushed, or dying. The most urgent need was to house the houseless, to feed the people, and to restore communications. My officers showed admirable presence of mind, and laboured unceasingly. There was no hesitancy or faint-heartedness on the part of any one. Temporary huts were run up in a few days, and a loan was offered from the Treasury to the bazar merchants with a view to the importation of grain. Looting, which had prevailed somewhat extensively on the night of the earthquake—and I am afraid it was white men who were to blame—was prevented. One of the earliest measures I took was to assign to every officer his own special duty in repairing damages and restoring confidence. Every officer, whatever his ordinary duties, was made available for the task of rendering assistance. An Examiner of Accounts was set to remove ruins ; Forest Officers and Accounts Officers were employed in clearing the roads ; the Officers of the Regiment supervised the work of their sepoys in building huts ;

SHILLONG CHURCH, BEFORE AND AFTER THE EARTHQUAKE, 1897.

To face p. 232.

Magistrates became foremen of coolie gangs ; and my Assistant Secretary was converted into a most efficient Conservancy Overseer. Every man was placed at his post, and all worked with their might. Above all, Major Neil Campbell, the Civil Surgeon of the station, and John C. Arbuthnott, the Deputy Commissioner—both of whom I am glad to say afterwards received a decoration for their services—never spared themselves, and day and night were continually at work, encouraging others and setting an example to every one by their sense of duty and self-devotion.

Of the Indian staff also I can speak in the highest terms. Although their own losses were great, they devoted themselves to the public service unremittingly and without complaining. It was due to their co-operation with the unwearying efforts of Edward Gait, my Chief Secretary, and to that officer's power of organisation that the records were salvaged with little loss, and that current work was promptly resumed. Not a single table or chair came out unbroken from the wreck of the Secretariat, and yet within ten days from the earthquake the office establishment was dealing with current cases.

After the first urgent need of shelter had been met, the task of re-opening communications was taken up. Telegraphic connection had been destroyed. The abutments of bridges had been shaken to pieces, and the superstructures had collapsed. Several miles of road had gone down the hillside, all roads were cracked and fissured, both longitudinally and laterally, and great chasms thirty feet in depth yawned open in places. Portions of the road were buried by huge landslips. Other portions, which ran along level ground, presented the rough appearance of a ploughed field. It will serve to illustrate the force of the shock when I say that all the stacks of metal on the roadside were levelled as though the metal had been spread by hand. The difficulty of re-establishing communications was enormous. It could only be overcome gradually; but it was done in a manner reflecting the highest credit upon Walter Nightingale, the Chief Engineer, and the other Engineers of the Public Works Department.

Assam is well known as a region of seismic disturbance, and earthquakes before this were not uncommon; but they had never been known on any previous occasion to cause widespread destruction. The area over which this earthquake was felt is prodigious. It was estimated on scientific authority to have "extended over a tract of nearly 1,500 miles in length and 1,000 in width, or about 1,275,000 square miles." The area over which the shock was destructive is believed to be unique, and the focus from which it radiated was in the neighbourhood of Shillong. The earthquake was said by the learned Japanese expert, Professor Omori, who was specially sent by his Government to inquire and report, to be due to a fault in the earth's crust about twenty miles below the surface and to be non-volcanic, and thus of a different type from those great cataclysms which have taken place at Krakatoa and in Japan itself. The character of the shock was everywhere much the same, though varying in degree—a sharp vibration accompanied by a rocking or heaving of the earth and a loud rumbling noise. In the hills, gigantic landslips plunged mountain-sides in ruin and buried villages beneath them. In the plains, the rivers were agitated, the water rising to a height of many feet; the banks crumbled and fell in, hurling whole hamlets into the stream; in many places geysers leaped forth, spouting up sand and innumerable jets of water. This eruption had such force that the covers of wells solidly embedded in mortar were

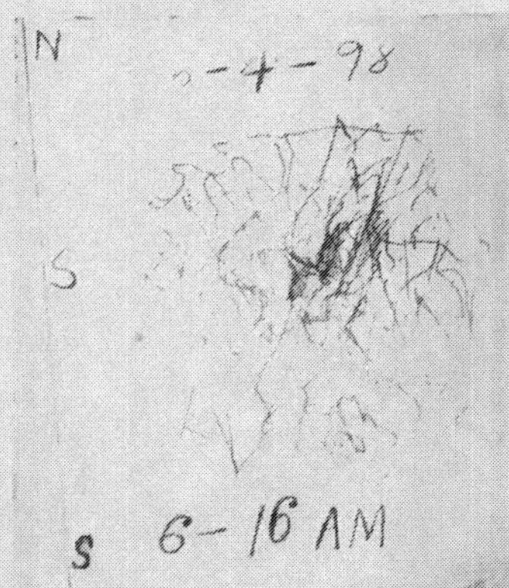

SEISMOGRAPHIC RECORDS.

These are reproductions of photographs showing the variations of the seismographic needle at Shillong, produced by the subsidiary earthquakes there on the 26th of April, 1898, and 5th of July, 1901.

The seismograph is an instrument fixed on the ground, consisting of a pendulum that remains steady throughout the shock, and acts as fulcrum to another very light pendulum which vibrates with the motion of the earth. A needle pivoted near the end of the latter pendulum, by reason of its position, magnifies the movements which it records, in a piece of smoked glass. The traced glass being placed over a piece of sensitised paper acts as a photographic negative, and gives such records as those reproduced above.

[To face p. 235.

tossed to a great distance, while the wells were choked with sand.

It is difficult to define the duration of the great shock ; but I do not think it lasted for more than three minutes, and the period of extreme intensity was probably limited to about thirty seconds. But this half-minute's disturbance of the earth's crust was sufficient to cover it with ruins. The fall of Government House, a large and straggling masonry building, must have been complete within ten seconds. But after the great disturbance definite shocks were incessant for about a week, and the earth tremor went on continuously for a longer period. In Shillong itself it was estimated that there were two hundred shocks a day for a few days after the 12th of June ; these had gradually diminished to twenty or thirty shocks a day by the middle of July. Then they became fewer ; but for at least two years after the earthquake we were accustomed to a daily shock. Occasionally these were of alarming intensity, but familiarity led to their being treated with contempt. My youngest son, out on a visit from home, was staying with us during the cold weather of 1898. We were on tour, and he was sitting reading in the veranda, while I was writing inside the official Circuit House. A somewhat severe shock occurred ; and it is a family tradition that as he sprang from his chair I called to him, "Don't be afraid, Bertie ; it is only an earthquake !"

Shocks had become rare when I left Assam at the end of April, 1902 ; but I may safely estimate that we acquired an experience of about four thousand quakes. Professor Omori had been good enough to explain to us that these after-shocks were merely the residual effects of the first big disturbance, subject to definite laws, and had nothing dangerous in their character. In fact, we were assured that they were absolutely necessary in the ordinary course of things, as by their means the disturbed earth crust was gradually settling itself into its final stable position, and that each after-shock meant the removal of one residual weak point. So we never minded them at all, and earthquakes became an accustomed element in the routine of life.

It was most fortunate that the big earthquake occurred when it did, in the afternoon, about five o'clock, when nearly everybody after a wet day was out of doors. Had it taken place at almost any other time—and needless to say had it happened at night—the mortality would have been terrible. As it was, one of the most remarkable features of a disaster so overwhelming and so widespread is the comparatively small number of deaths which it occasioned. The ascertained deaths numbered only 1,542 —a figure no doubt below the truth, as it was impossible at a season of floods and downpours of rain to collect complete returns. These were practically all due to falling houses, slipping mountain-sides, and the collapse of river banks ; in a few cases boats were swamped, and the occupants were drowned. Two cases were reported of persons having been swallowed up by the earth opening under them—as in the earthquake which swallowed up Korah, Dathan, and Abiram—but I decline to vouch for these, as nowhere does the earth gape open and close again.

The earthquake deaths were, however, immeasurably exceeded by the mortality from the epidemics that ensued. In Shillong—where there was a temporary but complete dislocation of the water supply—cholera, dysentery, and fever broke out in the Indian quarter, and much sickness, including a severe outbreak of enteric, laid many low in the cantonments and civil station. The connection between earthquakes and epidemic disease is a medical question of some obscurity, but I believe that this connection has been scientifically traced. Certain it is that in Assam there was the most appalling sickness throughout the province during the autumn of the earthquake year ; thousands, and tens of thousands, died from the most malignant form of fever, and the general mortality of the year was over fifty per thousand, or almost as high as that which prevailed in the regions of India where famine was then raging. It was the most unhealthy year of which there is any record.

The population at large, although completely cowed at first by the effects of such an unprecedented phenomenon, very soon displayed their usual patience and calmness, and resumed their occupations as though nothing had happened. The catastrophe was one which principally affected the few wealthy and well-to-do persons who reside in masonry dwellings. The poor, who live in mat huts, did not suffer so directly from the shock itself. Tea plantations were damaged in some places, but this great industry escaped as a whole without serious injury. The losses sustained by the province were, however immense. I am afraid that in the interests of the province I was not altogether wise in the studied moderation with which I reported our difficulties. Nothing could have exceeded the personal sympathy of Lord Elgin, and that was felt at the time to be a great support. But I venture now to say that we received no adequate assistance from the Government of India. When I went down to Calcutta at Christmas I bearded the Finance Minister in his den, but he would give me no satisfaction. I appealed to Cæsar, and got some concessions from the Viceroy, but they were quite insufficient for the needs of the province. It was not until I was leaving Assam, and had no control over the distribution of funds, that Lord Curzon placed supplies at my disposal. The finances of the province during the whole period of my charge were paralysed by the necessity of restoring public works to their former condition, and the dial of progress was set back.

As soon as I could leave headquarters and had made some provisional arrangements for sheltering my wife, whose nerves were badly shattered by what she had gone through, I proceeded on tour during August and September to examine with my own eyes the damage done by the earthquake in all parts of the province. This was a most interesting experience, and it was absolutely necessary that I should go, although the exposure I went through, following on what I had already undergone, resulted in my health being permanently affected. I was accompanied by Nightingale, the chief engineer, and could not have had a more cheery companion. We witnessed some wonderful sights. We saw a large native bazar which sank and was embedded in six feet of sand. We saw huge fissures, sixteen feet deep, as many wide, and a mile long. We found rivers completely silted up. In many cases we found embanked roads which had subsided to a level with the adjacent country. We visited a village in which forty-one persons, mostly Mohammedans, who were celebrating the *Mohurrum*, fell into the river owing to the subsidence of the river bank and were drowned. The appearance of the southern range of the Khasi Hills—the precipitous sides of which had been scarred as far as the eye could see by numerous and extensive landslips, resembling glaciers running down into the valleys—bore eloquent testimony to the tremendous character of the shock, and left no room for doubt that the centre or focus of the disturbance was to be placed among these hills.

The most permanent and disastrous consequence of the earthquake undoubtedly consisted in the raising of river beds and the obstruction of drainage channels. It so happened that the rainfall that year was quite exceptional, and we witnessed from the foot of the hills at Cherrapunji a downpour of eighty inches in three days. The little Cherra railway was destroyed and, though every effort to repair it was made, it was ultimately abandoned. A stray pony was utilising the broken-down terminus as a stable. With the aid of an elephant we traversed the course of the line. In places the rails had been forced upwards, as if by the expansion of the metal, and had formed a triangle with the ground, the apex of which was three feet above their former level. Occasionally the embankment had been washed away, and the rails and iron sleepers hung in mid-air.

From a place called Chhatak, the centre of the limestone industry, we embarked on a day of inspection in drenching rain. Starting at daybreak, in three small country boats, we arrived at our destination after a seven hours' journey. Our difficulties were serious, for the rapids were exceedingly violent, and one of the boats containing our luncheon was lost, while the occupants had a narrow escape, clinging to the boughs of trees till they were rescued. The channels were blocked with débris and silt, and immense quantities of huge drift timber had come down with the landslips. The beautiful orange-groves, which were so marked a feature of this tract, were a sea of ruin. The whole country was covered with sand, and the floods found no other way of outlet than over the surface of the plain. In one place where there had been a crystal pool forty feet deep and a noted resort for fishermen, I was able to cross without wetting myself above the knees. The return journey was accomplished in four and a half hours, and the shooting of the rapids among trees and snags, though dangerous, was accomplished with no further mishap.

From the same cause the floods of the Assam Valley rose to a height far exceeding any previous record. When I visited the town of Barpeta I found the inhabitants living on platforms and in boats ; cattle were perishing from starvation, and dead bodies were floating about. Dogs and ponies were like skeletons. I rescued one miserable pony, which was lying in water with its head only on dry land, and had not strength to raise itself. The police guard of honour to receive me was drawn up on the roof of a large country boat, which had been serving as a treasury and jail and guardroom. The first thing I did was to release the prisoners, all short-time men. The Magistrate's Court, his residence, and the Circuit House were up to their eaves in water, and the shops in the bazar and all private houses were in the same condition. Everywhere we found that the river beds had upheaved, so as to be almost on a level with the surrounding country. There was no natural escape for the water to run off. These excessive floods were directly due to this cause, and even up to the present time I hear of old channels not properly scoured out and no new channels formed. Many village sites therefore became uninhabitable, and the people were forced to move to other places. A great decrease of cultivation followed in what had been a very fertile country.

The following encomium was passed on the Assamese Magistrate of Barpeta by Colonel Maxwell, the Commissioner, whose sympathy with the people was the secret of his influence among them :—

"Placed single-handed, as he has been, in this isolated town, among a population thoroughly terrified and full of prophecies of approaching dissolution, he has never lost heart ; but by the cheerful disposition with which Nature has endowed him has been of much comfort to the subordinate officials and traders, and has carried on the routine duties of his charge without interruption."

I would make this eulogy a general one. The flag of Great Britain never ceased to fly on the Government House flag-staff, in the centre of wreck and desolation. It was the token of the spirit by which all my officers were animated. Everything that could be done by them was done—quietly, effectively, and promptly. When I left the province no trace remained of the catastrophe. Shillong was more beautiful than it had ever been. Houses, public buildings, churches, and jails had been rebuilt. The new roads and bridges were better than the old ones. The whirligig of time had removed from the province most of those who had borne the brunt of the shock. But the great earthquake will never be forgotten. Its memory will live beyond the lives of those men and women on whom it is indelibly impressed. It was a great calamity,

> "Quo bruta tellus et vaga flumina
> Quo Styx et invisi horrida Tænari
> Sedes Atlanteusque finis
> Concutitur."

CHAPTER XXI

UP AND DOWN THE FRONTIER

THE Assamese peasantry are pioneers of cultivation in a remote and unhealthy tract of country encumbered with forest and morass and intersected by torrential streams. They maintain a difficult struggle against the forces of Nature. But lately removed from the fear of the incursion of savage neighbours, they are still exposed to danger from floods and fevers, earthquakes, and the attacks of wild animals. They have few incentives to exert themselves in the reclamation of the wastes by which they are surrounded. There is no wealthy class among them upon whom they can lean in time of trouble. There is a general absence of the minor luxuries and superfluities of life which accompany the advance of material prosperity. The province passed through many trials during my time. Harvests were indifferent, and land was injured by sand deposit directly attributable to the earthquake. The people suffered from pestilence in an extraordinary degree, and a peculiarly malignant form of malarial fever, known as *kala azar*, or black death, sapped the life-blood of the race. The circumstances of the country were of a depressing character.

Assam has been called the Cinderella of India. I regret that the province is still in the position of the poor girl in her slovenly clothes waiting for the visit of the Fairy Prince, who I was fain to hope had at last appeared in the person of Lord Curzon. But that hope was dispelled. Lord Curzon arrived in India in December, 1898, and I was then down in Calcutta to bid him welcome and to say farewell to his predecessor. In March, 1900, he paid a long-looked-for visit to Assam. The only Governor-General who had ever been to the province before him was Lord Northbrook. It was a brief tour of inspection, but well arranged, and he threw an immense amount of energy into it. We traversed the whole length of the Brahmaputra in record time, which I imagine has not been equalled since, travelling day and night at much risk of running aground. No mishap occurred. There was a reception at Dibrugurh, a flying visit to some of the best tea gardens in the province, an inspection of the coal-mines at Margherita and of the spouting oil at Digboy. There was another reception at Tezpur, and more visits to tea gardens. We inspected the Assam Bengal Railway, then under construction, up to railhead at Lumding. A grand Durbar was held at Gowhatty. It all passed like a flash.

No one could have been kinder than Lord and Lady Curzon were to my wife and myself. Lord Curzon's vivacity, his store of anecdote, particularly of Parliamentary and Court reminiscences, and the frank openness of his manner, which seemed to conceal nothing, made his visit from the personal point of view perfectly charming. But he made no attempt to woo Cinderella. On the contrary, he said in reply to an address : "It is not fair of you to tax the Government of India with neglect ; as a fact it has always taken a very great interest in the province ; but the true secret of the woes of Assam is the same as that which Mr. Disraeli said was the true secret of the woes of Ireland. He said that Ireland lay under weeping skies surrounded by a melancholy ocean." In other words, as he went on to explain in graphic terms, the climate of Assam was the cause of its failure to prosper. There is, unfortunately, just sufficient truth in this to have made it an unpleasant reminder. Lord Curzon also said: "You complain of the want of pecuniary assistance from the Government, but, when I examine the accounts, I find that the annual balance is against Assam"; and he proceeded to make up that balance by debiting to Assam the prodigious losses which had been incurred by the mistaken alignment of the Assam-Bengal Railway, a measure of high policy in which local interests had received a very small share of consideration. In any case, these were not the cheering notes of encouragement poor Cinderella had expected to hear in the hour of her deepest depression. If I had been rash enough to posture before her as a fairy godmother, it was my misfortune rather than my fault that I could not introduce her to a Fairy Prince.

Nevertheless, although the resources at my disposal were always insufficient, I did something for the good of the province. I point to none of the features of my administration with more satisfaction than to the improvement in jail management. While raising the standard of discipline, I reduced the number of jail floggings by three-quarters, and brought Assam into a line with other provinces. I found, when I took charge, that the average rate of mortality in jails was sixty per thousand, a higher rate than in any other province in India. I determined that this should cease, and spared no exertion to improve the sanitary conditions of jail life. In 1900 the rate of mortality had fallen to 23·9 and in 1901 it was 23·2 per thousand. I could not have accomplished this without the cordial and humane co-operation of jail superintendents. I reorganised the civil police. I reconstituted both the Assam Commission and the Provincial Service on terms very favourable to their members. I prepared a scheme for the reconstruction of Local Boards. To the encouragement of education I devoted the best of my energies. I regard it as a great honour that my name should be associated with a first-class college which I inaugurated at Gowhatty. It had made a good start, even in my time; it has thriven since, and long may it flourish!

Much trouble was devoted by me to the elaboration of a scheme for gradually colonising the province and bringing vast tracts of cultivable waste lands under cultivation. Although my proposals were not accepted by the Government of India, they were, I think, among the most valuable of the contributions which I rendered to the province. I combated energetically the ravages of *kala azar* and remedied as far as possible a standing grievance from all parts of Assam known as *begar*, or forced labour. I improved communications, and encouraged both the railway system and river steam companies. In a general scheme for developing the resources of the province, I pressed forward a well-devised system of tramways as feeders to the main line of railway and to the river bank. Metalled roads cannot be maintained on account of the cost, and no earthen road is capable of standing regular wheeled traffic when the rainfall is as heavy as it is in Assam. The only way in which communication by land can be kept permanently open in a satisfactory form is by the construction of tramways. I had hoped to have seen these tramways stretching from either side of the main line of river and railway, and, although that hope has not yet been realised, I do not despair of its fulfilment.

I always recognised the importance of the tea

industry which had done so much to make Assam what it is, and boldly aver that few men have assisted that industry more than I did. As soon as I joined the province, at a time when the demand for tea land was pressing, I threw open large tracts of country for occupation. I revised the forest rules for the valuation of timber, which were represented to be a crushing burden, and by common consent removed all cause for complaint. I did my utmost to extend and encourage the local manufacture of tea-boxes. The Surma Valley Tea Association owes its existence to my initiative. I afforded every facility in my power to the planters of that valley for the recovery of their coolies who were alleged to have absconded for work on the railway—even, I am afraid, straining the law for this purpose. Although the resources of the Administration could ill afford it, I spent the public funds liberally in the furtherance of tea interests. I devoted my private funds to the same object. I gave every encouragement to planters to take up lands for ordinary cultivation in the neighbourhood of their gardens, and granted them leases on very favourable terms for the cultivation of new staples, such as sisal hemp, rhea, and rubber. I helped them in their endeavours to strike oil and coal and other minerals. I spared no pains to improve the conditions of coolie transit from the recruiting districts to Assam, and may boast that I improved them to the immense advantage of the industry. If I spoke plainly to offending planters, my bark was worse than my bite ; and I was more chary than any of my predecessors in resorting to the extreme measure of closing bad gardens to indentured labour. One of the principal merits of my colonisation scheme was the assistance it would have afforded to the tea industry by the repopulation of the province. And if my proposals for improving local communications by means of tramways had been carried out, the most important gardens all over the province would have been directly connected with the railway and the river.

It is a fortunate coincidence which smiles upon the ruler of Assam that the interests of the province are so deeply wrapped up in the welfare of the tea industry, that zeal for the latter in no way interferes with, but rather serves to supplement, the general advancement and development of the country. There was no collision, therefore, between administrative schemes which were impartially designed to benefit alike the humble tiller of the soil and the British capitalist. That was always a source of thankfulness. But there loomed all the time in the background, like a spectre over the Administration, the larger and independent question of the protection of the hundreds of thousands of helpless labourers, imported from other provinces of India, often transmitted more than a thousand miles by rail and river, to work on the tea gardens for inadequate wages and under penal provisions which Sir George Campbell, from his place as President of the Bengal Legislative Council, thirty years earlier, had not hesitated to describe as reducing the coolie to the position of a slave. Over this question—too large to be discussed or even referred to further till I can spare a whole chapter for the purpose—a storm of obloquy was shortly to descend on my devoted head.

Few spectacles are more beautiful than the distant view of the snow-clad Himalayas from the Assam plains. This great range of mountains extends from the extreme north-west frontier of India to the extreme north-east. It constitutes the southern boundary of the bleak and inhospitable raised plateau of Tibet. But between these snowy peaks and the frontier of British India there everywhere lies an intervening barrier of range upon range of mountainous territory, over which the British Government exercises little or no control. From every hill-station in the Himalayas a glimpse of these natural obstacles to further aggression may be obtained. But it is only as we leave Nepal and Sikkim and Bhutan behind and approach the frontier on the north-east, where the distance between the plains and the Abode of Snow is greater, and the intervening ranges increase in numbers and in ruggedness, that we find ourselves confronted by races wholly uncivilised and savage.

Short and squat, with protruding cheek-bones, of a Mongoloid type, strong and active like all hill-men, these savages are armed only with primitive spears, rude *daos*, or choppers, and occasionally with bows and poisoned arrows ; and there is scanty truck in life and nothing common in ideas or sentiment between them and the peaceful dwellers in the plains. Far away to the extremity of the frontier, until the boundaries of Assam march with the hills and forests of Upper Burma, these tribes are scattered—Akas and Dufflas, Apatanangs, Abors, and Mishmis—each of whom have many septs or clans among themselves —Khamptis and Singphos—living entirely separate from one another, and without any unifying influence among them of language or religion. The north-east frontier problem is therefore wholly different from the frontier problem on the north-west of India, where the handing on of the fiery crescent has ere now set the whole Afghan border in a blaze. Nothing of this kind could ever occur on the north-east frontier. Nevertheless, the existence of these savage tribes along the borders of Assam constitutes a source of anxiety from which it cannot be said that the Government of the province is ever altogether free.

In the days of the Assam Rajas most of these

tribes had acquired a right to levy from the villages in the plains certain petty dues, and it has been the policy of the British Government to commute this claim into money payments—or *posa* as it is called —which are made to the chiefs by Government only so long as they conduct themselves peaceably. It is found that this practice exercises a very restraining effect on the conduct of the tribes. In case of trouble another remedy is applied, known as a blockade, under which by means of frontier outposts and patrol all access to British territory is cut off. As the tribesmen are anxious to trade at our frontier marts this remedy also proves generally efficacious. But from time to time a frontier raid occurs in one direction or another; frontier patrols are ambushed and cut to pieces, or a village hamlet is sacked and its occupants killed or carried off; remonstrance is met with defiance, and the Local Government is unwillingly forced into a little punitive expedition against the marauders. A small force of military police, with perhaps a handful of native infantry, undertakes these reprisals, and the chastened tribe generally remains quiet for a term of years. These are petty affairs enough, but unfortunately they are not infrequent, and during the five and a half years of my administration there were two raids which were followed up by punitive measures. Such a sad case as that of my friend Noel Williamson, who was cruelly murdered in Abor territory in 1911, is unique, and I can recall no other case in which a British officer has lost his life at the hands of these sub-Himalayan tribes.

A far larger portion of my time was occupied by the affairs of the hill tribes who reside within the area of British territory. The hill tracts of Assam cover an area of about twenty-five thousand square miles, and have only gradually come under control.

Their history in the past has been one of continual raids into the plains, a perpetual harrying of border villages, and occasional onslaughts on tea gardens, where planters have been killed and coolies massacred. Reprisals have followed. At one time it was the fashion to make demonstrations or military promenades through the offending country; at another there have ensued periods of absolute non-interference; and eventually renewed outrages have resulted in the definite establishment of political control within the hills, terminating in absorption into British territory. In this way mountainous ranges within the province which were formerly inhabited by lawless and head-hunting savages have slowly merged into well-administered and peaceful tracts of country. Many a gallant British officer has lost his life in the process, but already in the days when I was in Assam complete order and quiet had been established. The pacification of and growing spread of civilisation among these tribes are among the noblest records of British rule in India.

> "Tu regere imperio populos, Romane, memento!
> Hae tibi erunt artes; pacisque imponere morem,
> Parcere subjectis et debellare superbos."

These great Virgilian lines proclaim the spirit in which my frontier officers lived and worked. First and foremost among them I place McCabe, the idol of his comrades, who perished in the earthquake. The names of others come quickly—Henry St. Patrick Maxwell, the sympathetic and worthy successor of Sir James Johnstone in Manipur; Alexander Porteous, who was not only a distinguished frontier officer, but one of the most conscientious and generous-hearted of men; Arthur William Davis and Albert Edward Woods, whose names are never to be forgotten in the Naga Hills; my old friend John

MAO NAGAS. SUBJECTS OF MANIPUR.

[To face p. 250.

Shakespear, who with indomitable enthusiasm and patience revolutionised Lushai Land ; and Francis Jack Needham, to whom I am knit with a bond of friendship during the whole period of my Indian service, and who rises to my mind as the very ideal of a frontier officer and gallant gentleman.

On the extreme eastern frontier of Assam is the tributary State of Manipur. Its early records are marked, not only by constant Burmese invasions but by internal wars of a savage and revolting type—a dark scene of blood and treachery. This evil reputation it was destined to retain, and one of the darkest and most tragic incidents of modern Indian history occurred at Manipur in 1891. One of the usual dynastic revolutions had taken place, and the Raja had been driven from his palace by his two younger brothers. The Government of India then decided to recognise the elder of these two brothers as Raja, but directed that the younger brother, known as the Senapati, or Commander-in-Chief, who had been the leading spirit in the revolution and was very popular with the people, should be arrested and deported from the State. This was the initial error in a series of distressing blunders for which there could be no adequate justification. Lord Lansdowne was Viceroy at the time, and the Manipur tragedy must always be held to cast a cloud on his reputation.

The Chief Commissioner was James Wallace Quinton, C.S.I., a man of high character and sweet disposition, and popular among all classes. With an escort of four hundred Gurkha sepoys he proceeded to Manipur to carry out the orders of the Government of India. He arrived there on the 22nd of March, and on the same day announced that he would hold a Durbar at the Residency at noon. At that hour the new Raja presented himself, but the Senapati sent his excuses and stated that he was too ill to attend. Mr. Quinton declined to hold a Durbar in the Senapati's absence, and informed the Raja that it would be held at 9 a.m. on the following day. But at the time fixed neither the Raja nor the Senapati appeared, and an ultimatum was then sent to the Palace that if the Senapati was not given up without more ado steps would be taken to have him seized by force.

Shortly before daybreak on the 24th of March troops were sent to arrest the Senapati in his house. They were resisted ; fighting became general and the Residency was attacked. In the evening a flag of truce was raised, and the Chief Commissioner attempted to enter into negotiations. A message was received to the effect that the Senapati would confer with Mr. Quinton. The Chief Commissioner, accompanied by Mr. Grimwood, the Political Agent, Colonel Skene, commanding the troops, Lieutenant Simpson, and his Private Secretary, Mr. Cousins, advanced unarmed to the main gate of the fort and disappeared within. About midnight a voice called from the fort, "The Chief Commissioner will not return," and immediately afterwards the Manipuris opened fire again on the Residency. It was then decided by the officers who had assumed command in the absence of Colonel Skene to retire towards Cachar, and effect was given at once to this infamous decision.

In the meantime the interview with the Senapati in the fort had taken place, but no conclusion was arrived at. The Chief Commissioner and his companions, who had started to return, were hemmed in by a menacing and angry crowd. Mr. Grimwood received a mortal wound from a spear, and Lieutenant Simpson, who immediately attacked the murderer, was slashed across the head with a *dao*. The party were detained for about an hour in a

THE DRAGONS AND CORONATION HOUSE, MANIPUR.

It was in this space in front of, and below, these Dragons that Mr. Quinton and his party were killed. The Dragons were destroyed by the British after the re-capture of Manipur and not a trace of them remains.

[To face p. 253.

small bungalow known as the Durbar Hall. From there they were brought out, bound hand and foot, thrown on the ground in front of the two gigantic dragons that stood before the Palace wall, and beheaded in the barbarous Manipuri fashion.

No time was lost by the Government in the dispatch of troops to avenge this unprecedented outrage. The Raja and the Senapati fled into the hills but were soon captured. All those principally responsible for the murder of the British officers were placed upon their trial. The Raja was sentenced to transportation for life. The Senapati and three others were hanged on the polo-ground. The Government of India declared that the Manipur State was forfeit to the Crown, but decided in their clemency to regrant it to a scion of a junior branch, who is the present Raja of Manipur.

This tragedy was the subject of a debate in the House of Commons at which I happened to be present. Sir William Harcourt moved for papers in a speech of studious moderation. I remember only one point he made. The Government of India, he said, accepted the revolution in Manipur as beneficial, but insisted upon the punishment of the Senapati, who had brought it about. This, he declared, "is as though the people of England had accepted the restoration of Charles II., but had ordered the execution of General Monk." Sir William was replied to by Sir John Gorst, then Tory Under-Secretary of State for India. The cynicism of his remarks and the transparency of their personal application electrified the House. He observed: "The Senapati was the man of the greatest ability and greatest force of character among the ruling family at Manipur. He was a man who was extremely popular among the people for his generosity." He went on to say that the Government of India had never encouraged men of that kind. They had always hated and discouraged independent and original talent, and had always loved and promoted docile and unpretending mediocrity. This was a policy they had inherited from Tarquinius Superbus. "Although in these days they did not cut off the heads of the tall poppies, they took other and more merciful means of removing any person of dangerous political pre-eminence to a harmless condition."

The debate was continued by George Curzon from the back benches, who repudiated Sir John Gorst, and in a long speech, which commended itself to his party, paved the way for his own appointment in a very short time to the Under-Secretaryship. Sir John, it may be added, never again held responsible office. For the rest I remember only Sir Richard Temple's declaration, amid cheers, that he was sure that after mature consideration the Indian Government would never stoop to justify the attempt to arrest the Senapati in public Durbar. It was reserved for the *Times* newspaper in a characteristic leading article the next day to defend the Government of India on the analogy of what Louis XI. might have done to Charles of Burgundy, or what the Duke of Alva did to Counts Egmont and Horn, and King Nebuchadnezzar to Shadrach, Meshach, and Abednego.

I visited Manipur twice: on the first occasion in January, 1898, when I came and went by the Kohima route through the Naga Hills, and again in November, 1901, when I accompanied Lord Curzon from Cachar. The Cachar route is the shorter, but in either case there is a long march over the hills of several days' duration. Both routes are of absorbing interest to one who has his heart in the administration, and both possess an attraction and romance of their own. If there were time to spare

I would always prefer the Kohima route, by the Hot Springs, the buried old city of Dimapore with its mystic ruins, and the weird and historic associations which surround every stage in the Naga Hills. As a spectacle nothing, I think, surpassed a great prairie fire I witnessed in 1898, when the whole country seemed a roaring and crackling blaze with men and cattle fleeing before it. But such incidents are common. The Cachar route, while it reveals here and there fascinating glimpses of fairy beauty, becomes almost monotonous in the density of its forest scenery.

There was nothing surprising in Lord Curzon's desire to visit Manipur. He was deeply interested in the sad episode which had occurred ten years before, and his march through Manipur enabled him to traverse the confines of Upper Burma to Mandalay. He enjoyed the trip to the utmost. At that time our official relations were gravely strained, but if possible his personal attitude was pleasanter than ever. We rode along side by side on two of the most beautiful ponies that could be found in Manipur. A really first-class Manipuri pony is a splendid little creature, about twelve hands in height, but with remarkable speed, courage, and endurance. Unfortunately, they are now very rare. We were a delightful party. There were Sir Hugh Barnes, Foreign Secretary ; Colonel Everard Baring, Military Secretary ; Colonel Fenn, R.A.M.C., Surgeon to his Excellency ; Captains Clive Wigram and Lord Suffolk, A.D.C's. ; and two of my own staff, Major A. E. Woods and Julian Cornes. We messed together in shanties prepared for the purpose at each halting-place, and Lord Curzon was the life and soul of us all. Most of the arrangements for the trip had been organised by Colonel Maxwell from Manipur. Not less than a thousand coolies were collected together along the route to carry our impedimenta, and comfortable little mat houses had been rigged up for each of us at every halting-place. The Surma Valley Light Horse supplied a mounted escort for our first stage, and at subsequent stages a full guard of honour was supplied by the 5th Bengal Light Infantry. The early morning general salute was occasionally a source of amusement and embarrassment. A detachment of military police under the command of Major Woods pervaded the whole route. Nowhere did any hitch occur. There was a public reception on arrival at the capital of the State, and on the next day a grand Durbar.

At Manipur there were the usual entertainments: Manipuri polo and hockey and Naga sports, and Manipuri and Naga nautches. I had seen all these before, and noticed that the crowds, though great, were no greater than on the previous occasion. Polo is the national game of Manipur. It was played there more than two hundred years ago. A dynastic revolution was once brought about by a quarrel over a polo pony. In the Manipuri game there are seven players on each side; there are no goal-posts, and a point is scored whenever the ball is hit across the back line of the opposing side. Among the polo players whom I saw in '98 were two veterans who had played before the Prince of Wales in Calcutta in a game of which I was also an eye-witness twenty-two years previously. Polo and hockey were both played with the utmost zest and were well worth seeing, but what I think interested me most was the immense concourse of spectators they attracted. On both occasions when I was at Manipur the crowd all round the ground must have been ten deep in many places, and it was highly critical and appreciative. It could not have been bigger in the late Raja's time, and this and other signs afforded evidence that

A GROUP OF MANIPURI POLO PLAYERS.

This and the two preceding illustrations are from photographs taken by an old Mahomedan, who was photographer to the late Maharaja. He was shot by our sepoys while they were firing on the Senapati's house in 1891.

bitter memories did not rankle much in the minds of the people.

I took my leave of Lord Curzon at Manipur ; he passed on in his tour to Upper Burma, and I returned to my own province.

CHAPTER XXII

INCEDO PER IGNES

FOR a period of nearly four years I lived on very amicable terms with the tea industry. I was identified with many active measures to promote its welfare. The newspaper press from time to time, the Indian Tea Associations, and the representatives of the tea industry in London afforded ample recognition of my zeal and exertions and personal popularity. My relations with the members of the planting community were of the most cordial nature. I do not think I was guilty of any bias, but whatever bias I had was a natural one in favour of the planters. My service was drawing to a close : it was my inclination and interest to say and do nothing to disturb the existing harmony. I am quite ready to admit that for at least three or four years my official Reports were drafted in the easy-going and optimistic vein which had been the general characteristic of the provincial Labour Reports. I have read all the Reports of my predecessors, and it is impossible not to be struck by the apologetic current which runs through them. I do not think that I or my predecessors are to blame for this, and I should have a mean opinion of any officer in our position who did not lend himself, according to his opportunities, to encourage the tea industry by word and action. That attitude of encouragement was the policy of all of us.

But my predecessors were more fortunate than I was in that no burning questions directly affecting the antagonistic interests of Capital and Labour arose in their time. Nor in the first instance did I start any such question. The proposal to raise the coolies' statutory wage emanated from the Government of Bengal. It devolved upon me, however, to inquire into it, to examine it from all points of view, and to probe the issues to the quick. In undertaking this investigation I learned many things of which a Chief Commissioner may remain, and often has remained, in ignorance. I was distressed beyond measure at the tale of suffering which came to my notice, and I felt it my duty not to conceal the truth. I reported on the facts. Although, when indignation is aroused against injustice and wrong, it is difficult to refrain from strong language, I wrote and spoke with moderation.

The Government of India decided on immediate legislation, and during the cold weather of 1900-1 I was residing on my yacht off Prinsep's Ghat in Calcutta as a member of the Viceroy's Legislative Council for the consideration of a new Assam Labour and Emigration Bill. I had been appointed on the Council in addition to my duties as Chief Commissioner of the province. My position was a difficult one. An acute issue had been drawn up between the interests of Capital and Labour. The labourers in Assam are an ignorant and voiceless community, and they had no organ to press their demands. On the other hand, the whole of society and all the newspapers of the British Press were united in their support of the tea industry. This term is used to denote the interests of the proprietors of the tea gardens, of the shareholders of companies, of the agents in

Calcutta and London, and of the employers of labour; and this customary use of the expression is a true indication of the fact that we are too apt, not only in language but in thought and action, to contemplate the interests of the industry exclusively from the capitalists' point of view. The capitalists were represented on the Council by many members of energy and ability; but there was no labour member to argue the coolies' cause, and I therefore felt it peculiarly incumbent on me, as representative and head of the province concerned, to state the case on their behalf as completely as possible and without reserve.

I cannot say that I derived much assistance from Sir Charles Rivaz, who was the Member of the Viceroy's Council in charge of the Bill, or any help at all from the Legal Member, Sir Thomas Raleigh, who presided by virtue of his office at our meetings in Select Committee. I do not pretend myself to be indifferent to the praise or blame of my own countrymen, and it was not a pleasant duty for me to take up an attitude which alienated from me their sympathy. But these two cautious officials who were responsible for moulding the policy of Government were the last men in the world who would venture, if they could help it, to incur personal unpopularity in the British Press, or with the powerful interests affected, or even with tea planters. So I was left to fight the cause of Labour single-handed and alone, and found myself during our discussions in a hopeless minority.

It may be said to have been fortunate that the Government was pledged to support the general principle of an increase in the coolies' statutory wage. But the members of the Council allowed the principle to be miserably whittled down in the course of our proceedings. The old law of 1865 provided for a monthly wage rate of Rs. 5 per man (a rupee being then worth two shillings, though in later days only one shilling and fourpence) and Rs. 4 per woman for the first three years of a labour contract, and Rs. 6 per man and Rs. 5 per woman for the fourth and last year. The Bill before the Council originally proposed to alter this rate to Rs. 6 per man and Rs. 5 per woman throughout the period of the contract. In all conscience this was a mild and moderate proposal. But in spite of my strenuous protest, this was modified in Committee to a graduated rate with annual increments only reaching the full rate of Rs. 6 and Rs. 5 in the last year. And finally in Council, in a moment of inconceivable weakness, Lord Curzon announced that he would acquiesce in a postponement of this graduated rate for two years owing to the depression in the market for tea. The result, therefore, was a decisive victory for the capitalist party in Council. I might have expected this all along, but the truth is that I hoped for better things from Lord Curzon and was bitterly disgusted at his timid attitude. I challenged him across the Council Board with the charge that he was stultifying his own policy, and he rejoined that I was exceeding the limits of decorous debate. I forced a division in Council on the question of this postponement, but was supported by only a few Indian members.

And yet no case could be more complete than that which I had made out. I had shown that the wages fixed for the labourer under the Act of 1865, even if he worked no overtime whatever, were higher than the average wages, including overtime and advances, actually earned by labourers during any one of the seventeen years preceding the introduction of this Bill. I had proved that the actual average rate of wages paid for ordinary unskilled labour in Assam was more than double that of the wage prescribed by law for indentured coolies. I had demonstrated that while an indentured labourer was expected to serve for Rs. 5 a month as an *adscriptus glebæ* in the remote wilds of Assam, the same man was in a position to earn in the vicinity of his own home a wage of from Rs. 6 to Rs. 10 a month. I pointed out that the present low rate of wage had never been sufficient to procure suitable labour for the Assam tea districts. This was admitted by Sir William Grey when he was Lieutenant-Governor of Bengal as long ago as 1868. Coolies of good physique and constitution, willing to emigrate to Assam under a penal contract, had never been obtainable at the statutory rates, and, to meet the demand, contractors were compelled to search far and wide for people who were in such a state of destitution that they were prepared to emigrate on any terms as a last resource. The recruiter was accustomed to lie in wait for wives who had quarrelled with their husbands, young people who had left their homes in search of adventure, insolvent peasants escaping from their creditors. In carrying on his business he had to display considerable activity and resource. He had to incur unpopularity and even physical danger, to bribe police underlings, and to run the risk of Government prosecution and punishment.

It was not surprising that for such difficult and dangerous work the contractor demanded a high rate of remuneration which the keen demand for labour enabled him to obtain. I showed that there was a regularly established business of buying and selling labour, and that employers were paying at scheduled rates for every labourer recruited under penal contract a sum varying from Rs. 120 to Rs. 150. I pointed out how these transactions were a great curse to the recruiting districts. In too many instances the recruiters resorted to criminal means, inducing their victims by misrepresentation or by threats to accompany them to a contractor's depôt or railway-station, where they were spirited away before their absence was noted by their friends or relations. The records of the criminal courts teemed with instances of fraud, abduction of married women and young persons, wrongful confinement, intimidation, and actual violence—in fact, a tale of crime and outrage which would arouse a storm of public indignation in any civilised country. In India the facts were left to be recorded without notice by a few officials and missionaries.

I had proved all this to the hilt. And although I lost the fight, the hard fact still confronted the tea industry that except in famine or destitution years they could not get the labour they wanted for their gardens. The rate of wage has since been slowly raised under the operation of economic laws—very slowly, however, for the ordinary principles of political economy have little application in the peculiar conditions of tea cultivation. In all avenues of business employers combine as much as they can to keep down wages: that is one of the normal points of antagonism between Capital and Labour; but in the Assam tea industry such combination is extraordinarily strong and effective, not only because the labourers are very ignorant but also because, being bound by a penal contract, they are unable to strike for an increase of wages. If they were to strike they would be sent to prison. It was long before a rise of wages was forced on employers by the impossibility of obtaining labour at the old rates. But there must eventually be a limit beyond which they could not allow the price of coolies to rise, and as that limit was reached so an unwilling industry was at last compelled to accept an increase in the rate as inevitable.

In the meantime the scene of battle shifted to the question of the actual condition of the labouring population. The *Times* newspaper, always to the front where there is an opportunity of advocating the interests of British Capital in any conflict with those of Labour, sent out a Special Correspondent to India, who published a series of astounding statements on the condition of the tea coolies in Assam. "The labourer," he told us, "has been withdrawn from the fierce battle of the millions amid the storm and stress of varying seasons into the constant shadow of prosperity and peace. Henceforward he has nothing to fear. He is protected from famine, from fraud, from violence, from usury, from all manner of external ills. For him and for his like alone among the poor of India the problem of life is solved."

Is life in a tea garden, then, an earthly paradise? That is not only not the fact, but the very reverse is the fact. The managers of the great majority of gardens are ordinarily humane and kindly-hearted gentlemen, and in their gardens the coolies are well cared for. But it would be a gross exaggeration to imply that even in such gardens the lot of the labourer is a happy one. He is not a free man, and he lives far from his home in an unwholesome climate on a miserable pittance. There remains a not inconsiderable residuum of gardens in which the coolie is protected from neither famine, nor fraud, nor violence, nor indebtedness, nor from any manner of external ill. There are black sheep in every fold. The managers are Britons, and they have the virtues of their race. But they are not exempt from the failings of a common humanity. They are neither saints nor knaves. As was said of Golyer's Ben :—

> "He warn't the best man that ever you seen,
> And he warn't so ungodly pizen mean,
> No better nor worse than the rest."

They have their good side and their bad, and it

was my misfortune to turn the searchlight on to the latter. I had no alternative but to do so. Unless the fullest publicity is given to the defects of an abnormal labour system, it is hopeless to look for a remedy. It was impossible for me to express the conviction that the gravest abuses were prevalent on tea gardens without at the same time substantiating it by the production of evidence. I never indulged in any vague or indiscriminate comment. I never described the condition of tea coolies as Sir Bampfylde Fuller did, in an unpublished memorandum, as that of beasts in a menagerie. If I extenuated nothing, I set down naught in malice. I wrote my last Labour Report for 1900. It was a tale of misery and wrong which it was my duty to unfold from my seat in Council and in that Report.

It is needless to say that it was only a small percentage of abuses which could come to my knowledge. But I had cases brought to my notice where contracts of sickly and unfit labourers were cancelled for the purpose of keeping down the rate of mortality among contract labourers, and of others where deaths had been treated as desertions for the same reason. I knew of cases where it was the practice to expel sickly coolies who had become unfit for labour. I have seen with my own eyes a Government hospital full of sickly and dying coolies whose contracts had been cancelled and who had just been expelled from his garden by one of the oldest and most respected tea planters in the province. I have seen dead and dying coolies lying in the ditch by the roadside and in the bazar. I knew of cases in which coolies in the fourth year of their agreement were not paid the higher rate of salary to which they were entitled. In other cases, rice was not provided at the statutory price and the subsistence allowance prescribed by law was not paid to sick coolies or pregnant women. Advances were often illegally debited against coolies on account of subsistence allowance or sick diet, as well as on account of rewards paid for the arrest of deserters, and labourers were thus bound hand and foot to the garden service. In some instances only a few annas (or pence) found their way into the hands of a coolie as wages in the course of a whole year, the managers having deemed that they were justified in making deductions right and left so long as they kept their labourers in good condition like their horses and their cattle.

I reported a case in which a coolie woman, who had escaped from a garden, was recaptured and flogged—the manager was fined Rs. 500 (£33) by the Magistrate—and another in which a coolie who was suspected of helping others to abscond was flogged. Towards the close of my service in the province a case came to light in which coolies were confined for days in what was described as a "prison-house" in the garden and were mercilessly beaten, three having their arms broken. I must add that these bad cases did not occur on bad gardens only. Some of the worst were reported from gardens which yield a good dividend and are under the control of most respectable London boards of management.

I confess that to a large extent these facts were revelations to me, forced on my attention by the circumstances of the particular inquiry into wages on which I was engaged. But in the face of what they reveal it is amazing that any one should venture to affirm that the labourer on Assam tea gardens lives "in the constant shadow of prosperity and peace." What is to be said in reply to the fact that every year many thousands desert from their gardens, some of whom in their ignorance and misery cross the frontier, where they become slaves and occasionally victims to sacrifice among savage tribes? What is there to be said in reply to the figures of coolie death-rate? During the seven years preceding the date of my Report the rate of mortality among Central Provinces adult emigrants into Assam was 72·5, 85·9, 84·1, 83, 65, 55·6, and 48·3 per thousand. During the thirteen years from 1887 to 1889 inclusive the death-rate among indentured tea coolies of all classes had averaged 53·2 per thousand; and it must be remembered that this was the mortality among adults in the prime of life. I do not envy the mental twist which enables any one to arrive at the conclusion that the lot of these unfortunate immigrants, perishing far from their homes and under a system of compulsory labour, at twice and four times the normal rate of mortality, was a happy one.

Many thousands of coolies imported from remote parts of India were employed on railway construction in Assam. They were horribly neglected and many died. Their condition was miserable, no doubt, but they were free men, they emigrated voluntarily, and were paid liberally. The penal laws which regulate the supply of labour to the plantations in Assam were not needed in their case. But it is an obvious reflection that a reasonable prospect of obtaining labour by the operation of the ordinary laws of supply and demand cannot be very far off when it is found that other employers of labour are able to get what they require without resort to the penal laws. The question is one of wage only. When Ceylon is able to recruit its labour supply from India under a healthy system, when the Dooars and Chittagong tea gardens, the coal-mines at Ranigunge, the jute mills in Calcutta, and the Railways and Public Works Department in Assam are able to do the same, there is no longer any reason why the tea gardens in Assam should continue to be bolstered up by a system of indentured labour which experience and moral sense alike condemn.

It is no small satisfaction to me to reflect that the action I deemed it my duty to take in protesting against the operation of a special labour law for providing labour in the tea districts of Assam was not without its beneficial effect. The annoyance of being persistently described as a "malignant slanderer" is, after all, a trifle in the face of the removal of many of the abuses to which I have referred. I do not pretend to say that those abuses were altogether removed: they never can be swept away so long as human nature remains what it is. But my action was undoubtedly instrumental in effecting a marked improvement, and I do not think that any of the benefits I was able to confer on the industry can compare in importance with this. It has been a pleasing task to my successors to chronicle an improvement in the management of Assam tea gardens, an amelioration in the condition of the coolies, the betterment of their health, and the rise in their wages. The industry was warned in time to set its house in order, and to co-operate with the efforts of the officials to raise the standard of comfort and happiness among the hundreds of thousands of poor and helpless creatures entrusted to its care.

More than one Labour Commission has been appointed since I left the province. The Report of the Commission of 1906 was a state paper of considerable importance, for it was an authoritative and definite pronouncement in favour of the termination of the system of indentured labour which has now prevailed in Assam for nearly half a century. The system has not yet ceased, but at least one step has been taken. In my time the coolie was bound down, not only by penalties under the law but by physical subjection to his employer, who, on a labourer attempting to run away, was empowered to seize him and bring him back to work. That provision of the law has been repealed. It cannot fail to follow that the whole of the legislation which deprives the labourer of his status as a free man will also cease ere long to disfigure the Indian Statute Book.

There remains the vital question of the relations between employers and labourers, and of the administration of justice in cases of collision between planters and coolies. I regret that this is another matter on which I am compelled to make the admission that I did not take the initiative myself. I knew what a storm of anger and irritation it would arouse. But Lord Curzon had not been more than six months at the head of affairs when he wrote to me an official letter, in 1899, inviting my attention to the many cases of collision between managers and coolies which had recently occurred on tea gardens. It was observed that these cases seemed to indicate that there was something seriously wrong, and it was inquired whether in my opinion they were due to the class of coolies employed or to the class of managers or to any other determinable cause, and whether any remedial measures could be suggested. I confess that I replied in the apologetic vein which had become the established practice in the province and contented myself with quoting and endorsing the opinion of my predecessors, and especially of Sir Dennis Fitzpatrick, that "there must be a certain amount of harshness and oppression at times, possibly even of downright cruelty, on the one side, and of turbulence, conspiracies, and maliciously concocted charges on the other. This, unfortunately, is human nature, as displayed among all classes of men, and happily we have criminal courts strong enough to deal with it. But, speaking generally, the relations between employers and the labourers seem to be fairly good."

It is to Lord Curzon's credit that an evasive answer of this character did not at that time commend itself to him. He directed that a special report should be submitted to him of every case of collision between employers and coolies, and for a long period there was a continual shower of letters from him, official and private, commenting on cases and condemning the bias of Magistrates. On one occasion I received a warning, and very properly I think, against a natural tendency to protect and screen my subordinates when I was afraid that their conduct was likely to bring them into trouble. If the truth is to be told, I rejoiced at the receipt of these letters which could only strengthen my hands, and I felt that at last there was a strong Viceroy in power who would not hesitate to vindicate justice and uprightness, and punish wrongdoers.

I quote a few extracts from one of these official letters, which could only strengthen my hands, and to three reports I had submitted on specific cases. Lord Curzon wrote through Sir John Hewett, at that time his Secretary in the Home Department :—

"The cases reported in your letters have been carefully considered by the Government of India. In the first case, a native gentleman of respectable family was grossly assaulted without provocation by the European manager of a tea estate. The sentence on the accused was a fine of Rs. 60 [£4] or one month's rigorous imprisonment in default. In the second case six coolies were convicted of committing an assault described by the Assistant Commissioner in his judgment as 'not a serious one and not premeditated,' the person assaulted being an European assistant manager of a tea estate. In this case the principal offender has been sentenced to nine months' rigorous imprisonment and the remainder to three months' rigorous imprisonment.

"The Government of India, I am to say, fully concur in your criticisms on these sentences, the disparity between which is both striking and deplorable. . . .

"The case referred to in the third of your letters under notice relates to a complaint of indecent assault brought by a native woman employed on a tea garden against the European manager of the garden, and has resulted, for want of evidence, in the dismissal of the case without the framing of a charge against the manager. His Excellency in Council desires, I am to say, to fully endorse your criticisms with regard to the mismanagement of this case. It is in his opinion scandalous that the Inspector, who was directed to submit his report within ten days from the 6th of December, should have omitted to commence his inquiry until the 29th of that month, and have submitted his report only on the 15th of January, 1901; that the Subdivisional Officer should have kept the report until the 15th of February, without passing orders on it; and lastly, that in consequence of the procedure adopted by the Magistrate, the appearance of the accused in Court should have been deferred until the 22nd of April, a period of exactly five months from the date on which the offence is alleged to have taken place. The neglect to exercise supervision on the part of the Deputy Commissioner over his subordinates during the progress of the case seems to the Governor-General in Council equally blameworthy. These officers should be informed of the opinions that are entertained of their conduct by the Government of India.

"The Governor-General in Council has read the accounts given in your letters under reply with regret, and directs me to draw your attention to the increasing frequency of cases of dispute between European managers and the labouring community on tea estates. In Mr. Monahan's letter, dated the 4th of September, 1899, it was contended that such cases were on the decrease, and it was observed: 'The Chief Commissioner is quite satisfied that the cases of collision between managers and coolies in tea gardens are proportionately fewer and less serious in character than they were in previous years.' Twenty-one such cases appear to have been reported by you to this office in 1900, and fifteen have been reported in the present year. His Excellency in Council is unable to reconcile the sanguine tone taken in that letter with these figures or with the facts which repeatedly come before his notice in connection with cases such as those now under discussion. With reference to the tendency noticed in the second of your letters under consideration to pass excessive sentences when coolies are charged with committing offences against their employers, I am to say that his Excellency in Council considers that the inequality in the administration of justice thus indicated is an abuse which cannot be allowed to remain unchecked, and that, should instances of similar partial administration of the law continue to occur, the Government of India will not hesitate to take drastic action in the matter."

A letter of this kind did not seem to indicate any vacillation of purpose, and Lord Curzon's private letters to myself, which I cannot quote, were couched in even more decisive terms. My course of conduct was clear. But I was never blind to the acute difficulties of the situation. I had not forgotten the experience of my old Chooadanga days. I had at my elbow a wise mentor in the person of my Secretary, Francis Monahan, who was my right-hand man in all this time of stress and storm, and to whom I am under innumerable obligations. I was never oblivious of the peculiar difficulty which besets a Magistrate, a member of a small European community in a distant land, who may be playing polo or bridge or billiards with a planter one month, or who may be serving under him as a trooper in the Light Horse, and who in the next month may be called on to try and punish him for cruelty to a contract labourer. I do not know what I should have dared to do in this delicate and thorny matter without the consciousness of support from Simla. I might perhaps have shrunk from casting myself into the Curtian Gulf. But with the Viceroy at my back —*te duce, Cæsar!*—I had no cause to hesitate, and I published in my Report for 1900 a summary of cases of collision between planter and coolie which had occurred during the year, and concluded with the following remarks, which I deem it fair to myself to quote in full :—

"Mr. Cotton has taken the pains to refer at some length to these cases, principally because they illustrate the fact to which he drew attention in a previous Annual Report that there is an undoubted tendency among Magistrates in Assam to inflict severe sentences in cases in which coolies are charged with committing offences against their employers, and to impose light, and sometimes inadequate, punishment upon employers when they are convicted of offences against labourers. The position of Magistrates in Assam is certainly a very difficult one, and it is impossible for them to be altogether uninfluenced by their environment and their natural feelings towards their fellow-countrymen who are employed in the development of an important industry ; but this renders it all the more necessary for them to be on their guard against any display, or apparent display, of partiality. About four years ago the Chief Commissioner received a representation on behalf of the tea industry protesting that insufficient sentences were being passed by Magistrates in cases in which coolies were concerned. He replied that he did not share the opinion of the Association, and he must now emphatically declare that he has never come across a case in which coolies were inadequately punished. On another occasion a deputation complained to him of the hostile attitude of a certain Magistrate; but Mr. Cotton has only to say that this officer, whom he believes to be a conscientious officer, has appeared to him to display undue leniency more than once when planters have been arraigned before him for punishment. It is impossible to read the accounts of the cases of which an abstract has been given above without feeling that justice has not been always well and truly administered between man and man. During the current year the same tendency has been observed in a marked degree, and special orders have been passed with reference to the sentences inflicted in particular cases."

It was evident from the resolutions passed at the various meetings of planters held in the province and published in the newspapers as well as from the agitation conducted in the Press that the personal irritation against myself, which was so marked, largely took its rise from these observations. They were the storm-centre round which the tempest rolled. I regret that it should have been necessary for me to record them, but I cannot withdraw or modify a single word. They contain nothing that I was not amply justified in placing on record; they substantially coincide with what I had separately reported to the Government of India, and they are expressed in more moderate language than had been used by the

Government of India and myself in our official correspondence. The utterances of Lord Curzon on this subject had been far stronger than my own. The time, in my judgment, had fully come when it was necessary that comments of the kind should be made publicly.

All the available floodgates of abuse in the Anglo-Indian Press were opened. I was assailed with extraordinary virulence. I was charged with malignity, inveracity, and dishonesty, my motives were impugned in the most shameful manner, and one journal loudly clamoured for my dismissal from the public service. It was not for the first time that I had stood forward as the champion of the oppressed, and had trod on the corns of powerful interests. But I had never raised such a storm against myself as on the present occasion. The head and front of my offending was no more than that I had ventured to direct attention to defects of a serious character in the conditions under which the cultivation of tea was carried on in Assam. The tea industry and the planters as a body had become so intolerant of Government control and interference that they had come to regard a derogatory word as an insult, and the official who uttered it as an enemy. A section of the community had set itself up in an attitude of defiance of the Administration because I ventured to expose in fearless terms that everything connected with the industry was not *couleur de thé*. The position taken up by the tea industry was one fraught with dangerous consequences. There is an obvious line of argument in this direction which I do not deem it necessary to pursue. I content myself with saying that it is likely to become a very serious element in the political situation in India if the non-official European community should from one cause or another find reason to believe that officials who are confronted with facts damaging to an industry in which European interests are involved may be induced to keep silence for fear of being overwhelmed by a whirlwind of invective.

The most illustrious of Bengal officials—Sir Frederick Halliday and Sir John Peter Grant—had been attacked with equal virulence more than forty years previously for doing their duty. But the Viceroy of their day stood by them, and time has triumphantly vindicated their reputation. There was no Viceroy to stand by me. In the face of a rising storm of unpopularity from his own countrymen, Lord Curzon quailed. In a published letter to the Indian Tea Association on the 5th of February, 1902, he saved his own skin but deliberately flung me to the wolves. In regard to the treatment of coolies, he was "content to accept the opinions which have in the past been held to justify a conclusion favourable to the employers." He was "further of opinion that in dealing with the relations of the planters with their coolies and with the cases of criminal violence which have come before the courts, the Chief Commissioner's remarks have the effect of implying a wider condemnation than is deserved." The words of Sir Dennis Fitzpatrick and others of my predecessors whom I had quoted in 1899 were reproduced with approval, and Lord Curzon went so far as to say: "The Government of India are reluctant to believe that the Hon. Mr. Cotton can be correct in his rejection of the views expressed by an unbroken series of his predecessors and endorsed by himself."

I confess that I rubbed my eyes when I read this passage, so completely at variance with the whole tenor of the correspondence between Lord Curzon and myself for the previous two years or more. "Put not your trust in princes or in viceroys," was the only reflection I could make. But the substance of Lord

Curzon's decision came as no surprise to me, for I knew what to expect of him. I had already received an intimation that the sooner I vacated my appointment the more convenient it would be for the Government of India. I had no desire to make any protest. My health was at the time very much broken, and in any case I should have been compelled to seek an interval of rest. So it came about that I applied for and obtained leave from the end of April to the end of October, when my thirty-five years of service would have expired and my Indian career, unless I had been promoted to higher office, would, under the rules in force, have automatically closed.

I am afraid that I shall find it impossible to avoid the imputation of egotism, but it is no more than the literal truth when I say that I left India accompanied by demonstrations of popular sympathy and regret which had never before been accorded to a provincial Governor. From every district in Assam I received addresses, and was the centre of public receptions which must ever remain among the memorable events of my life. It would need a man cast in a sterner mould than I am, and a heart more insensible to emotion than mine, not to feel deeply and indelibly the kindness I have always experienced at the hands of the Indian people. Certain it is that in Assam, everywhere, wherever and whenever I mingled, as I did, with all classes and communities of the people of the province, not during my last year only, but always, men and women, the rich and poor, the old and young, vied with one another in the warmth of their greetings, and, when I left them, in the affectionate cordiality of their farewell. I retain as a treasure in my family all the addresses I received, and not the least interesting among them is an address contributed from all parts of the province by the women of Assam.

My departure became, like Lord Ripon's had been, but of course on a smaller scale, a triumphal progress. There were crowded deputations at every railway station, and on arrival at Calcutta the Sealdah Terminus was crowded to suffocation. In Calcutta we were the guests for a night or two of our old friends Mr. Justice and Mrs. Ameer Ali. A magnificent reception was accorded to me in the Town Hall, and an address, enshrined in a costly and beautiful casket, was presented on behalf of the people of Bengal. Throughout the long railway journey from Calcutta to Bombay there were further deputations at every railway station where we halted, and in Bombay itself—where I had only a couple of hours at my disposal to catch the steamer—I was simply swept away by the wave of popular enthusiasm from men with whom I had never had personal relations, but who showed in this remarkable demonstration their sympathy with my public career. These Calcutta and Bombay addresses are also among my most precious possessions.

Lord Curzon once confided to me that he was not very anxious to get an extension of his service in India, but that what he would like would be a potential voice in the selection of his successor. That is a privilege which, so far as I am aware, has never been enjoyed by the satrap of an Indian province. It was certainly not accorded to me, and I was succeeded in Assam by Sir Joseph Bamfylde Fuller, who was the Secretary of the Government of India under whose signature Lord Curzon's repudiation of my Assam policy had been issued.

CHAPTER XXIII

UNMUZZLED

ALL voyages by a P. & O. steamer are very much alike. I have always found them pleasant, but they recur to one's memory like the slides of a kaleidoscope. I have no clear recollection of any one voyage, except the first, which differentiates it from any other. One meets a number of interesting persons, but it is impossible to say on which voyage you met them, and you probably never see them again. I have travelled with Blondin, and have seen him cross from mast to mast on a very swaying cable in the Indian Ocean. He confessed to me that he did not very much enjoy that trip, but at the same time declared that he was quite as much at home on the tight rope as I was on the cuddy stairs. I travelled with Sir Edgar Vincent on his first appointment to Egypt, and thought what a splendid-looking young fellow he was. I have played whist with ambassadors, and even with Lord Kitchener before he was known to fame. A bit slovenly and unkempt I thought him, and very unlike the paragon he has become, but I noticed that even then his companions treated him with respect. On two occasions I journeyed with Valentine Baker Pasha, a heavy and silent man, *quantum mutatus* from the dashing Colonel of the Tenth Hussars. I have been accosted by William Howard Russell, of the *Times*, with a "Bonjour, Monsieur le Marquis," having been mistaken for a French nobleman with whom I played more than one good game of chess under the blue Mediterranean sky.

On our return from India in 1902, our most imposing fellow-passenger was Prince Ch'ing, who, with a large suite, was coming to England for King Edward's Coronation. Their beautifully coloured satin robes were the envy and admiration of all the ladies on board. The Prince was met at Marseilles by the Chinese Minister at Paris, and peeping through a window I witnessed the Kowtow ceremony which took place in the saloon. At Port Said our steamer was joined by Captain Tristram Speedy, whom I had not seen for many years. Captain Speedy was a remarkable man, of immense height and very varied experience in India, Abyssinia, and the Straits Settlements. He had once been guardian and tutor of Prince Alamayu, son of King Theodore of Abyssinia. He was now ill and suffering severely from rheumatism, which made him lame—a very different man from what he had been. But he gave a lecture to us on Abyssinia, extraordinarily good, and illustrated with splendid powers of mimicry. At its close I congratulated him, and Speedy replied: "Many thanks! Yes. But I found it hard work all the time standing on one leg." Then I said: "*Stans pede in uno.*" But poor Speedy did not take the point.

I arrived in England in May, 1902, in shattered health myself. But I picked up sufficiently to be able to attend the investiture ceremony held at Buckingham Palace in June, when His Majesty the late King Edward conferred upon me the dignity of a Knight Commander of the Star of India. I owed this honour to Lord Curzon's recommendation. It had been conferred on my predecessors, and an exception could hardly have been made in my case. But, with his customary courtesy, Lord Curzon had intimated to me that he intended to recommend me for the distinction in a letter which referred in very eulogistic terms to the services I had rendered in India. And in August I had the satisfaction of being present at His Majesty's Coronation in Westminster Abbey as the official representative of Assam. In October I formally tendered my resignation of the Indian Civil Service, and my official career was closed.

I was now free, if my health permitted it, to enter into English political life, and, after some desultory negotiations with other constituencies, was accepted by an unanimous vote as prospective candidate in the Liberal interest for the Eastern Division of the City of Nottingham in the spring of 1903. I assiduously nursed that constituency for a period of more than two and a half years. Though I had come in the first instance as an absolute stranger to the city, I very speedily made innumerable friends, and when the General Election came round in January, 1906, was quite as well known to the constituency as the sitting Member, Edward Bond, who had then represented the Division for ten years. But I must not anticipate events. My campaign in Nottingham, a crusade in Press and platform against the expedition into Tibet, and a return visit to India to preside over the Indian National Congress held at Bombay in December, 1904, were the most important events which occupied my leisure time until I was in due course elected to be a Member of Parliament.

There is a glamour about Tibet. It is the land of mystery and romance, and no Englishman had penetrated to the forbidden city of Lhasa since Thomas Manning, the Chinese scholar, the friend of Lamb, and the prince of eccentrics, had interviewed the Dalai Lama in 1811. The last Europeans to visit Lhasa had been the French Lazarist priests Huc and Gabet, in 1846. Scores of travellers from the West—French and Russian, Swedish and American, Belgian and British—tried and struggled in vain, and none ever got to Lhasa. The Tibetans are just as much opposed to the admission of Russians within their territory as they are to the approach of other Europeans. Prjevalsky was no more successful than Bower or Littledale. Sven Hedin had an escort of Cossacks, but it availed him nothing. The Tibetan policy of isolation is dictated by political motives; their tactics, peaceful but so far successful, had aimed at the exclusion of all white men of whatever nationality. In Sven Hedin's words: "They have not fallen victims to specious representations about the growth of commerce—that is to say, the importation of tobacco, spirits, opium, and firearms. They say in effect, 'Away with all your luxuries, with your steel, your gold, your silver! All we want is to be left in peace in our own country.'"

The imputation of Russian intrigue anywhere is generally sufficient to rouse the indignation of Englishmen. And so the Russian bogey was deliberately trotted out in the case of Tibet. Even as Calverley detected a Senior Wrangler in every perambulator he encountered in the Backs, so the attitude of Lord Curzon was always persistent to discern Russian intrigue in every innocent movement of Oriental politics. It was enough for Lord Curzon to know that a Mongolian Buriat, with his domicile in Russian Mongolia, had acquired a great personal influence over the Dalai Lama, and had visited St. Petersburg. But there never was a tittle of evidence to show that Russia had really been intriguing in Tibet. Read Sven Hedin's volumes, and you will learn what impenetrable natural barriers intervene between the Russian boundaries and Lhasa. Nor could there ever be any danger to British India through Tibet. The invasion of India from Tibet is a physical impossibility, and there is no record of any army having at any time attempted to raid India across the Himalayan passes. The Russian bogey was a simple snare and a self-made delusion.

In addition to this hollow pretence of Russian intrigue in Lhasa, it was put forward as a justification for an expedition from British India into Tibet that it was necessary to compel the Tibetans to adhere to treaty obligations which they were said to have broken. It was conveniently forgotten that there never had been a treaty to which the Tibetans were a party, and that Lord Lansdowne's agreement of 1890—the only treaty bearing on the subject—was a "Convention between Great Britain and China relating to Sikkim and Tibet." In point of fact, it could never be denied—although Lord Curzon endeavoured to do so—that China was the acknowledged suzerain of Tibet, and that if the Convention had been broken the responsible offender was not Tibet but China. In any case, there was no valid or true statement ever put forward showing how the terms of the Convention had been broken.

I opened my campaign in the columns of the *Times* in November, 1903, when a British armed mission first crossed the frontier. In those days the *Times* was honourably distinguished by the liberality and hospitality it offered to the expression of views diametrically opposed to its own. It so happens that my views are almost invariably opposed to those of the *Times;* and, if that paper at any moment were to express approval of what I had said or done, I should involuntarily be disposed to ask myself if I had said or done something particularly foolish. I therefore gratefully acknowledge my obligations to the management, which freely placed its columns at my disposal and published what I had to say prominently and in large type. This was a courtesy extended to me by the Editor for a period of more than four years. After that it was curious to notice that I was gradually relegated to small type and generally to an obscure corner of the paper, while personal attacks on me from anonymous contributors would find publication in the large type and prominent place I had formerly enjoyed. And now at last I have been barred by the Editor altogether from his columns. I am sorry for that, but I cannot complain, for if the Editor finds my contributions of an exceptionally pestilent or worthless character it is obviously within his discretion to exclude them. I have referred to this matter only as an interesting personal literary experience, which may or may not be unique in journalism, and to record my acknowledgments—which I do very sincerely—for the generous hospitality the *Times* afforded me in former days.

The use of the *Times* in my Tibetan campaign was invaluable. I was able to state the case against the invasion of Tibet in the most prominent and public manner possible, and, though I fought practically single-handed, there can be no doubt that my letters attracted considerable attention. I wrote to many other papers also, and embarked on a general lecturing tour in all parts of London and England on the subject. The late Lord Spencer asked me to go and see him at Spencer House, and I coached up other noble Lords and Members of Parliament over the matter. I attended the Tibetan debates in the Lords and Commons, but they seemed to me as unreal as the Manipur debate had seemed twelve years before. My Lords and Gentlemen were slaves of the Blue-book—small blame to them, considering the profusion and confusion of the information therein supplied—and had no mastery of its contents. Fortunately the Government of the day, acting, I cannot doubt, largely on Lord Lansdowne's advice, was firm in resisting the pressure put on it from India to establish a permanent British Residency at Lhasa. But the "pacific mission," as it was then called, was allowed to proceed without let or hindrance.

On the 31st of March, 1904, occurred a terrible incident which effectually roused the moral sense of England. The Tibetans had strictly confined themselves to pacific remonstrance. But, at a little place called Guru, on the line of march, they met their doom. A "huddled crowd" was safely penned up, with our troops on three sides of them and our guns commanding the only line of retreat. Our troops proceed to disarm this motley crowd of monks and husbandmen of their old matchlocks and swords. The Tibetans were simple enough to resist, and that was the signal for the massacre to begin. "It was," in the words of the *Times* Special Correspondent, "such a target as is not offered twice in a lifetime." The chance was not missed; the Tibetans could not run, and we literally mowed them down. The slaughter went on long after the pen was emptied. To quote the *Times* again, "Punishment is the word . . . there was nothing for the mission escort to fear except the crossing bullets of their own companions." That is the story of a massacre in which a "pacific mission" murdered some seven or eight hundred unresisting monks. It was not warfare: it was butchery.

After that incident Lord Curzon was practically left without sympathisers in this country. The peaceful mission was converted into a force of armed raiders, who advanced in spite of such feeble opposition as the Tibetans could offer, and in due course took possession of Lhasa. But the Dalai Lama had flown and sought a refuge in Russian Mongolia. A treaty was extorted from the Lamas who remained. They agreed, under pressure put upon them, to pay an indemnity of £500,000, which they had no more means of discharging than the man in the moon. The expedition returned to British India. And then began a new phase in the operations. The opportunity of China had come at last, and the diplomatists of the Celestial Empire did not fail to avail themselves of it. China refused to adhere to the treaty unless her suzerainty over Tibet was properly recognised. And the amount of the indemnity having been reduced to £166,666, China, as suzerain, offered to make herself responsible for paying it within three years. The demand of China was acceded to, the reduced indemnity was paid by China, and British troops withdrew from the occupation of any part of Tibet.

The subsequent situation at Lhasa is the natural aftermath of the British raid. The Anglo-Chinese and Anglo-Russian Conventions having, in spite of Lord Curzon, recognised the suzerainty of China in unequivocal terms, it was inevitable that China should assert her authority by drastic measures, quite inconsistent with her long past record, aiming at the establishment of an effective power in Tibet which would render nugatory all attempts to dislodge it. Before the raid the power of the Ambans or Chinese Viceroys at Lhasa was supported by a force of not more than two hundred Chinese troops. Since the raid a more aggressive policy has been adopted, and the garrison at Lhasa is now said to amount to two thousand men. The climax was reached when this force approached Lhasa, and the Dalai Lama fled again from his sacred palace, just as he had fled when its sanctity was invaded by British troops. He then sought security in Mongolia and in China; he has now sought and obtained the protection of the British Government in India. The situation is a piquant one, but it is the direct consequence of our own interference with Tibet. It is more than piquant, for it is very embarrassing to the British Government, upon whom have been forced the most delicate and tactful negotiations with China regarding Tibetan affairs in which we have no real concern.

I had always intended to revisit India, but the opportunity occurred earlier than I had expected. In the course of 1904 I was offered and accepted the Presidency of the Twentieth Session of the Indian National Congress, which was to be held at Bombay during Christmas week. Accompanied as I was by Sir William Wedderburn, I knew that we should be warmly welcomed on our return to India, but I had no idea of the reception which actually awaited us. During the whole of the long drive from the jetty to Malabar Hill, where we were very hospitably entertained, ours was a veritable regal progress. The crowds in the streets with their deafening cheering, the windows and verandas crammed with spectators, the tram service blocked, and every tramcar we passed with its clerks and mill-hands on their way to work rising in their seats and shouting, ladies and children overwhelming us in our carriage with garlands and flowers, people of all classes, from Sanyasis or religious hermits to respectable shopkeepers and merchants, all joining in vociferous welcome, in every variety of picturesque garb and head-dress—all this constituted a demonstration of profound significance.

When the Congress met, the scene was not less remarkable. An enormous *pandal*, or continuous tent, had been prepared, and therein was seated an audience of not less than twelve thousand persons. Of these, one thousand were duly elected delegates from all parts of India; the remainder were local visitors who had paid for their seats. They included about five hundred Indian ladies. The scene, with its bright colouring and animated faces, was extraordinarily interesting. The delegates were all men of distinction, and leaders of thought and opinion in their own provinces. The elected Members of Council from every Presidency were there in full numbers, and no profession or religious creed was unrepresented. Some had travelled thousands of miles to attend this Congress. Officials were not allowed to attend, even as visitors, but there were present two Judges of the Bombay High Court—one a Mussulman and the other a Hindoo—who had before their appointment to the Bench been Presidents of former Congresses. It is impossible to conceive of a more influential and representative gathering than was there assembled.

No human voice could have made itself audible through all the recesses of that vast assemblage. But there was no disorder, and unabated enthusiasm prevailed from first to last. The resolutions put had been carefully drafted by a special committee of delegates, and all were carried with acclamation without a dissentient voice. Bal Gangadhar Tilak was there, and he had his following, but there was no division then of the community into Extremists and Moderates. All were Moderates. The Chairman of the Reception Committee, Sir Phirozeshah Mehta, K.C.I.E., opened the proceedings. He was followed by Surendranath Banerjea, who moved that I should take the chair. I then delivered my Presidential Address, and the day's proceedings closed.

The two following days were devoted to the discussion of resolutions which comprised within their scope the most important political and economic problems of the Indian Empire. There was the

INDIAN NATIONAL CONGRESS GROUP, BOMBAY, DECEMBER 1904.

Front Row. From left to right. Dinshaw Edulji Wacha (ex-President), Sir William Wedderburn, Bart. (ex-President), Sir Phirozeshah M. Mehta, K.C.I.E. (ex-President), Sir Henry Cotton, K.C.S.I. (President), Samuel Smith, M.P., Surendro Nath Banerjea (ex-President), and J. N. Ghosal.

Second Row. From left to right. F. J. Latji, H. A. Wadia, N. M. Saker, R. K. Cama, the Hon. G. K. Gokhale, M. Viraraghava Chariar, the Hon. G. K. Parekh, Shamrao Vithal, S. C. Sarbadhikari, and Hasan Budrudin Tyabji.

To face p. 288.

question of the larger employment of Indians in responsible positions in the public service. This was supplemented by a comprehensive resolution pressing for the extension of primary education, due provision for instruction in manual training and in scientific agriculture, and especially for the establishment of at least one central, fully-equipped Polytechnic Institute, with minor technical schools and colleges in every province. Other resolutions dealt with the economic situation and the indebtedness of the peasantry. Another protested against the injustice of charging the cost of the India Office in London to the revenues of India, and declared that the salary of the Secretary of State for India should be borne on the English estimates. Then came the question of the position of Indian emigrants in British colonies, which was spoken to by four Indian gentlemen from South Africa, who described from their own experiences the hardships and injustice to which Indians were subjected in Natal and the Transvaal. The question of Indian finance was ably treated by Mr. Gokhale in a speech which would compare favourably, both in delivery and matter, with the best utterances of our legislators in the House of Commons. But the general excellence of the speeches, the moderation of their manner, the logic of their argument, and the soundness and correctness of their English style could not fail to have roused the admiration of any English listener. They were in themselves an object-lesson on behalf of the cause they advocated.

Another resolution urged that the people of India should be allowed a larger voice in the administration and control of the affairs of their country by an enlargement of the Legislative Councils which should be empowered " to divide on all financial matters coming before them, the Head of the Government concerned possessing the power of veto," and "the appointment of Indian representatives (who shall be nominated by the elected members of the Legislative Councils) as members of the Indian Council in London and of the Executive Councils of the Government of India and the Governments of Bombay and Madras." The Tibetan expedition and a forward frontier policy generally were roundly condemned. A protest was recorded against the constant increase in military expenditure and against the proposed Partition of Bengal, which was then arousing the utmost indignation and dismay among the inhabitants of that province.

This was generally admitted to have been the most largely attended and successful Congress gathering ever held in India. The enthusiasm was wonderful, and nothing could have exceeded the roar of applause which accompanied Sir William Wedderburn and myself when the proceedings terminated. I left at once for Calcutta, and there was again the familiar scene of popular demonstrations at every halting station on the railway. The Parsi refreshment contractors for the railway made themselves responsible for providing me with princely hospitality along the whole of my railway route as far as into Assam. In Calcutta I was the guest of my old friend the Maharaja of Durbhunga. Acting on a suggestion which Lord Courtney had made to me in England, I wrote to Lord Curzon asking permission to lay the Resolutions of the Congress before him. This Lord Curzon would not agree to, and I regret his refusal, for it tended to add to his unpopularity. But he received me privately with his old courtesy.

I attended one or two public meetings in Calcutta: one was a monster protest against the contemplated Partition of Bengal, and it is indicative of the public feeling on the subject that my speech, which took more than an hour to deliver and for which I had no notes, was reported verbatim on the next day in all the Calcutta newspapers—an effort of journalistic enterprise which at that time, I think, had not been equalled in the local Press. My Indian friends entertained me at a sumptuous banquet in the Town Hall, and in the same edifice an address was presented to me on the 10th of January. Even the *Englishman* newspaper, my bitterest critic and opponent, remarked that "in the annals of the historic Town Hall there has never been another such gathering, the reception being colossal in its greatest sense."

From Calcutta I extended my visit to Assam as far as Gowhatty, where I met with another great ovation from my Indian friends, but marked inattention from my successor in the government of the province, which was reflected by the local subordinate officials. I was left to put up at the public dawk bungalow. I found that the marble bust of me by my old friend Armstead was not allowed to rest in the Cotton College, for which it had been intended, but had been removed to another building. This is a replica by the artist's own hand of the original bust which I had lately seen loaded with garlands in the Calcutta Valhalla.

In the beginning of December, 1905, the long-expected resignation of Mr. Balfour's Government took effect, and on the 8th of December Sir Henry Campbell-Bannerman became Prime Minister and lost no time in forming the most memorable Administration of modern times. On the 8th of January, 1906, Parliament was dissolved, and a General Election immediately followed. I had not allowed the grass to grow under my feet in East Nottingham. My opponent, the sitting Member, Edward Bond, was a most courtly gentleman, and our relations during the contest were always of a friendly character. Bond had been a Liberal in his younger days, and found considerable difficulty in assimilating the new Chamberlain propaganda. He was, therefore, not very popular among the ardent Tariff Reformers of the lace city. But he made one mistake in his campaign, and that was when he allowed himself to attack my Indian record. That attack recoiled on his own head. For my part I was floating along very comfortably on the wave of enthusiasm which resulted, as every one knows, in the greatest Liberal victory throughout the country that was ever won. The issue was never in doubt. When the walls of Jericho had fallen in the defeat of Mr. Balfour and all his colleagues in Manchester, the hoardings of my constituency were posted with "Follow Manchester and Vote for Cotton!" In the result I was returned by 6,020 votes to 4,290, a majority of 1,730 compared with a Tory majority in the 1900 election of 779. In all three divisions of Nottingham the Liberals were elected by record majorities. In the great national triumph Nottingham had played her part with credit, and I had attained what was then, for me, the great ambition in life, a seat at Westminster.

CHAPTER XXIV

IN THE HOUSE

WHEN I entered the House of Commons, I was in my sixty-first year. Is that too old to embark on a new career? I had been warned that it was, and I remember how Lord Curzon, in one of his most friendly moods, had cautioned me while I was in India against any lurking ambition I might have in the direction of Westminster. Every old Anglo-Indian in Parliament, he said—and he quoted names in support of his assertion—inevitably gravitated into a parliamentary bore. I appreciated his advice though I did not act on it. I was not afraid of becoming a parliamentary bore, but I always felt a reasonable doubt whether my long bureaucratic training had not disqualified me from holding my own in the rough-and-tumble arena of public life. I think I overcame that difficulty to some extent, and, though it is obviously true that no one late in life can hope to start on a parliamentary career with the same chances and prospects as a younger man, I did not feel myself too old at sixty. I was under no illusions. I knew what to expect, and the result was more than to surpass my expectations.

I was a Member of the House for only a short time, but within four Sessions there was crowded an amount of unceasing and engrossing occupation, novel associations, fresh opportunities, political and social activity, and new friends which would have made the period memorable in the life of any man. I threw myself heart and soul into the work: I was one of the most regular attendants in the House, both in committees and at debates; my record of attendances at divisions was among the best; I did not miss a division on the Licensing Bill of 1908, and on the great Budget of 1909 only those in which I was forced by ill-health to be absent; I did my duty like a young man at all-night sittings, and I remember on one occasion when I came home fagged out at eight o'clock in the morning and had just enjoyed the luxury of a hot bath, I got a telegram from the Whips enjoining again my immediate presence. Off I rushed and, driving furiously into Palace Yard, was accosted by the policeman on duty: "Please, sir, House is up: rose about half an hour ago."

In truth the life was a most exhilarating one, and nothing that I had ever experienced in the course of a long and active public service could compare with the excitement and enjoyment of those four glorious Sessions. Everything in and about the House and connected with its traditions and amenities was of absorbing interest. It is pleasant to be in the hub and focus of all political movement: to be in daily contact and companionship with men whose names are household words: to take your share in the bustle and buzz of the Lobbies: to be able, when you will, to seek the sacred seclusion of the library and smoking-room: and, not least, to meet and entertain constituents who listen with bated breath while you point out to them this great luminary or that, as he passes by and perhaps honours you with a nod or word of recognition, which you are conscious exalts you in some indefinable way in their estimation. There is a charm in tea on the Terrace during the summer months that may not easily be equalled; and a sense of importance steals over even the humblest representative in the Grand Inquest of the Nation when the division bell rings, and you slip off with an apology to your friends for your temporary disappearance to attend to the call of duty.

I plead guilty to having been a great devotee of the Members' smoking-room. One of the magnificent suite of library rooms was reserved for smokers, and it was there I used to sit when I had need to study Blue Books or Hansard, or to write letters. The facilities for letter-writing in the House are innumerable. There is a quiet little room upstairs off the Opposition Gallery; the Aye and No Lobbies are furnished with many large writing-tables, and it is rarely indeed that they are vacant; the library itself is, I suppose, the finest writing-room in the world; and the inner apartment of the Members' smoking-room is consecrated to correspondence, but more often, I confess, to draughts and chess.

The former of these games is, I verily believe, the only recreation in which the members of the Labour Party ever indulge, and there were three or four of them, whose names wild horses would not induce me to betray, who were very regular in their attendance for some part of nearly every day solving the problem of unemployment with the aid of draughts. But chess of course easily dominated over draughts among Members generally. The best player in the House, in my judgment, was W. Watson Rutherford, the Tory Democratic Member for one of the divisions of Liverpool. But there was very little to choose between him and Bonar Law and Atherley-Jones, and thereafter, at some interval, players like Dr. V. H. Rutherford, Leif Jones, Lord Morpeth (now Earl of Carlisle), George Hardy,

George Wardle, and many others. The late Sir George Newnes—a great patron of chess and once a very good player—was in my time an extinct volcano. But the breeziest spirit in the chess-room and the most lightning-like of players was Henniker Heaton. I cannot imagine what chess in the House of Commons without his cheery and enlivening presence has now become. It was chiefly due to his initiative that we got up annual tournaments with a combined team from Oxford and Cambridge, followed by a chess dinner in the evening, which we all hugely enjoyed.

But let no one suppose that we wasted an undue amount of time on these frivolities. It is a poor heart that never rejoices, and I am sure that even the most exacting constituent would not desire that his unfortunate Member should sit for ten or twelve hours together listening to debates. I deem that I sat out my fair share. I was nearly always present at prayers, and remained in the House until the adjournment. My seat was on the Ministerial Front Bench below the Gangway, and as near to the Gangway as I could get it. This gives one a post of vantage, as it were; it is easy to get in and out of the Chamber: just a bow to the Speaker, and little more than half a dozen steps, and you are at once in freedom below the Bar. These front seats are also very convenient for all-night work. You have room to stretch your legs, and also to rest your head and perchance to sleep in a degree of comfort which none of the back benches affords.

I never, if I could help it, was absent from my seat during the hour for Questions, with which for four days in the week the proceedings of the House begin. That is generally the most interesting period of the day's sitting. I put my Indian questions down for Tuesdays and Thursdays, but there was always something at Question Time which I would not willingly have missed. Following Questions, up to tea-time, there are generally statements made and speeches delivered from the Front Benches ; but about half-past four a drowsy feeling is apt to crawl over one, and I was ever ready enough to slip out to tea. The tea-room at that moment is a crowded and animated centre of political gossip. Men pass in with their *Westminsters* and *Globes*, but they do not find time to read them in peace or silence. No one, perhaps, would have dared to disturb Sir Henry Campbell-Bannerman or Mr. Balfour, but a kindly smile, if you were bold enough to take your seat at their table, would put you at your ease. I always enjoyed my tea half-hour. After that, one would drop in again to the Chamber to see what was going on, and oftener than not drop out very quickly to get through one's letter-writing. Dear me ! The number of letters we had to write was sometimes prodigious.

I generally lunched and nearly always dined in the House. It is good to be conservative in habits, whatever views you may hold in politics, and I invariably sat in one place at lunch and in another at dinner. Irishmen were often my luncheon companions. There was dear old Sam Young, with a twinkle in his eye and bright and lively in spite of his burden of nearly ninety years ; and a very young colleague who once pointed out to me with silent awe the seat in which Parnell had sat. At dinner I took my place at a large round table in the first dining-room, which supporters of the Government were prone to frequent. There are separate tables reserved in that room, one for the Front Bench Members of the Government, another for the Opposition, and at a third John Redmond used to preside, surrounded by Members of his party. Rather an exclusive arrangement I thought, but undoubtedly it had its conveniences, and smaller fry would never dare to intrude their presence among the Olympian gods. But in the smoking-room after dinner all caste barriers were removed, though in the House in which I sat Liberals so enormously preponderated that they would form a majority in every part of the smoking-room as well as everywhere else. It was at this hour that we would woo the goddess Caissa for a friendly game over a good cigar, and then return to the debate until the rising of the House. I think that in my experience the eleven o'clock rule was more often honoured in the breach than in the observance, and "Who goes home?" used to peal through the corridors more frequently than any of us cared for during the small hours.

It is not for me to say whether I fulfilled Lord Curzon's anticipation by gravitating into a bore. Except on one or two occasions I never spoke in other than Indian debates and, though unfortunately it is still true that an Indian discussion will empty the House, those who were interested in India, and did remain, would always listen with attention to any one who spoke with authority on the subject. In my first speech, when I seconded an Amendment to the Address, I spoke at far too great length, but I did not perpetrate that blunder a second time and all my other speeches were brief enough. It was, however, during Questions, and not in debate, that I was able to make felt whatever influence I possessed. It is never quite satisfactory for a Minister to be conscious that his interlocutor knows a great deal more about the subject of a question than he does himself. And that, from the nature of the case, was invariably the predicament of the Indian Secretary and Under-Secretaries during Question Time. The dreaded supplementary would come in and they would be nonplussed. The putting of supplementaries is an art in itself—for there is always Mr. Speaker as well as the Minister to reckon with—but I acquired considerable practice in it, and the Parthian shot went home.

Never could there have been a Prime Minister who excited greater enthusiasm among his supporters than dear old "C.-B.," as we always called him. This enthusiasm did not date from any remote period, but it crystallised around the famous Albert Hall speech which he delivered, after forming his Ministry, in December, 1905. From that moment he had the party at his feet. It was not eloquence nor even ability which won him this unique position. It was his courage and his earnestness and the transparent sincerity of his life and Liberal creed. We believed in him and loved him, and he moved in the House of Commons like a King among us all. Moreover he knew, or seemed to know, everybody, and I am sure there were none of us who did not get a kindly word or smile from him as we passed him in the Lobbies. He bound the party together by the sympathetic magnetism of his nature.

His successor, Mr. Asquith, is endowed with a far higher order of ability and debating power. He shares also, in an unequal degree, the human element without which there never was a great leader of men. But his House of Commons manner to the Members of his own party does him an injustice, and, while the matter of his speeches will rouse echoing cheers, there does not always follow the applause from the heart which accompanied the utterances of C.-B. It cannot be expected, of course, that all natural gifts will combine together in one man—and there is probably no man in the House of Commons more gifted by Nature and careful training than Mr. Asquith—but there is an indefinable something wanting in him in respect of the personal touch between Minister and Member which C.-B. pre-eminently enjoyed, which Speaker Lowther shares, and Mr. Balfour may claim, although in smaller measure, to possess.

It is not wise to leave too much to the Whips, and there was a tendency to aloofness among the Twice-Born on the Front Bench which appears to be a characteristic of Ministers. Perhaps this is the normal attitude of a parliamentarian promoted to Ministerial office. But I think it was aggravated in my time by the unprecedented party majority which inclined Ministers to be careless in securing or conciliating the goodwill of their followers. There were exceptions, no doubt, but in many a case the personal relations between a Minister and a humble supporter among the rank and file on the back benches bore more than a superficial resemblance to those between the archangel Michael and a marine ascidian. The exceptions are so agreeable that I am disposed to chronicle some of them by name, and I mention in particular Sydney Buxton at the Post Office; Lewis Harcourt as First Commissioner of Works; John Burns, Haldane, and Birrell as Cabinet Ministers; Sam Evans as Solicitor-General; Jack Seely in the Colonial Office; and the late Mr. Buchanan and the Master of Elibank in the India Office, who were all models of courtesy and ready accessibility. No one knows better than I do that it is difficult to break down the barriers of officialdom and caste, but the example of C.-B., whenever it was followed, was worth its weight in gold.

Second only to the Prime Minister, Lloyd George and Winston Churchill were undoubtedly the most powerful forces on the Ministerial side of the House. Lloyd George himself happened to be at his worst during the delivery of his magnificent Budget—it took him five hours to read, and the greater part of it should have been relegated to an explanatory memorandum—but the substance of that statement and the ability with which, aided by skilful lieutenants, he piloted its provisions through Committee established for him a parliamentary reputation which nothing can impair. It may be the boast of Lloyd George, as it certainly should be of Winston Churchill, that he has seldom elicited cheers from the Opposition Benches. Mr. Churchill enjoys in a special degree the advantage of being *anathema maranatha* to the Opposition. Looked upon as a traitor to his own order, he inspires the members of the opposing benches—whom he knows too well —with a peculiar sense of dislike which is an equivalent source of strength to him, and more, by reason of the encouragement it suggests among his own supporters. So whenever Churchill was up the House would fill, and there were more cheers and counter-cheers than when any other Member spoke.

Mr. Balfour had been thrown out at Manchester and did not take his seat as Member for the City of London until a little time after the new House had assembled. He then laboured under enormous disadvantages. He had been Head of the late Government with overwhelming battalions : now he was coming back discredited, with a miserably small following, and was personally unknown to a majority of the Members of the House. When he reappeared there was a prejudice against him which he did not fail to recognise. I watched him closely, and admired the tact and good temper and masterly adroitness with which he triumphed over all the difficulties of his position. For one who is easily sensitive to the personal grace of any man, it was enough to look at Mr. Balfour and come under the glamour of his smile to fall a victim to his charm. As Leader of the Opposition, he towered head and shoulders above all his colleagues, and there was no second.

> "Unde nil majus generatur ipso,
> Nec viget quidquam simile aut secundum:
> Proximos illi tamen occupavit
> Austen honores."

Once only did I see Mr. Balfour annihilated in debate, an occasion on which the Nemesis of his own wrongdoing wrought an irreparable blow to his reputation. Never do I remember the House of Commons to have been in such an electrical condition as it was on the night of Tuesday, the 2nd of November, 1909. It was known that the Lord Advocate, Mr. Ure, intended to make his reply in the House to the gross insults which had been heaped on him by Mr. Balfour outside its walls. The Chamber was packed, and Mr. Ure when he sprang to his feet was greeted with a roar of applause, again and again renewed. His speech was the finest and most dignified vindication of personal honour that can be imagined, and the scene was indescribable when he sank back into his seat with the memorable words: "Accusations such as these, couched in language such as this, happily find no parallel in the history of this country since the days when it was open to a man to defend an attack upon his honour with his own right arm." The whole of the Ministerial Benches rose and cheered until they could cheer no more. I had been observing Mr. Balfour narrowly during all this scene, and he was overcome by it. I had no sympathy for him, and yet it was a painful sight to contemplate his discomfiture. He rose to reply, a broken man. I thought he was about to express his apologies to Mr. Ure, and to the House. But, no! In a few halting words he refused to apologise and sat down. The storm was over:

Mr. Asquith wound up the debate, and Members streamed out in a more indignant and excitable frame of mind than on any other occasion in my experience.

The recent death of Sir Charles Dilke is a grave loss to Liberalism and progress. There was no Member of the Government, in charge of whatever portfolio he might be, who was not aware when Dilke was listening to him that he was addressing a man who was even more fully equipped than himself on every question of detail, difficulty, or doubt. His seat was the corner one on the Front Bench below the Gangway, and I therefore sat very near to him and was associated with him in his capacity as Chairman of the party of advanced Radicalism in the House. He was not an orator or even a great debater, but he enjoyed a perfect command of words which poured forth from the fulness of knowledge. He was beyond comparison the most prominent and most able private Member of the House of Commons.

Nearly all Members have their mannerisms, and Sir Charles Dilke's was to stand on one leg while he spoke, continually tapping the floor with his other foot. Like many old Members, he wore his hat while seated, and was most punctilious in regard to all the customs of the House in such matters as bowing and touching his hat when referred to by any other speaker. He was always dressed in a frock-coat, and generally wore straps to his trousers. But his most marked peculiarity was his extraordinary restlessness, and it was often pathetic to notice his frequent going in and coming out, hurrying through the Lobbies, visiting his locker, and exchanging hasty comments with his friends.

His special knowledge of India related to military matters, and his memory was marvellously accurate on the intricate questions arising out of North-West

Frontier complications. But in all recent Indian troubles he took a lively interest, and followed sympathetically the attitude which I and those who acted with me felt bound to take in defence of liberty and justice, supporting us by his vote in the Division Lobby. Sir Charles Dilke's voice was always to be heard on behalf of suffering and oppressed nationalities, and his speeches on all issues relating to the rights and protection of indigenous populations were storehouses of wise and high moral policy. The poor, the suffering, and the weak in all countries and climes have been deprived by his death of the services of a fearless champion whose mantle is not likely to fall on the shoulders of any other so well qualified as he was to advocate their cause.

What shall I venture to say about Lord Morley of Blackburn—John Morley as he was then—Secretary of State for India? Like all other Liberals, I came into the House with an almost idolatrous admiration for his services to the Liberal cause, and I shared the feeling which prevailed in India that at last a good time was coming, when grievances would be redressed and an era of contentment, such as had not been known since Lord Ripon's day, would follow. The shock, therefore, was all the greater when it was found that he was as absolutely in the hands of the permanent officials of the India Office as his predecessors had been before him. Perhaps I had not realised, as I might have done, the helpless situation of a new-comer altogether ignorant of Indian affairs, and consequently dependent on his advisers in everything. It may be that I had not sufficiently appreciated that it would need more than ordinary confidence and courage to take a line of action which would bring him into conflict with his own Secretaries and the veteran Members of his Council. The truth is that he was overwhelmed by the unexpected character of the problems that beset him and the magnitude and complexity of conflicting interests to which he had never before devoted a day's attention. He was not prepared to be confronted in the House of Commons by half a dozen Members, sitting below the Gangway as his own supporters, who were each and all of them experts in their own sphere, and ready enough to tender their advice, which was almost invariably antagonistic to that of his own permanent officials. And yet it was always a marvel to me that he should so easily have surrendered at discretion and abandoned the principles of a lifetime. It was pitiful to see him while he was in the House, dodging us in the Lobbies, and avoiding interviews when he could, and shrinking from any personal explanation away from the Front Bench, where he was always well primed with official replies. And he must have found it very painful himself, as an old and stalwart Liberal Member of the House of Commons, to hear his recantations invariably cheered from the Opposition Benches amid the depressing silence of his own followers. Although, therefore, it came as another shock, I can hardly say it was a surprise when we heard that Honest John Morley, the *dulce decus* and " end 'em or mend 'em " of our young days, had preferred to become a Viscount and moved to the serener atmosphere of the House of Lords.

In the House of Commons there are always innumerable groups organised for this purpose or that and among one or another party, and it was inevitable that the great Liberal Party should consist of many groups of Members. I belonged to several of these, and always to the section associated with the Extreme Left. Dilke was our leader in most directions, Sir John Brunner, Josiah Wedgwood, George Greenwood, Leif Jones, and Sir Thomas Whittaker in others. Taxation of land values, temperance, economies in naval and military expenditure, secular education, colonial self-government, protection of aborigines—it is probable that I was identified with what some people would describe as every fad that was discussed in the Committee Rooms of the House. So be it : yet after all we were the stalwarts of the party, and within our ranks was always to be found the salt of the Old Guard which did not surrender.

It was natural, perhaps, that I should assume the foremost place in what was known as the Indian group. Around me there were other sun-dried bureaucrats : Hart-Davies, a retired Judge from Bombay and Sind, who had supplemented his Indian experience with wide travel and observation of men and manners ; C. J. O'Donnell, who had held the high office of Commissioner in the distressful Province of Bengal ; the late Donald Smeaton, who had been for many years Financial Commissioner of Burma, and had sat with me on the Viceroy's Legislative Council ; and Sir John Jardine, who had been for a long time a Judge of the High Court in Bombay. These men supplied sufficient weight of authority ; but authority is of no use in the House of Commons without battalions to support it ; and it was fortunate, therefore, that we were sustained by a little gathering of ardent and devoted Liberals, among whom Frederic Mackarness will always come first to my grateful memory as one who never feared any obloquy or abuse or alienation from his friends in the manful struggle he maintained, both in and outside the House, on behalf of the elementary civil rights of personal liberty and justice. Associated with him were Dr. V. H. Rutherford, dowered, almost above other men, with a detestation of wrong, who visited India himself during one winter to see the people with his own eyes ; G. P. Gooch, Wedgwood, Sir William Collins ; the late Felix Cobbold, whose death was a sad loss; Percy Alden, Philip Morrell; W. P. Byles, a true friend; C. E. Price, G. Greenwood, Arnold Lupton, E. N. Bennett, J. M. Robertson, the late J. Galloway Weir, and many others below the Gangway. We had also the support of *viri pietate graves* like Sir Charles Schwann and Sir Herbert Roberts, who had deservedly won baronetcies from the Government and had rendered long and faithful service to the cause of India, but who, when the crack of the Whip was heard, could rarely screw themselves into giving an anti-party vote.

But our movement, active and watchful as it was, would have been valueless without the solid phalanx of the Labour Party at our back and the guerilla outposts on the Irish Benches to safeguard us when our ammunition was exhausted. I do not know what we should have done without the flashing wit of my dear friend Swift McNeill and of Willie Redmond and Jerry McVeagh, which poured forth so readily from their sympathetic Nationalism; and the support of men like Long John O'Connor and Hugh Law, whose warm hearts drove them to speak as well as vote in India's cause. We could always count on a good Irish vote. But it is to the Labour Party that we were most indebted. None of my associations with the House of Commons are more pleasant to recall than my intimate and friendly relations with the members of the Labour Party. One doughty champion there was who early emerged from its ranks and signalised himself by his eloquent and effective interference in Indian questions—James O'Grady, a busy man if ever there was one in the House, but he spared no time or trouble for the purpose. There followed quickly in his footsteps an even more famous warrior, who had qualified himself for the duty by a personal visit to India. Even as Elijah the Tishbite was greatest among the prophets of Israel, so Keir

Hardie is enshrined in the hearts of his followers as the greatest of prophets and teachers in a later day. No one since the time of Fawcett has rendered such service to India in the House of Commons ; and of all the friendships I have made in the House I am proudest of the hand of fellowship with Keir Hardie. And last, but not least, was Ramsay Macdonald, the handsomest Member of the House of Commons, who has also visited India, and is by common consent the ablest mouthpiece of the party of which he is now the leader. The Labour Party would always go solid with us into the Lobby ; and so from one source or another our composite Indian group could generally command a total vote of seventy or eighty Members, men whose motto was, with James Russell Lowell :—

> "They are slaves who fear to speak
> For the fallen and the weak :
> They are slaves who will not choose
> Hatred, scoffing, and abuse,
> Rather than in silence shrink
> From the truth they needs must think:
> They are slaves who dare not be
> In the right with two or three."

CHAPTER XXV

NIAGARA AND AFTER

FROM whatever point of view we may regard him, Lord Curzon must always be one of the most notable of Indian Viceroys. His abilities, his restless energy, his masterful character—a personal magnetism which all who have come into contact with him feel—mark him out among the run of ordinary public men with uncommon distinction. Happy indeed was he in his opportunity to be appointed in the prime of life and vigour to the splendid office he was able to hold for nearly seven years. I remember when I met him on his arrival in India, a day or two before his fortieth birthday, keen and glowing with a sense of responsibility and power, and resolved to pluck bright honour from the sphere of government on which he had been launched by Fate. He was well equipped for his task. His great natural gifts had been matured by a close local study of the problems of the East, and there was no lack of confidence on his part to apply them to the goal of his aspirations. He loomed large before the British public on a scale unequalled by any of his predecessors ; his name was on all men's lips ; he surrounded himself with associations of unprecedented pomp and circumstance ; there was no department of the administration that he did not reform, and there was no frontier or angle of the Indian Dominions on which he did not leave his mark. And yet he failed ! He closed his Indian career with a sense of disappointment and baffled hopes, with a feeling, it may be, that he had done something to attain his ends, but with the consciousness of general failure and mortified ambition. He might have been a great Viceroy ; why is it that he was not?

The cause of his failure is not far to seek. Lord Curzon is an autocrat. He believes in a bureaucracy ; he believes in officialism ; and, above all, he believes in himself. His zeal is for the people, but it is for the people in the abstract ; his desire is to govern well, but it is not to govern through the people or with their aid. Everything for the people, but nothing by them or through them. The bureaucracy knows what is best for the people ; that was the keynote of his Government.

Lord Curzon had no sympathy with the aspirations of the educated classes of the Indian community ; he refused to listen to their voice, and seized every opportunity to weaken their influence. He is too much an admirer of his own race to make a successful ruler of a foreign people. He believes in Englishmen alone. He would think it his duty to notice any representations from a body of European planters or merchants. But he would vouchsafe no recognition to the most reasoned memorials of large and representative Indian bodies. His object was avowedly to strengthen British rule in India, but he was indifferent to the only means by which that end can be attained. He was incapable of realising the truth of Lord Salisbury's warning that those are the truest friends of British rule in India who win the confidence of the people by kindness and sympathy, and that those are the worst enemies of British rule who alienate their affections by unsympathetic treatment.

He once said, in an address to the Bengal Chamber of Commerce, that when he contemplated the enormous possibilities of Calcutta he almost felt as if, when he laid down the post of Viceroy, he would like to become Chairman of the Calcutta Corporation. He could not imagine a higher duty or a more beneficent aim. He said: "I should require ten years of office, sufficient cash, and a free hand—give me these commodities, and I would undertake to make this city the pride of Asia, and a model for the Eastern world." It may occur to some that, given these commodities, it would not need the genius of the heir of Kedleston to accomplish the task. Most men of some administrative training are capable of doing a good deal in the direction of improvement when they are practically unlimited as to time and are subject to no financial check and to no control. But the expression is typical of Lord Curzon's turn of mind: Give me a free hand and Fortunatus's purse, and I will show you how the world should be governed!

It is an easy thing to exercise irresponsible authority, but it is a sublimer function of Imperial dominion to lead and guide and train the people of a country to manage their own affairs and to afford scope to their political aspirations. Lord Curzon is one of those who labour under a constitutional incapacity to adapt themselves to such an idea. However great may have been his energy and activity in working through official agency, it is the more to be deplored that he should have lacked the higher quality of evoking the powers of the people by affording them opportunities for their exercise, and of raising them from a condition of mere passive subjection to a capacity for the discharge of their legitimate responsibilities.

The failure of Lord Curzon's viceroyalty was due

to his own limitations. His will must be law ; otherwise he would resign. His superiors, as well as his subordinates, must be his instruments, otherwise he would resign. He was a great organiser, but nothing more. His ideal was a wise and beneficent Governor-General at the top, a set of provincial authorities perfectly amenable to his touch below, and a cut-and-dried policy at hand for everything.

Lord Curzon found India friendly to himself. The country was dissatisfied and disappointed with the colourless features of Lord Elgin's reign. It welcomed a new Viceroy whose early utterances inspired hope. He left India in a condition moody and disturbed, and only refraining from overt symptoms of disorder because her people are instinctively law-abiding and were patiently waiting for the advent of a Liberal Secretary of State and a Liberal Viceroy, under whom they expected to see the undoing of the mistakes committed during dark years of reaction. Lord Curzon had weakened and discouraged the beneficent scheme of local self-government which Lord Ripon introduced and did so much to foster ; he had officialised the Universities, and as far as possible the whole system of popular education ; he had substituted a system of nomination to Government service in the place of competitive examinations ; and he had announced a practical declaration of race disqualification for the higher public offices. The end in view was to officialise the Administration by every means in his power, and this sinister aim was known to be underlying the project which raised such universal and bitter opposition—the Partition of Bengal.

A growing sense of Nationalism is the most marked feature of modern Indian life—not only nationalism as a whole but that feeling of patriotism in the provinces which is the source of emulation and progress and binds together the units of a great Empire. In no part of India is that patriotic sentiment more firmly rooted than in Bengal ; and the secret of the antagonism to Lord Curzon's policy of partition is the consciousness that this disruption was designed to enfeeble and, as far as possible, shatter the independence and power and influence of the most prosperous and advanced province in India. The scheme of partition was not without its attraction to the members of the Civil Service, who saw before them a glittering vista of additional offices and emoluments. But it was repugnant in the last degree to the inhabitants of the country affected, in whom there is a sense of patriotic pride in their province, their ancestry, and their future. Whatever may be said to the contrary, they were convinced, and are convinced, that the object of the partition was to undermine the feeling of solidarity among them. The measure was carried out against their will and in spite of their protests. They held innumerable public meetings and demonstrations : their local Press was unanimous : they exhausted the resources of constitutional agitation.

At last they fell back on new methods, which resulted in the organisation of a *Swadeshi* or patriotic movement, the object of which is to foster national manufactures and industries, and to prevent the consumption of foreign goods. The original source of this movement was the hope that it would operate on Englishmen through their pockets, and induce Lancashire to compel the Government to pay some regard to local opinion in Bengal. As this hope died away, the movement broadened in its character and tendencies until it became, as it is now, the most practical and visible form in which the national impulse of the country finds expression. The movement is one to which it is hardly possible to make any reasonable objection on principle, but it is obviously antagonistic to British interests, and the process of boycotting British goods led insensibly to methods which must occasionally bring those who are employed on the boycott within the meshes of the law. It was a cause, therefore, of no surprise to find that in the eye of Anglo-Indian officialism *Swadeshi* grew very speedily to be identified with sedition.

The Partition of Bengal took effect on the 16th of October, 1905; Lord Curzon vacated the Viceroyalty on the 18th of November; and a Liberal Government came into power in England in December. These dates, following swiftly after one another, are important. India was in a phase of extraordinary excitement. There was a buoyant rebound of public opinion after long years of depression. Large numbers of educated men felt towards John Morley as to a master, and their heart, as Mr. Gokhale declared in his Presidential Address at the Benares Congress at Christmas, "hoped and yet trembled as it had never hoped or trembled before." A Liberal Government was at last in power, with the reverent student of Burke, the disciple of Mill, and the friend and biographer of Gladstone as its head in the India Office; now would their wrongs be righted and their grievances redressed. Above all, it was felt in Bengal, where the Partition was such a fresh and rankling sore, that inquiries would surely be made which would lead to its reversal or modification. There was a ferment in the country of expectation and anticipation.

A golden opportunity presented itself to the new Secretary of State. A Liberal Cabinet did not hesitate to grasp the nettle in South Africa, and achieved there a success which posterity will point to as the greatest administrative triumph of the Empire since the restoration of peace to Canada.

There was an equal, if not greater, chance ready to Lord Morley's hand in India. We, the Indian group of Members in the House of Commons, depicted it to him in glowing colours. We might charm never so wisely, but he would not hearken. The iron was hot, but he would not strike. The precious moments slipped by, and there was nothing done. When I was pressing him in the House on as early a date as the 25th of February, 1906, Lord Morley admitted that the Partition of Bengal "was and remains undoubtedly an administrative operation which went wholly and decisively against the wishes of most of the people concerned." But it was "a settled fact." Therefore no action could be taken. "India should now be allowed to take breath, and we should move very slowly." These were the commonplaces he had learnt from the permanent officials in the India Office, who had lived all their lives like the ostrich, with their heads buried in the sand.

In the meantime, the hourglass had run out. My successor in Assam was an officer who would probably have distinguished himself as a Lieutenant-Governor if he had been appointed to any other province in India than Eastern Bengal. But he was ignorant of the Bengali people and of their language. He was appointed at a time of crisis, when they were in a state of acute irritation. It was a critical situation which Sir Bampfylde Fuller had to face. On the one hand a thoroughly discontented people, and on the other an intensely patriotic movement which it was incumbent on him to guide and control. He might have adopted a policy of tact and conciliation. There are no people within the British Empire whom it is more easy to govern than the Bengalis. It is very easy to win their hearts by sympathy and kindness. But he preferred to follow a policy of repression. Public meetings were forcibly dispersed; the military police were called out; a system of espionage was established; a racial and religious antagonism between Mohammedans and Hindoos was stirred up in a province where no such feelings had existed within living memory; and there was a cruel and systematic persecution of schoolboys in the criminal courts, and otherwise, for their participation in the *Swadeshi* movement. The popular exasperation was daily rising, and a state of things had come about which was quite intolerable. The Lieutenant-Governor would take no warnings, and pursued his own way to his undoing. As the result of a difference of opinion between the Governor-General and himself, he resigned.

Lord Morley had now become uneasy at the Indian outlook; but he was already so accustomed to official spectacles that soon he was unable to see at all without their use. Again and again we brought the true facts to his notice; we implored him to re-open the question of the Partition of Bengal; it was not too late; still there might be peace and quiet where peace and quiet had reigned for generations. But no! The stern official reply came as a sledge-hammer to our appeals. It was a "settled fact." And so the tide of disorder, which it might have been so easy to quell, rolled on from bad to worse, and it was aggravated, both in the House of Commons and in the public Press, by means of persistent exaggeration and misrepresentation. Officialism in India always has control of the Press cables, and things came to such a pass that seven British journalists in Calcutta, connected with different newspapers and holding varying shades of political opinion, raised a formal protest against the misleading accounts of the situation which were being telegraphed to England.

The Mohammedans of Eastern Bengal are almost all descended from low-caste or aboriginal Hindoos who long ago embraced Islam in hope of social improvement or from hard necessity. There was never any cause for quarrel between Hindoos and Mohammedans as such. As simple cultivators they live side by side, and speak the same language. For the first time in history a religious feud was established between them by the Partition of the province. For the first time the principle was enunciated in official circles: Divide and Rule! The hope was held out that the Partition would invest the Mohammedans with "a unity they had not enjoyed since the days of the old Mussulman viceroys and kings." The Mohammedans were officially favoured in every possible way. "My favourite wife" was the somewhat coarse phrase used by Sir Bampfylde Fuller to express his feelings. The High Court in Calcutta was constrained to censure the racial bias judicially displayed by a District Judge. The opportunity was taken by evilly disposed persons with their headquarters at Dacca to scatter emissaries through the country preaching the revival of Islam, advocating the wildest extremes, and proclaiming to the villagers that the British Government was on their side and would exact no penalty for violence done to Hindoos. No steps were taken by the authorities to check this dangerous propaganda. Riots followed, lives were lost, Hindoo shops were looted, Hindoo temples were desecrated, and many Hindoo women were carried off. Some towns were deserted, women spent nights concealed in tanks, and general terror prevailed throughout the country-side.

An official excuse was at once put forward that the national boycott of foreign goods was the cause of the disturbances. But there was no vestige of foundation for such an explanation. The ill-feeling which had made itself manifest between Hindoos and Mohammedans affected only the limited area in which the emissaries of fanaticism had done their work. The judicial inquiries that were held conclusively proved that the object of the rioting was to molest the Hindoos, and had nothing to do with any boycott. And yet Lord Morley was put up to reply in the House of Commons: "The situation in Eastern Bengal was strained owing to the bitterness existing between Hindoos and Mohammedans consequent on the attempts made to compel Mohammedans by violence to abstain from purchasing foreign goods." There could be no more grotesque instance of the power officials have of misleading their chief.

The curtain of unrest then rose in the Punjab. This was the beginning of the campaign against Indian journalism which for the first time disclosed editors of newspapers sentenced to hard labour for many years and removed from court to jail in fetters. Political agitators convicted of rioting were punished with long terms of imprisonment, and a youth among them was sentenced to be flogged with thirty stripes. On the 3rd of May, 1907, prosecutions were instituted against three barristers and three other lawyers of the Rawalpindi Bar for complicity in disturbances which had taken place in that city. Lurid telegrams were sent home, and a statement was made by Lord Morley in the House of Commons imputing the most violent and seditious language to these lawyers. Bail was refused to them, and their trial dragged on for five long months while they were in prison. At last, on the 1st of October, they were all acquitted by the special judge appointed to try their case, who declared that there was not an iota of evidence to justify the prosecution and characterised the evidence adduced as "suspicious, if not fabricated."

Then suddenly and without warning and like a

bolt from the blue we heard that Lala Lajpat Rai, a gentleman of independent position and high character and antecedents, whose acquaintance I had made at the Bombay Congress in 1904, and one Ajit Singh, a callow youth of twenty-two years of age, had been arrested and deported without charge or trial under the provisions of an old Regulation III. of 1818. This incident was the turning point of our agitation in the House of Commons. There were very few Members sitting on the Liberal benches who did not realise that it was a gross outrage on the first principles of their political creed to arrest, deport, and detain indefinitely in custody "for reasons of State" any "individuals against whom there may not be sufficient ground to institute any judicial proceeding." I took the lead with Frederic Mackarness in besieging Lord Morley with questions and in driving him from corner to corner in his replies. We had the sympathy of the party at our back, and the facts of the case were on our side.

In connection with Lajpat Rai's case the following supplementary questions and answers are recorded in Hansard of June 11, 1907:—

SIR HENRY COTTON asked the right hon. gentleman whether he had any information in his hands to confirm the statement he made last Thursday to the effect that the speeches of Lajpat Rai were very greatly dominated by sedition and that they were published broadcast even on the floor of that House.

MR. MORLEY: I must really ask my hon. friend to accept it from me that I am very unlikely to make statements on the floor of this House without having provided myself with fair and reasonable confirmation.

SIR HENRY COTTON: Will the right hon. gentleman lay the facts of the case on the Table of the House?

MR. MORLEY: I think anything more injudicious, from the point of view of Government and of law and order, than that which the hon. gentleman suggests cannot be imagined.

Lord Morley's replies were received, as usual, with

Opposition cheers. As for me, I could only sit in silence; but I recalled to my mind the words used by John Morley in the House on April 24, 1902, on the occasion of the arbitrary detention of a certain Mr. Cartwright at Capetown. The official reason given by Mr. Secretary Brodrick for that detention was: "Mr. Cartwright's views are anti-British and it is not deemed desirable by the authorities in South Africa to increase the number of persons in this country who disseminate anti-British propaganda." Dissatisfied with further answers he received, Mr. Morley moved the adjournment of the House. During the debate he characterised Mr. Brodrick's reply as "the most outrageous and indefensible answer ever given within these walls since Simon de Montfort invented Parliament"; and in the course of his remarks he applied the following adjectives—illegal, unconstitutional, tyrannical and arbitrary impudently absurd and preposterous—to the action of the Government in detaining a man "for some other reasons which they do not disclose." Such is the difference between a Liberal leader in Opposition and the same man when placed in due course as a Minister on the Government Front Bench!

The charges made against Lajpat Rai in the House of Commons have since been deleted by Lord Morley from his published speeches. It was impossible to substantiate them, and after six months' imprisonment the two deportees were unconditionally released.

In the meantime the Government resorted to action which should obviously have been taken in the first instance. They proceeded to probe the causes of the discontent. It was found that they were exactly as Charles O'Donnell and I had declared them to be from the first. The grievance in the Punjab was occasioned by heavy increase in land taxation, and especially by arbitrary procedure in connection with the enforcement of water rates and the colonisation of new lands brought under cultivation by the extension of irrigation. A Colonisation Bill, which gave effect to a number of measures which were strongly resented, had been passed into law with the more haste because, as the Lieutenant-Governor declared from his place in Council, "any delay in legislation would only increase the agitation." But the discontent prevailed among a population which furnishes the Indian Army with some of its most valuable soldiers. The Government of India were alarmed lest the native troops should be affected by it. They took prompt action. Remissions of the land tax were allowed, water rates were reduced, inquiry was ordered into the complaints of the colonists, and the Viceroy refused to allow the provisions of the Colonisation Law to come into operation. The immediate result of these concessions was the pacification of the Punjab.

Alas that no similar remedies were applied in Bengal! If they had been extended to that province the same result would have followed, and it was still not too late. But the native army is not recruited from Bengal. There were no words of conciliation there, no prospect was held out of any modification of the Partition, and no concessions were offered. In place thereof there arose a bitterness of feeling between the officials and the educated classes which aggravated the position to breaking-point. The bitterness of this feeling was reflected from Bengal to other provinces. A general crusade against "sedition" was promoted all over India under the Penal Code, in the course of which scores of journalists and literary men were sentenced to long terms of hard labour, instead of confinement as first-class misdemeanants, to which by the law of Great Britain political offenders are entitled. Many and many were the appeals we made to Lord Morley to bring the procedure in this respect into line with the law of England. It was pointed out that these men of culture and educational distinction were herded with the most degraded criminals, made to labour at the severest tasks, and marched through the public thoroughfares in fetters and chains. In vain ! Lord Morley refused to allow any mitigation of this harsh treatment.

The indignation in India provoked by the treatment of political offenders was augmented beyond endurance by the long sentences passed in so many cases by the Courts. An unfortunate "Assistant Secretary to the *Swadeshi* Steam Navigation Company" was twice over sentenced by the District Judge of Tinnevelly to transportation for life (reduced on appeal to six years) for making seditious speeches ; another man was sentenced by the Judge of Allahabad to seven years' transportation (reduced on appeal to five years) for "dispatching a seditious telegram," and the same wretched man was sentenced by the same judge to five years more for "disseminating a seditious leaflet." The editor of a newspaper in Madras was sentenced to five years' transportation for "publishing seditious articles." Another Madrasi was sentenced to five years' transportation for "exhibiting and commenting upon seditious photographs in a railway carriage." A newspaper editor was sentenced by the Allahabad Judge to "seven years' transportation on each of three charges, the sentences to run concurrently, for publishing seditious articles." Another editor, a highly educated man, was sentenced by the Judge of Nagpore to two and a half years' hard labour "in respect of a Marathi pamphlet containing speeches of Arabindo

Ghose," the said speeches being subsequently declared by a competent Court of Justice in Bengal to be free from sedition. And in another case a Mohammedan editor was sentenced by the Magistrate of Aligarh to two years' hard labour (reduced on appeal to one) for "publishing a seditious article," the said article consisting of comments on the methods of education in Egypt.

More recently, the publication in Sind of a pamphlet entitled "*Swadeshi* Movement or Opinions of Patriot Tilak"—a pamphlet published through inadvertence and which the proprietor of the press brought to the notice of the Magistrate of his own accord after stopping further delivery of copies to the publisher—was punished by a sentence of five years' transportation, with a fine of Rs. 500, on the translator and publisher; and sentences of three years' transportation, with fines of Rs. 1,000 in each case, on the unfortunate proprietor of the press and the printer. Men have been prosecuted and imprisoned in the Punjab for publishing extracts from the writings of the late Professor Seeley and William Jennings Bryan, and I remember a Bengal case in which an editor, who was told by the Court that he would be treated "leniently" if he pleaded guilty, received a year's hard labour for following the advice. It may be added that in Bengal particular irritation was created by the frequency of judicial floggings administered to schoolboys for trivial offences.

I brought nearly all of the cases I have enumerated to the notice of the Secretary of State, but in not a single case, however savage and vindictive the sentence might be, was the clemency of the Crown invoked.

The tension of public opinion broke all bounds at the Indian National Congress held at Surat in

December, 1907: the so-called Extremists put the Moderates to rout, and the Congress separated in a state of confusion without transacting any business. No symptom of popular unrest could have been more acute. But up to this time the orderly and peaceful habits of the people exercised such control over them that there had been no exceptional resort to outrage or methods of violence. A remarkable tribute, be it said, not only to their law-abiding qualities but to the influence which the National Congress movement—always based on constitutional principles—had been able to maintain. Now at last the strain gave way in that feeling of resentment which in all lands drives men to acts of passionate despair. Nothing could be more deplorable for India than the sporadic outrages which then began and have disfigured the face of the country—not in Bengal only but in Bombay and Madras and even in London—during the past three years. Nothing could be more criminal, more insensate, and more deserving condemnation and punishment. But is there any country in the world where similar antecedents would not have led to similar consequences?

The result was an official panic which found its echo through the official mouthpieces of the India Office in Parliament. One repressive act of legislation followed upon another. In 1907 a Seditious Meetings Act was passed which prohibited public meetings being held for the consideration of any political object except by the permission of the District Superintendent of Police or a Magistrate. It also forbade any individual to deliver a lecture or make a speech on any political subject in a public place except by leave of the police or Magistrate. In 1908 the first Press Act was passed. There were already in existence, under the ordinary criminal law, stringent provisions against sedition and violence of any kind. But the new law gave Magistrates the power to confiscate any newspaper held by them to incite to violence, and it was no longer necessary to proceed for trial before a properly qualified tribunal. In the same year was passed a Criminal Law Amendment Act which enabled the most serious charges to be formulated before a Magistrate against a man in his absence. It deprived him of the right of trial by jury and of the right to bail. The same Act gave the Executive Government power to declare, without warning, any association of persons to be an unlawful association, to dissolve it, and to treat any of its members or subscribers as liable to criminal prosecution. In 1910 a second and more arbitrary Press Act was passed, giving the Executive power to prohibit the publication of newspapers except under heavy money securities, and to confiscate newspapers already in existence which are deemed to be objectionable. The largest powers were also given to confiscate literature and to open letters. The result of this legislation is that there is not a single Indian newspaper which now dares to write with freedom on political subjects. Or, if it dares, it does so with the sword of Damocles hanging over its head.

In 1908 there came the startling news that the provisions of Regulation III. of 1818 had been again resorted to, and that nine Bengali gentlemen had been taken from their homes, deported, and confined in jail without charge or trial. Two at least of these were known as men of the highest character. No indication was given as to when, if ever, they would be charged, tried, or released. Indeed, Lord Morley declared in the House of Lords that they "were being summarily deported without trial and without charge, and without intention to try or charge." Another storm of indignation burst in the

House of Commons, but not one word of satisfaction or even of explanation could we obtain. It was at first denied that these men were confined in jail, so incredible did it seem to the Under-Secretary that such a procedure could be followed. But it was too true. And in prison they remained for fourteen months. They were not even informed by the Government of what they were suspected. But it was generally understood, and I made this assertion in the House without contradiction, that the only reason why the most highly respected of them were deported was that they were strong advocates of the *Swadeshi* movement. It was not alleged that they were members of a revolutionary movement. And in the speech in which he announced their release Lord Minto not only specified no charge against them but said he believed the Government were face to face with an anarchical conspiracy against the British and European communities, thus suggesting that the *Swadeshi* movement with which the deported men were supposed to have been connected had, through their absence, been superseded by a criminal one, and that the Government had actually released them in order to invite their co-operation against this new danger. The stupendous blunder of these deportations was becoming every day more generally admitted.

As was implied in Lord Minto's speech, the repressive energies of the Government were now concentrated on the vigorous extirpation of what were described as "conspiracies against the Crown." With this end huge prosecutions were worked up, and cases brought into Court. On the Bombay side of India success attended the prosecution of Savarkar, who was convicted and sentenced, as his brother had been before him, to transportation for life and confiscation of all his property. But in Bengal, with the partial exception of the Alipore Conspiracy case (in which the principal accused, Arabindo Ghose, was acquitted), almost all the important criminal cases that came before the Chief Justice and his colleagues in the High Court ended in the complete breakdown of the prosecution and the utter discomfiture of the police. More scathing condemnations of the methods employed by an untrustworthy and unscrupulous police to promote the prosecution of so-called political offenders have never been pronounced by the judiciary. And in case after case in which the police were severely censured by the High Court the Executive did not take the smallest step to punish their misconduct.

In the Midnapore Conspiracy case 154 persons were arrested as conspirators and bail was refused. Eventually twenty-seven of these were committed for trial before the District Judge. When Mr. Sinha, the then Advocate-General, appeared on the scene, twenty-four of these unfortunates were set at liberty. Three only were convicted at the Sessions, and they were released, on appeal, by the High Court. The Chief Justice recorded a famous judgment, in which he ventured to say that he hoped what the Court had said about the conduct of the police would receive proper notice from the Government. It will hardly be believed, but yet it is a fact, that these police officers whose conduct was the subject of judicial stigma were not only promoted by the Government, but their names appeared in the King's Birthday Honours List as the recipients of titles. More recently damages and costs have been decreed by Mr. Justice Fletcher of the High Court in a civil suit instituted jointly against these police officers and the district Magistrate for conspiring together against one of the accused in the above case who had been arrested and imprisoned with most improper motives.

It is noteworthy that the costs of the defendants in this suit were defrayed by the Government and that the Government is about to pay the cost of an appeal.

In what is known as the Howrah Gang case (of conspiracy) forty-six persons were placed on trial. The preliminary inquiry against them was held for a period of eighty-six days *in camera*. They were committed to a special tribunal of three judges of the High Court on the 1st of December, 1910. Four hundred and fifty Crown witnesses were examined. One of the accused, the bread-winner of his family, died during the trial, one was found to be insane, and the case was dropped against five at various stages of the hearing. The remainder were detained for a whole year in custody during inquiry. On the 18th of April, 1911, thirty-three were acquitted, and six, who were already under conviction for another offence, were sentenced to various terms of imprisonment. It would be repeating a twice-told tale to go on through the other cases of this conspiracy campaign. The one bright feature that shines out in the sordid record is the impartial and judicial independence of the Calcutta High Court under its Chief Justice, Sir Lawrence Jenkins.

During this long and painful period of coercion and prosecutions Lord Morley was actively employed on his own official reform scheme for infusing an Indian element into the Executive Councils in India and into his own Council at Whitehall, and for enlarging and broadening the basis of the Legislative Councils in India. The scheme was a very poor thing as it emanated from the Simla workshop; then it was improved in England by Lord Morley, who issued a most admirable dispatch to the Government of India on the 27th of November, 1908. Eventually it came into full operation at the end of 1909, subject to grave and vital flaws which deprive it of most of its attraction to the educated classes, through whose insistence alone any scheme at all came into being.

The Indian Councils Act of 1909, to which I was glad to lend my parliamentary support, was a mere skeleton measure ; it was clothed with flesh and blood by means of rules and regulations framed by the Government of India. Under these rules, the electors as well as those eligible for the Legislative Councils are limited to members of municipal and district boards. The Government has a right arbitrarily to prohibit any one from becoming a member. A further wedge has been driven in between Mohammedans and Hindoos by giving the former electoral privileges which are denied to the latter.

Still, with all its defects, what is known as the reform scheme of Lord Morley would have been welcome at any other time. It was put forward as a measure of conciliation and it contains within it many features of a popular character. But it was handicapped from the start. "I know not," said Edmund Burke, speaking of the measures of the British Government in America—"I know not how the angel of conciliation will work in concert with the angel of repression. Standing by itself I could answer for the angel of sweetness and conciliation. In the bad company in which it is found, I cannot." And so I can cite one quotation from an Indian newspaper which briefly summarises Indian opinion : "Until Mr. Morley frees India from the nightmare of executive tyranny, people are hardly disposed to attach even a featherweight of importance to his academic reforms." Here we have the case in a nutshell. While a policy of strenuous coercion was being pursued, the people of India were in no mood to listen even to an angel of light.

CHAPTER XXVI

CONCLUSION

I HAVE now little more to add, for the record of these memories is drawing to a close. My parliamentary life was a short one, but my attitude was, I may venture to say, always consistent and straightforward. I place this *Apologia* for my Indian policy before the judgment of the public. I claim to have grasped the unrivalled value of the opportunity which presented itself to a Liberal Secretary of State. I foresaw the unequalled danger which would inevitably follow if that opportunity were neglected. In season and out of season, through good and evil repute, inside the House and out of the House, I lost none of the chances I could get in pressing on to Lord Morley's hands the master-key of the situation with which he was confronted. I had high hopes when I entered the portals of Westminster: I believed that I saw before me an era of happiness and contentment such as our Indian fellow-subjects had not enjoyed for nearly a generation. Although those hopes were early dashed and it soon became apparent that there would be no reconsideration of the reactionary tendencies of Lord Curzon's policy, and no prospect of allaying the festering sore which the Partition of Bengal had created, I did not lose heart. Although it cannot be otherwise than a most painful duty to one who is as convinced and faithful a follower of a Liberal Government as I am to place himself in opposition to the administration of a department of that Government because it abandons Liberal principles, I did not shrink from taking that responsibility upon myself.

I remember to have heard Lord Morley say in the House of Commons: "We are all agreed that it is best and wisest to exclude India from the field of our ordinary party operations." Words of this kind are always used by men who desire that there should be no breach of continuity in our Indian Administration, whether it be a Liberal or a Tory Government in power. They are always used by men who do not desire Indian questions to be discussed in Parliament. When such words are used the unanimity between the Front Benches is wonderful. And yet it is obvious that they connote the gravest dereliction from Liberal principles. They may be true if we are to regard "our ordinary party politics" as an ignoble struggle for office. But they are not true if they mean that the principles of Liberalism are not as applicable to Indian as to English affairs. Speaking as a good party man, I am prepared to find under a Tory Government a policy of race and class domination, of disregard of the people's wishes, of aggression abroad and repression at home. But when a Liberal Government comes into power, I confess that I expect to see a negation of this policy.

As soon as it became apparent that there was to be no negation of Tory policy, there was no longer any question as to my personal attitude in regard to Indian matters. I was in the House of Commons to advocate Liberal principles everywhere and in everything. I was there to vindicate the elementary principles of freedom of speech and of writing, and the indefeasible right of British subjects to be heard in their defence before being sent to prison. I was there to protest against the infliction of cruel penalties upon political offenders. I was there to support what Mr. Gladstone had once declared to be the duty of a Liberal Government—"the systematic enlargement of the liberties of the Indian people." It is needless to say that this was an unpopular attitude to assume. How often have I not been told that it was "the rôle of a Little Englander, unpatriotic, disloyal, and seditious!" The group with which I acted soon became a target for abuse from the sharpshooters in the public Press, and we had few defenders even among our own party organs. In my own case I suffered the additional penalty of alienation from many old Anglo-Indian friends to whom I had been, and still am, most warmly attached. I was made the subject of obloquy, not in the Press only but through the Post Office, and became the recipient of shoals of obscene letters and offensive postcards. I was the victim on more than one occasion of the scurvy form of practical joke which consists in sending forged orders to undertakers, coal merchants, furniture dealers, and other tradesmen to supply goods. And some there were whose moral sense sank so low as to dare deliberately to associate my name with murderers and assassins.

Fais ce que dois, Advienne que pourra! That is the motto of the old knightly banner which for so many centuries has braved the battle and the breeze in scorn of calumny. That is the motto which with a clear conscience and a fearless spirit I invoke on behalf of my friends and myself in our justification.

* * * * *

Now I am no longer in the House and am not likely to seek again for a seat in Parliament. I lost my health as a result of attendance to my duties during the arduous Session of 1909, and when the General Election came round—into which we were forced by the Lords' rejection of the Budget—I was lying on a bed of sickness and unable to take any part in the contest. The strain on the system, already weakened by exposure and hardships during my later years in India, had led to a complete collapse. I placed my resignation as a candidate in the hands of my Committee, but they were unable to accept it. My friends worked splendidly on my behalf—in a way for which I have ever felt gratitude and admiration—but in the untoward circumstances and with a millionaire, who did not hesitate to spend his money, as my opponent, it is not surprising that I should have lost my seat, although only by the small margin of 152 votes out of a total poll of 11,602 voters.

I do not desire to quit this subject without another grateful acknowledgment to my old constituents in Nottingham. They always rallied round me with a degree of personal kindness and affection which has linked me to their city with such a bond that time will never sunder it. They cordially recognised and endorsed the services I endeavoured to render to India while I sat in Parliament as their representative. When I was compelled finally to decide not to become a candidate again, they presented me with an illuminated address and costly gifts, which are treasured with the many Indian tributes I already possess, and will be handed down with them as heirlooms in my family.

Although my parliamentary life has closed, my interest in politics, and in Indian affairs in particular, is unabated, and I can still in my retirement take up the tangled skein of circumstance, and watch the current aspect of changing turns of policy as closely as I could when I was an active figure in public life. I look back on the period during which a Liberal Government has been in power with a profound realisation of the disappointment which has ground itself into the heart of a people who had been accustomed to associate with Liberalism the broad and sympathetic temper of Ripon. At the same time, I recognise that there are now gleams of hope to which India has long been a stranger. There are signs—slight they may be, and no bigger than a man's hand—but signs unmistakable of a welcome change of front indicating a determination to suspend the protracted series of political prosecutions. This new departure is attributed to the sagacity of Lord Hardinge. Charges in more than one grave case have been withdrawn, and prisoners have been discharged.

The salutary effect produced on public opinion by this magnanimity is already most encouraging to a further development of clemency. I dare not augur too much from what has been done, but I do entertain a hope that we have at last beheld the dawn of a new method of campaigning along the lines of unalloyed conciliation and sympathetic treatment. If there is anywhere a safe and sure guarantee of British rule in India, it is to be found in a contented people. If we are willing to govern that wonderful country on liberal and sympathetic principles, to show deference to popular wishes, opinions, and aspirations, to encourage and foster the national sentiment of the people, and to unite the educated classes of the community with ourselves in the administration of their own affairs and in formulating a policy in which all can join in furtherance of progress—in this case we need have no cause for anxiety. The best protection of India must always rest on the loyalty, confidence, and affection of the Indian people. The surest way to prevent unrest is to take away the matter of discontent. Remove the causes of discontent and there will be no sedition. And assuredly never were times more auspicious than the present for the inauguration of such a campaign as this.

A real occasion of national rejoicing is approaching. Expectations are again strung high, and popular sentiment is again deeply moved. Another golden opportunity presents itself to those who are ready and willing to grasp the olive-branch of peace. There could be no more fitting attribution to the Coronation of His Majesty the King-Emperor at Delhi than the redress of grievances, above all a modification of the Partition of Bengal, and a general amnesty to political offenders. If the King's Proclamation breathes a new spirit in official policy and infuses a new hope and new life among the people, all will be well. Then, indeed, would fly away "Anarchy" and "Conspiracy" like birds of evil omen, and panic-mongers would die a natural death. And then would at last be fulfilled the prophetic words of Queen Victoria in her gracious Proclamation to her Indian subjects more than fifty-three years ago: "In their Prosperity will be our Strength; in their Contentment our Security; and in their Gratitude our best Reward."

INDEX

INDEX

W

Y

Z